ST. LOUIS

[FOR THE RECORD]

URBAN
TAPESTRY
SERIES
TOWERY
PUBLISHING, INC.

[CONTENTS]

Library of Congress Catalog-in-Publishing information may be found on page 509.

Mark McGwire's 1998 baseball feat—70 home runs—would undoubtedly have energized any city.

But it really galvanized St. Louis and made clear to outsiders certain things about the city. Among the

qualities revealed are St. Louis' basic good-naturedness, its appreciation for history, its standing as

a baseball city. McGwire's record-breaking run couldn't have happened at a better place, where fans

were simultaneously so passionate, so knowledgeable, so appreciative, and so civil about it all.

To have an encore performance in 1999—with McGwire hitting 65 home runs—only added to his

stature among the city's baseball legends.

Long before Mark McGwire focused additional attention on St. Louis, people in the know had

been saying for years and years that this is the

best baseball city in America because nowhere

else can you find, as one writer put it, such a

combination of passion and civility among fans.

Opera—is located in a big outdoor amphitheater; the Muny is where Cary Grant appeared as a stock performer in 1931 under his real name, Archibald Leach. Every year, they have a full lineup not of opera, but of musical theater featuring name entertainers as well as local talent, a tradition that has held since the Muny was born.

Forest Park is also home to what many people consider to be the finest zoo in any big city in the country. It draws more than 2.5 million visitors a year. It was founded back in 1913, with one of its first inhabitants being the already endangered buffalo, along with some exotics left over from the 1904 World's Fair. From the beginning, it was one of the first zoos to show animals not in cages, but in natural surroundings (where possible). Hence the zoo trains, which putter along through natural, open exhibits.

Thousands of St. Louisans love to just stroll in Forest Park—there are dozens and dozens of good places to walk (and jog)—and if you come out on Lindell Boulevard on one side of the park, you see stately old homes that you imagine might have been the setting for *Meet Me in St. Louis*. This is where the pope's parade took place during his visit to the city in January 1999.

Another point of civic pride and near-religious devotion is Ted Drewes Frozen Custard. There are two locations—one on South Grand in south St. Louis, the other on Chippewa Street along the old Route 66. I grew up in New York, and I have visited a number of places in the United States and around the world, so I make no false claims when I say this—the best ice cream I have ever had is the frozen custard at Ted Drewes. They call their ultra-thick offerings "concretes" to describe how thick they really are, and they bring them out and turn them upside down with a spoon stuck in them to prove it. The

concrete may be the highest-calorie-per-serving item one can possibly consume—short of just eating a

can of Crisco. It tastes unbelievably good—so don't worry about it.

If I knew that I was going to the electric chair, I would, as a last meal, have them bring over a couple of

cheeseburgers from O'Connell's—a south St. Louis pub that serves quite possibly the world's best ham-

burger. I'd follow that up with a pistachio concrete and a vanilla milk shake from Ted Drewes—and expire a

happy man.

Another renowned burger is found at a popular rock-and-roll bar called Blueberry Hill in University

City. Here, you can get a pretty good idea of how

deep and diverse the contribution of St. Louis is to

the world stage. Blueberry Hill itself is, foremost, a

bar and restaurant with a fine jukebox and more brands of beer than anyone can keep up with. Joe Edwards,

the owner, collects stuff he likes, from favorite icons from his childhood (metal lunch boxes featuring the

likes of Batman, Superman, the Lone Ranger, the Beatles, Howdy Doody) to more substantial items like

Chuck Berry's Gibson guitar. Berry himself is a regular, performing monthly in the Duck Room downstairs.

But it's outside the bar, on the St. Louis Walk of Fame, that you see the names commemorating the city's

cultural heritage, enshrined in the concrete. The Walk of Fame is maintained by a nonprofit organization

that awards the brass stars and bronze plaques to those who have somehow contributed to the city's heri-

tage. The list is, even for those who live in St. Louis, pretty incredible. It pays to take a look at a few of the

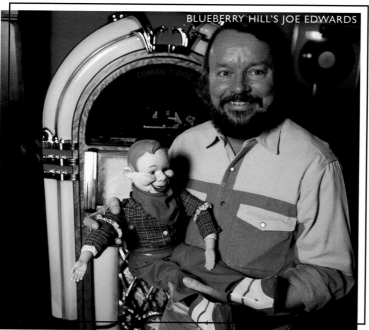

BLUEBERRY HILL'S JOE EDWARDS

names, just to show the depth and variety of talent

that I'm talking about.

There are, naturally, a host of baseball and sports

legends: Cool Papa Bell, Yogi Berra, Lou Brock, Dizzy Dean, Bob Gibson, Stan Musial, Branch Rickey, and Red Schoendienst.

There are writers and journalists: T.S. Eliot, Maya Angelou, William Burroughs, Kate Chopin, Stanley Elkin, A.E. Hotchner, William Inge, Bill Mauldin, Marianne Moore, Howard Nemerov, Joseph Pulitzer, and Tennessee Williams.

There are musicians, actors, and entertainers: Josephine Baker, Chuck Berry, Miles Davis, Phyllis Diller, Buddy Ebsen, Redd Foxx, John Goodman, Betty Grable, Dick Gregory, Scott Joplin, Kevin Kline, Vincent Price, Leonard Slatkin, and Tina Turner.

And how could we forget Ulysses S. Grant, Charles Lindbergh, Masters and Johnson, and Marlin Perkins?

Hey, if it was good enough for them (for all or part of their lives), it's good enough for me. ❡

COMPLETED IN 1965 AS A monument to western expansion, St. Louis' famed Gateway Arch is also a reminder of the optimism and determination of those who settled in and built a great city.

BUILT ON LAND DONATED BY city founder Auguste Chouteau, the Old Courthouse was the tallest building in St. Louis until the late 19th century. Deeded to the National Park Service in 1940, it is now part of the Jefferson National Expansion Memorial, which includes the Gateway Arch.

© DARIN IPEMA

© BRENT REED

HAVING SURVIVED THE wrecking ball to sing, laugh, and roar another day, these gems front some of the city's more architecturally interesting buildings. The Greek mask (OPPOSITE) has its home on the Kiel Opera House, currently quiet, but looking for new occupants.

WHEN THE FOX THEATRE opened in 1929, it was the second-largest movie theater in the United States; 50 years later, it was a leaky, messy home for pigeons. In 1982, the "Fabulous Fox" reopened— every piece of brass, marble, glass, and bronze polished, every gilded lily regilded. Its look has been described as Siamese-Byzantine with a touch of Egyptian, Babylonian, and Indian thrown in for good measure.

ST. LOUIS

EVEN THOUGH THE CONTI-nental Building (LEFT) has been closed for more than 20 years, it has been the subject of many renovation ideas, a New York art exhibit titled *Abandoned Skyscraper,* and its own Web site. Adornments on lesser-known buildings wait their turn for attention.

AN EAGLE'S PERCH ATOP THE Civil Courts Building shows the quiet side of a busy city center.

ST. LOUIS

NOT CONTENT TO STAY IN-doors, mythic creatures grace many St. Louis buildings and landmarks.

DEDICATED TO "OUR SOLDIER–
Dead" in 1936 by Presi-
dent Franklin D. Roosevelt, the
Soldiers Memorial Military
Museum is the centerpiece of
a plaza across from City Hall.
The Greek Revival, limestone-
and-marble building houses
war artifacts and is the starting
point for the city's Veterans
Day Parade.

FROM THE CIVIL COURTS Building (OPPOSITE LEFT) to the War Memorial (RIGHT), a variety of statues around the city pay tribute to heroism and honor.

MORE THAN 100 MILITARY and civilian units of all kinds march in the Veterans Day Parade. Chilly November weather can't keep spirits down as vets strut their stuff down Market Street.

ONCE THE CITY'S TOP COP, Mayor Clarence Harmon (RIGHT) still can't resist a parade. Veterans, cute kids, and the ever present Shriners in tiny cars make for a good time.

SOME 100,000 TOMBSTONES of Georgia white marble dot the hills of Jefferson Barracks National Cemetery, whose 309 acres are tended by veterans. Shot down in Vietnam, Lieutenant Michael Blassie's body had been interred in the Tomb of the Unknowns in Arlington, Virginia, until being moved to the cemetery in July 1998 after DNA testing made his identity known (TOP).

74   ST. LOUIS

IN 1804, THE DISCOVERY Expedition—featuring the heralded explorations of Meriwether Lewis and William Clark—left nearby St. Charles, returning two years later to St. Louis. Clark eventually died in the area; his grave in Bellefontaine Cemetery fittingly overlooks the Mississippi River not far from its confluence with the Missouri. But neither man has been forgotten. In celebration of the bicentennial of their expedition, reenactors are preparing to re-create the trip.

80

THE MISSISSIPPI AND MISsouri rivers were the superhighways of the frontier era, bringing a wide variety of folk to the area—from river rat to silk and lace sophisticate. The Lewis and Clark Heritage Days celebration in St. Charles relives all aspects of life on the frontier, from cooking and sewing to black powder shooting and tomahawk throwing.

GEOFFREY SEITZ IS A LOCAL authority on old-time fiddle music, an important aspect of community life in the time of the French settlers. He keeps the tradition alive with his championship fiddle playing and expert craftsmanship as a violin maker.

THE TOP-RATED ST. LOUIS Symphony is almost as beloved as baseball's Cardinals. One reason may be that the symphony—America's second oldest—likes to get out of Powell Hall and into the community, where it performs 400 free concerts and workshops each year in informal settings. Two symphony-sponsored schools aim to cultivate a love of music in young people, as well as a future audience.

Roots music—a blend of folk, country, and blues—has a firm foothold here on the banks of the Mississippi. Singer-songwriter Jay Farrar (OPPOSITE) and his band Son Volt have a loyal, local following and are developing a national reputation, as well. Vintage instruments keep any sound authentic, and Jimmy Gravity keeps them in good repair at J. Gravity Strings.

88   S T . L O U I S

S T. LOUISANS MARCH TO MORE
than one kind of beat. The
battle of the bands at the Greater
St. Louis Marching Band
Festival draws nearly 50 high
schools to the Trans World
Dome. For those with a more
global rhythm in mind, the
Japanese and African arts
festivals are two of the many
ethnic fairs that celebrate the
diversity of the community.

St. Louis

WITH ITS BRICK ROW HOUSES and ornate wrought iron, Soulard is a little bit of old Europe in the near south side. Once densely packed with immigrants, the historic neighborhood is still a blend of rich and poor, educated and working class, rehabber and longtime resident. While sometimes at odds, all want to ensure that their neighborhood remains vibrant.

GEYER AVE
10TH ST

HISTORIC
SOULARD

THE SOULARD FARMER'S
Market of today had its
beginnings in 1779, when
farmers brought their produce
to the city and circled their
wagons into an impromptu
marketplace. Generations of
shoppers and vendors have
visited the two-acre site, which
is owned and operated by the
City of St. Louis, making it the
first publicly owned market
west of the Mississippi.

S OULARD FARMER'S MARKET features an eclectic array of food—from freshly caught channel catfish to exotic spices and decorative vegetables. Low prices attract gourmet and fixed-income shoppers alike, and on any given Saturday, up to 20 different languages can be heard as customers wind their way through rows of stands.

THE ST. LOUIS SCIENCE Center calls itself the "playground for your head," and has been wildly popular, drawing 15 million people since its makeover in 1991. Interactive exhibits on everything from 1950s science fiction to dinosaurs to a physics playground engage visitors, who discover that science is anything but boring.

AMONG THE MANY THINGS IT is known for, St. Louis' pivotal role in aviation history is especially significant. In 1927, a group of influential businessmen financed Charles Lindbergh's solo transatlantic flight to Paris (OPPOSITE). The next year, James S. McDonnell (second from left in bow tie, with the Mercury Seven astronauts), began his aircraft company. Now part of Boeing, locally based McDonnell Douglas was a leader in aeronautical engineering. The company's *Freedom 7* capsule launched Alan Shepard and America into the space race.

▼ © JONATHAN POSTAL / TOWERY PUBLISHING, INC.

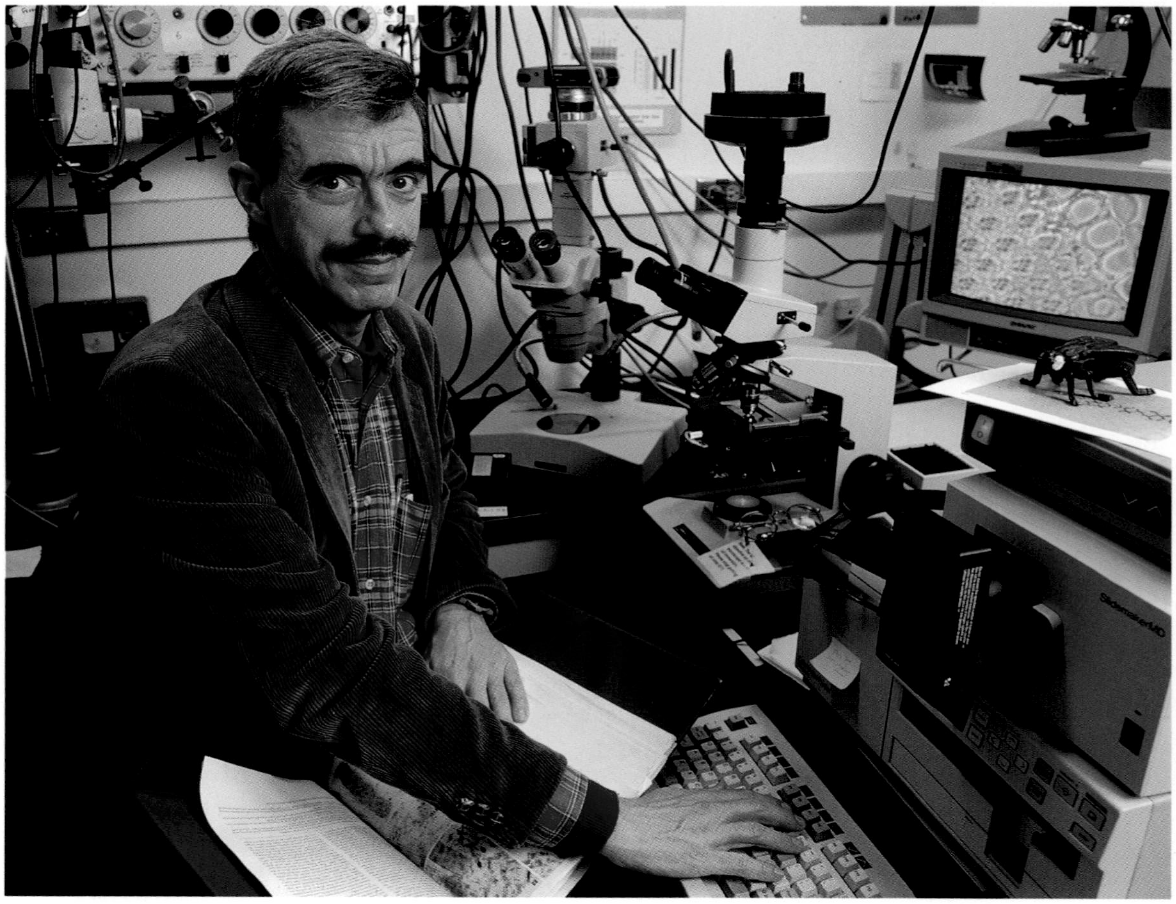

▼ © JONATHAN POSTAL / TOWERY PUBLISHING, INC.

$$\frac{}{a^2} = \frac{8\pi G}{c^2}(\rho_m + \rho_r)$$

$$\frac{-a^2}{a^4} = \frac{8\pi G}{3c^2}\left(\frac{\rho_{mo}a_0^3}{a^3} + \frac{\rho_{ro}a_0^4}{a^4}\right)$$

$$= \frac{2\alpha_m}{a^3} + \frac{\alpha_r^2}{a^4}$$

$$\alpha_m \equiv \frac{4\pi G}{3c^2}\rho_{mo}a_0^3$$

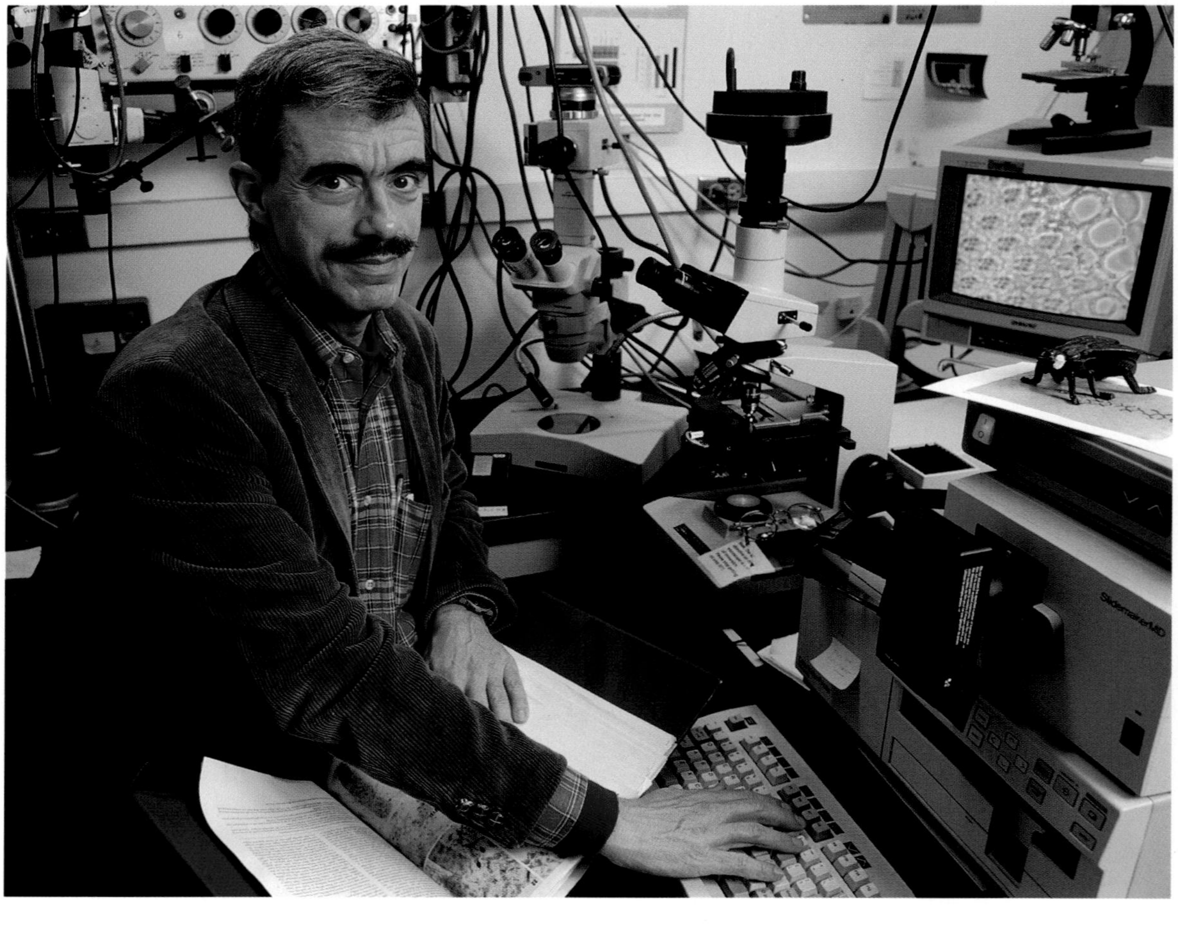

$$\alpha_r \equiv \left(\frac{8\pi G}{3c^2}\rho_{ro}a_0^4\right)^{1/2}$$

Mixed Matter/Radiation Universes

SAINT LOUIS UNIVERSITY, founded in 1818, was the first Catholic university in America to have a graduate school, as well as schools of philosophy, divinity, medicine, law, and business. Today, cutting-edge research and instruction in biotechnology, life, and physical sciences has continued, attracting students and faculty from around the world, including Ian H. Redmount, assistant professor in the Parks College of Engineering and Aviation's Department of Physics (OPPOSITE TOP), and Dr. William Stark with the university's Department of Biology (OPPOSITE BOTTOM).

Webster
UNIVERSITY

WORLD
HEADQUARTERS

THE ST. LOUIS METRO AREA is home to 12 colleges and universities. Among its oldest are Saint Louis University (OPPOSITE) and Webster University (BOTTOM). Historic Washington University's Francis Field (top) was the site of the 1904 Olympic Games and the Pike (amusement area) of the 1904 World's Fair ran through its campus.

THE UNIVERSITY CITY LIONS, which stand atop entry gates on either side of Delmar Boulevard, have become the insignia of this inner ring suburb. In the early 1900s, Edward G. Lewis headquartered his *Woman's Magazine* in what is now the City Hall (OPPOSITE), planning the early development of the city, which he had hoped would become a utopian community of thinkers and artists. People debate whether he was a visionary entrepreneur or a con artist, but either way, University City has become a progressive and culturally rich community.

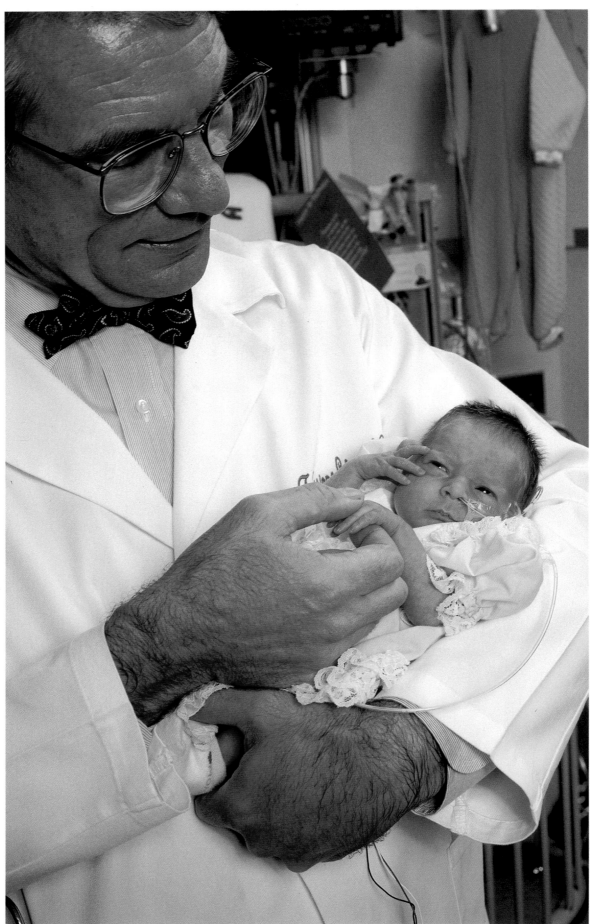

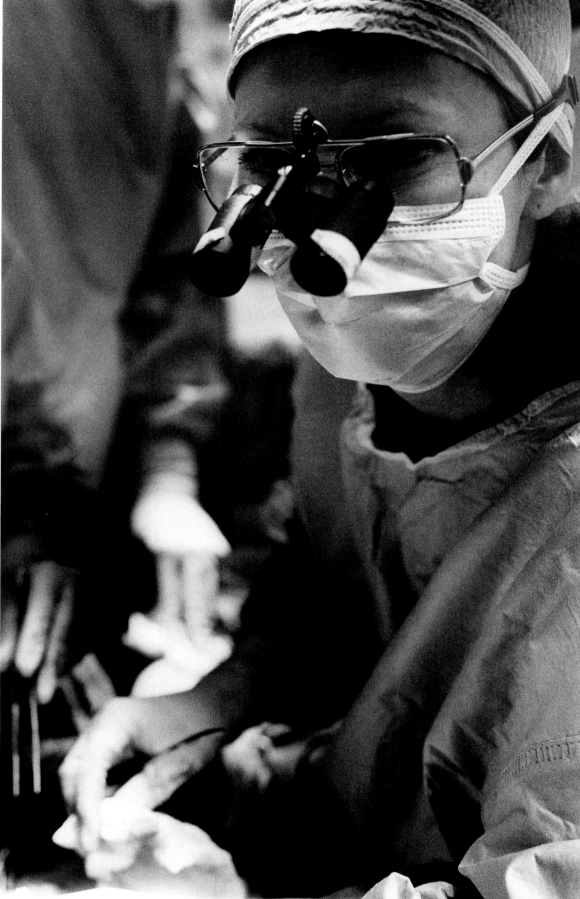

BJC IS ONE OF THE LARGEST integrated health care systems in the United States, with more than 25,000 employees, 100 ambulatory care sites, and 13 hospitals. Two of its hospitals, Washington University Medical Center's Barnes-Jewish and St. Louis Children's, consistently rank in the top 10 nationally for teaching and research. Children's highly rated neonatal ICU and its pediatric lung transplant program care for young patients from around the nation and the world.

126

ST. LOUIS FIRE CHIEF NEIL Svetanics (OPPOSITE) was *Fire Chief* magazine's Fire Chief of the Year in 1998. Five days after he joined the department as a trainee in 1962, St. Louis had one of its biggest fires. Convinced he had made the right career choice, he stayed on, becoming chief in 1986. Svetanics has worked to pass a fire detector ordinance and to reduce accidents by changing the way that fire trucks respond to alarms.

128   ST. LOUIS

LARGER-THAN-LIFE NATIVE turtles roam the grounds of Turtle Park (OPPOSITE), much to the delight of visitors. Baby turtles emerging from giant eggs complete the scene in this whimsical creation by sculptor Bob Cassilly. The ancient reptilian ancestors across the way at the St. Louis Science Center remind us that all creatures may not have been so friendly.

DURING THE GOLDEN AGE OF steam, up to 170 boats docked on the St. Louis levee. Their day may be gone, but some still linger, either as tour boats, restaurants, or casinos. The *Admiral,* once the largest inland steamer in the United States, plied the Mississippi near St. Louis on day and evening excursions. Its 140,000-square-foot interior housed ballrooms, an arcade, restaurants, and a steam calliope. Today, it is permanently docked as the home of the President Casino.

146

ST. LOUIS SITS IN A RIVER valley on the edge of the plains with nothing between it and the jet stream. Weather can change quickly and drasti-cally—all four seasons can be experienced in a matter of days. Though the area often features spring-like temperatures in January, sudden blizzards can dump more than a foot of snow, catching unsuspecting residents off guard.

148

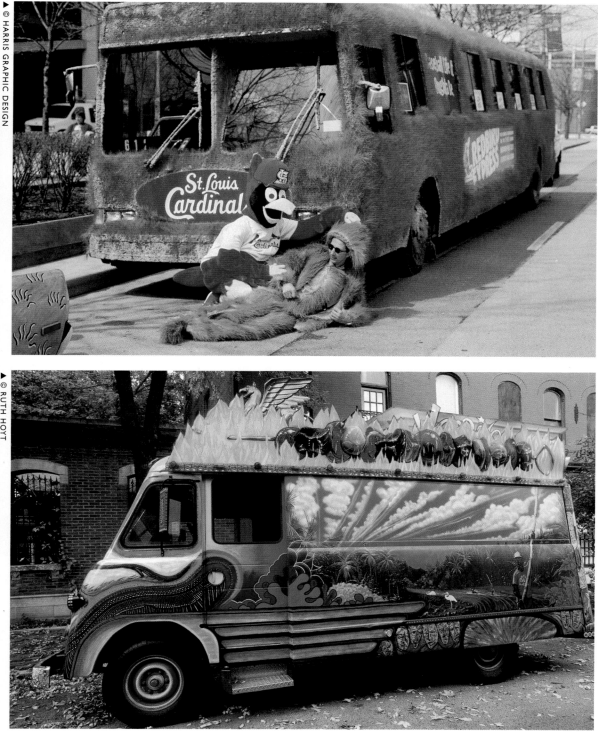

ART CARS ABOUND IN ST. Louis. When the baseball Cardinals wanted to celebrate the new natural turf at Busch Stadium in 1996, they hired New York performance artist Gene Pool (aka the Grass Man, aka Bill Harding) to help. It took 150 pounds of seed to cover a special Redbird Express bus—a quarter acre in all—with living grass (TOP). Other not-so-organic vehicles can be found at the Venice Café (BOTTOM), home of the local art car scene that was captured in the documentary *Wild Wheels*.

THE VENICE CAFÉ IN THE Benton Park neighborhood is the brainchild of local artist Jeff Lockheed and friends (ABOVE). The three-story, brick building is studio, gallery, coffeehouse, restaurant, and nightclub—a bohemian mall of sorts. Lockheed created his first art car by attaching hundreds of plastic baby doll parts to his father's old pickup truck. Sculptor Mark Coughlin (OPPOSITE) relied on welded steel and found objects for his piece, *Loudmouth Bass Band*.

LOCATED ON 116 ACRES OF rolling hills in southwest St. Louis County, Laumeier Sculpture Park hosts an annual contemporary art fair that attracts some 23,000 visitors and 150 artists from around the country. Donald Lipski's piece *Ball? Ball! Wall? Wall!* (BOTTOM) is made up of 55 steel marine buoys and is part of the park's more than 75-piece permanent collection.

162

© RAY MARKLIN

© RAY MARKLIN

ALEXANDER LIBERMAN'S
The Way (OPPOSITE) is the
best-known piece at Laumeier
Sculpture Park, founded in 1968
to promote a variety of forms
of contemporary art. George
Greenamyer's *Fire and Ice* performance piece (TOP) was a
popular winter solstice event at
Laumeier, but St. Louis' unpre-
dictable winter weather prompted
park officials to end the annual
festival in 1992.

DOWNTOWN IS NO LONGER the only place for office buildings. A growing number of companies are locating in the open spaces of the county, employing modern architecture that blends into the landscape.

166

TOWER GROVE PARK ON THE near south side is a treasure trove of Victorian elegance. Modeled after English walking parks, its wooded, winding paths take visitors past sculptures, fountains, gazebos, bandstands, and reconstructed Greek ruins (very stylish in the late 1800s). Real Greek ruins can be found at the St. Louis Art Museum (OPPOSITE), whose fountain is a favorite wishing spot.

INNSBROOK ESTATES IS ST. Louis' favorite getaway spot. Just one hour west of town and recently incorporated as a city, its many lakes—dotted with A-frame, Swiss-style chalets—and quiet seclusion have made it a haven from hectic city life.

170

UNLIKE THEIR FAMOUS CLYDES-dale cousins, Missouri mules are unaccustomed to the glare of cameras and tourists–although they seem quite willing on occasion to strike a pose for posterity's sake. In their off time, the famous Anheuser-Busch show horses (OPPOSITE) reside on Grant's Farm, which was once owned by Ulysses S. Grant and is now the Busch family estate.

ST. LOUIS

VISIONARY ZOO DIRECTOR George Vierheller's philosophy was that "a zoological garden should not be a penitentiary." That was in the 1920s when most zoo animals were kept in cages, and for Vierheller, that just wouldn't do. The bear pits were among the first to show animals in natural surroundings. Continuing in that spirit, the zoo is undertaking an ambitious, $55 million reworking of its hippo and elephant habitats, putting less distance between people and animals.

ST. LOUIS

CIRCUS FLORA–MODELED after a 19th-century, one-ring European circus–features the talents of performers from the renowned Flying Wallendas to the locally based St. Louis Arches (LEFT), whose tumbling feats of skill and daring are showcased during the event's annual two-week run, and as part of the Everyday Circus at City Museum.

© DOUG CALDWELL

© BILL BOYCE

© DOUG CALDWELL

FATHER TIME
WISHING ALL
A HAPPY
FAIR ST. LOUIS
GOD BLESS AMERICA

GRAND OLD FLAGS ABOUND
at Fair Saint Louis, the
country's biggest Fourth of July
celebration. Three days and
nights of revelry draw more
than 1 million to the riverfront, undaunted by blistering
temperatures and sudden
thunderstorms. Paul Pagano
(TOP RIGHT), also known as
Father Time, is a staple at area
parades in his red-white-and-
blue step van, with its public-
address system resounding
Kate Smith's *God Bless America*.

FAIR SAINT LOUIS HAS ITS roots in the Veiled Prophet celebrations, which began in 1878 when civic-minded businessmen brought costumes and floats from New Orleans in hopes of creating a fall version of Mardi Gras. Today, the Veiled Prophet Parade continues as part of the fair, which was moved to July 4 in 1981.

DURING THE COURSE OF THREE nights, more than 12,000 pyrotechnic effects light up the night sky over Fair Saint Louis.

FOUNTAINS AND PUBLIC sculpture abound in St. Louis. *Meeting of the Waters* by Swedish sculptor Carl Milles (THIS PAGE) was originally titled *Wedding of the Rivers*, but virtuous citizens were shocked at the bride's and groom's absence of clothing. Milles refused to modify his work, but consented to a title change for the fountain. Today, the happy couple and their attendant river nymphs welcome visitors to Union Station. The less controversial fountains of Six Flags over St. Louis proved to be a magnet for one youngster (OPPOSITE).

BUILT TO RESEMBLE A medieval walled city in France, St. Louis' Union Station was a transportation marvel of its age. In 1894, it was the world's largest railroad terminal. At its peak, it handled 290 trains a day, moving immigrants, soldiers, and passengers—22 million in the 1940s—through St. Louis. Reopened in 1985 after a $150 million makeover, it is home to a hotel, restaurants, cafés, shops, live music, and a lake with pedal boats. Some 5 million visit each year.

THE GRAND HALL AT UNION Station had fallen into such disrepair in the 1970s that it was used as a set in the apocalyptic film *Escape from New York*. Today, its gilded walls and stained glass have been restored to their original glory.

OFFICES

SHOPS

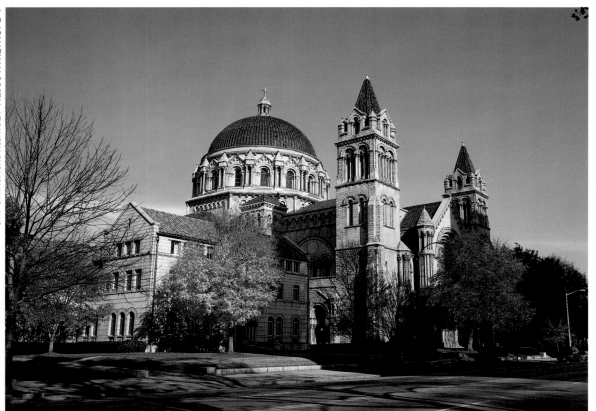

In a city as old as St. Louis, new can be a relative term. The New Cathedral, officially titled the Cathedral Basilica of Saint Louis, was built in 1907 (PAGES 204-207). Its Byzantine interior is home to the world's largest mosaic collection—83,000 square feet, 41.5 million pieces of glass, 8,000 colors—and was crafted by 20 artists between 1912 and 1988. In 1997, the New Cathedral was designated as a basilica by the Vatican because of its beauty, history, and significance as a center of worship.

CATHOLICS CAME TO FRENCH-dominated St. Louis to escape religious persecution in the 13 colonies, and, in 1834, built the first Catholic cathedral west of the Mississippi. The Basilica of St. Louis, King of France is the formal name for what most call the Old Cathedral (OPPOSITE).

THE SHRINE OF ST. JOSEPH (OPPOSITE) was the site of a verified miracle in 1862 when a dying man was healed there. Its Altar of Answered Prayers was built in 1867 after parishioners prayed to St. Joseph, asking his intervention during a cholera epidemic. Across town, St. Francis Xavier Church (LEFT) — also known as the College Church — is the main place of worship for Saint Louis University.

ST. LOUIS

CATHOLIC AND NON-CATHOLIC alike lined the streets to catch a glimpse of Pope John Paul II during his visit here in January 1999. An order of contemplative nuns, the Holy Spirit Adoration Sisters (known as the Pink Sisters because of their bright pink habits), spent eight months praying for warm weather during the visit. Winter stopped in its tracks for two days as pope-watchers basked in the warm, sunny weather — and meteorologists scratched their heads.

THE 46-FOOT-HIGH SIGN FOR the old Airway Drive-In in suburban St. Ann (OPPOSITE) was just too pretty to demolish when the facility closed. Today, its majorette twirls her baton over shoppers at the Airway Centre. Less decorative perhaps, but no less artful, the bright lights of the city—from parking markers to the red letters of the Anheuser-Busch sign—point the way.

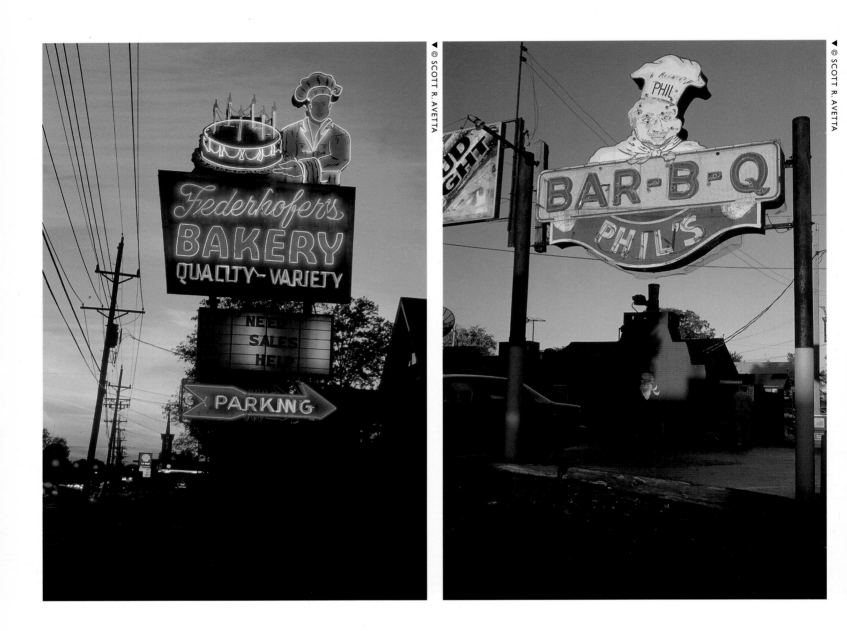

Local wisdom dictates that the older the sign, the better the food. Landmarks like Federhofer's Bakery and World's Fair Donuts continue to crank out the hometown favorites, drawing customers back to the old neighborhoods from franchise-dominated suburbs.

ST. LOUISANS LOVE FATTY, greasy foods like gooey butter cake and pork steaks, which may be why the city has such a large Tums factory. The A.H. Lewis Medical Company began manufacturing its Nature's Remedy here in 1905, followed by Tums in 1930. The five-story building is on the National Register of Historic Places and is one of the last manufacturing plants in downtown St. Louis. Now owned by SmithKline Beecham, it delivers 8 billion Tums to tummies each year.

A NHEUSER-BUSCH ISN'T THE only name in town when it comes to drinking. The 34-foot-tall neon Vess soda bottle continues to tout the "billion bubble beverage" that's been made here since Vess Jones invented Whistle soda in 1916. In nearby Collinsville, it was a different liquid treat that caught the attention of residents. Unable to bear the loss of the town's icon–a 100,000-gallon bottle of ketchup (or catsup, if you prefer) from the shuttered Brooks manufacturing plant–citizens raised almost $80,000 in 1995 to have the 170-foot-tall structure restored to its "tangy-est," old original self.

BEHIND THESE WALLS AWAIT some of the delicacies favored in St. Louis—brain sandwiches, for example. Enjoy with beer and good company.

ST. LOUIS IS A CITY OF CULINARY delights, like Piekutowski's Sausage Shop (TOP AND BOTTOM LEFT), a favorite of Pope John Paul II's. In 1969, when he was still known as Cardinal Karol Wojtyla, the pope visited St. Louis and craved sausage from his hometown of Kraków. He was able to find it at Piekutowski's and, in keeping with tradition, the eatery made a special batch for him upon his 1999 return visit to the city. When it's chocolate St. Louisans get a craving for, they head for the Crown Candy Kitchen (top right), whose copper fudge pots have been churning out confection since 1913.

THE BREW HOUSE OF THE Anheuser-Busch facility was part of a $500 million upgrade that keeps this National Historic Landmark in operation. Inside, five-story-tall wrought iron hop vine chandeliers have been restored, reminding visitors of a more elegant time. This 100-acre beer drinker's mecca has daily tours that end at the tasting room for free samples of St. Louis' most famous product.

IN THE SHADOW OF THE BREW-ery at Lemp Avenue and Pestalozzi Street stands the Venice Cafe, a restaurant, nightclub, bar, and art gallery, although it's hard to tell where the art begins and the gallery ends. Scavenged junk from demolished buildings and pop culture icons have become fountains, pillars, and wall hangings. Dedicated to more than the visual, the café is also a site for poetry slams.

ST. LOUIS NATIVE CHUCK Berry's Gibson ES-350T— "the guitar that rocked the world"—hangs on display, not in a rock-and-roll restaurant franchise, but in St. Louis' one and only Blueberry Hill. A friend of owner Joe Edwards', Berry (OPPOSITE) performs live in the Duck Room in this anchor of the University City Loop. Known for its burgers, jukebox (2,000 selections), and intellectually witty bathroom graffiti, Blueberry Hill has even appeared in an *Archie* comic.

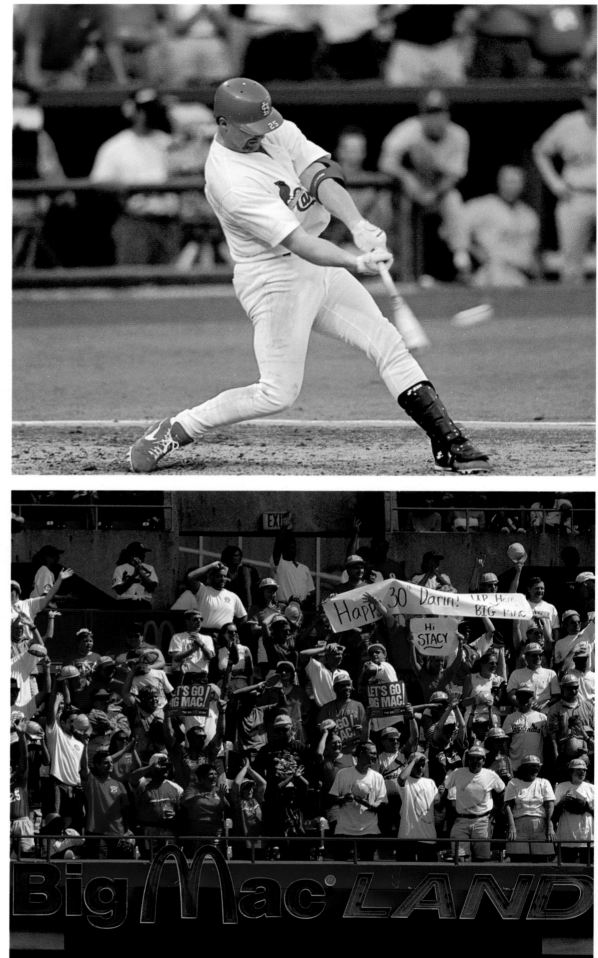

THE 1998 SEASON WAS magical for both the city and its baseball Cardinals, who drew more than 3 million adoring fans to the ballpark. Although they were 13 games out of first place, no one seemed to care as Mark McGwire pounded shots into the left field bleachers—dubbed Big Mac Land—and the town was in a two-month-long jubilant stupor as he chased and eclipsed Roger Maris' home run record. When the season ended—70 home runs later—some $60 million had been pumped into the region's economy.

244

FOR 51 OF ITS 100-PLUS seasons as a baseball town, St. Louis had two major-league teams, the American League Browns and the National League Cardinals. The old adage "first in shoes, first in booze, and last in the American League" was disproved in 1944 when the Browns faced the Cardinals in the World Series. While the Cards remain, the eccentric Browns became the Baltimore Orioles in 1953.

246

YOU MIGHT SAY BASEBALL in St. Louis has a religious following. Fans have been flocking to the ballpark in record numbers for years to see such teams as the Gas House Gang of the 1930s (ABOVE). Since 1954, the voice behind the team has been Hall of Fame broadcaster Jack Buck (OPPOSITE, BOTTOM LEFT). The storied Cardinals franchise has a rich history that has led it to win more World Series (nine) than any other National League team and 15 National League pennants.

372

ST. LOUIS

I N 1953, AUGUST A. "GUSSIE" Busch Jr. bought the St. Louis Cardinals and their home stadium at Sportsman's Park. Though officially owned by the Anheuser-Busch brewery, the Cardinals became his pet project and, by 1966, a new, $20 million stadium had been built– privately funded by the business community, including $5 million from Busch. Though the brewery sold the team in 1996, Gussie will always be remembered as its most colorful owner.

C ARDINAL FANS ARE A TOLER-
ant, appreciative bunch
who come in droves to Busch
Stadium whether or not the
Cardinals are winning. Cold
winter months are spent day-
dreaming of baseball; spring
training is eagerly anticipated
and closely watched, so that
by opening day, the faithful—
peanuts and Cracker Jacks in
hand—fill the ballpark to its brim.

252

IN ADDITION TO ITS BASEBALL fervor, St. Louis used to be a football Cardinals town, too. But when the city wouldn't build a new stadium, the team took its ball and went to play in Phoenix in 1988. Not to be daunted, die-hard football junkies, working on the "if we build it, they will come" theory, pushed through construction of the $280 million, publicly funded Trans World Dome and made the Los Angeles Rams an offer they couldn't re-fuse, moving them here in 1995.

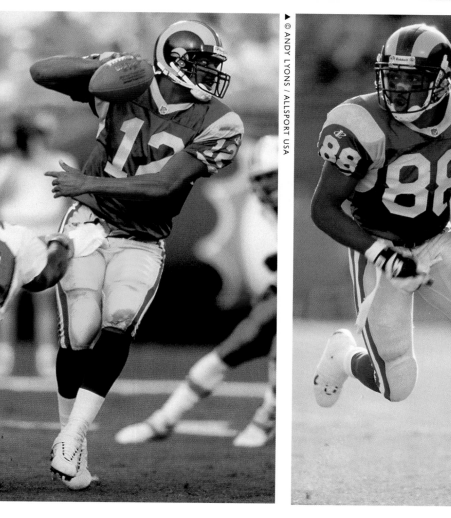

HOCKEY CAUGHT ON QUICKLY when St. Louis got its NHL franchise in 1966. The Blues went to the Stanley Cup play-offs in their first three years of play and to postseason play for their first seven. A solid core of fans developed, and Blues hockey games, now played at the new Kiel Center, are still one of the hottest tickets in town.

ST. LOUIS IS HOME TO PRO AND amateur boxing legends like Sonny Liston and the Spinks brothers. Terronn "Tramp" Millett (RIGHT) is one of the newest on this impressive list, winning the International Boxing Federation junior welterweight title in 1999. He fights out of the Pagedale Boxing Club, a gym in a converted garage run by his parents, Faye and Coot Millett. Ed Mahone (OPPOSITE), a former Golden Gloves heavyweight champ, trained with the Milletts, while Radford Beasley (LEFT) fights out of Jim Howell's North County gym.

ST. LOUIS

ST. LOUIS' SKIES PLAY HOST TO many events throughout the year. The Great Forest Park Balloon Race and the Gateway Kite Club's annual Great St. Louis Kite Festival draw thousands to the park, while air shows at Fair Saint Louis transfix riverfront audiences with daring feats of sky jinks.

264

WAY BEFORE SOCCER MOMS and minivans, St. Louis parents were taking their kids to practice for a variety of sporting events. Long a hotbed for amateur soccer, the area has supplied players for many championship college teams. Football and Little League baseball have their place on the field, as well, and you can always find a rambunctious game of Frisbee at any given park, on any given day.

FROM CHARITY GO-CART AND cross-country races to city-side events, St. Louis has its share of competitive activities.

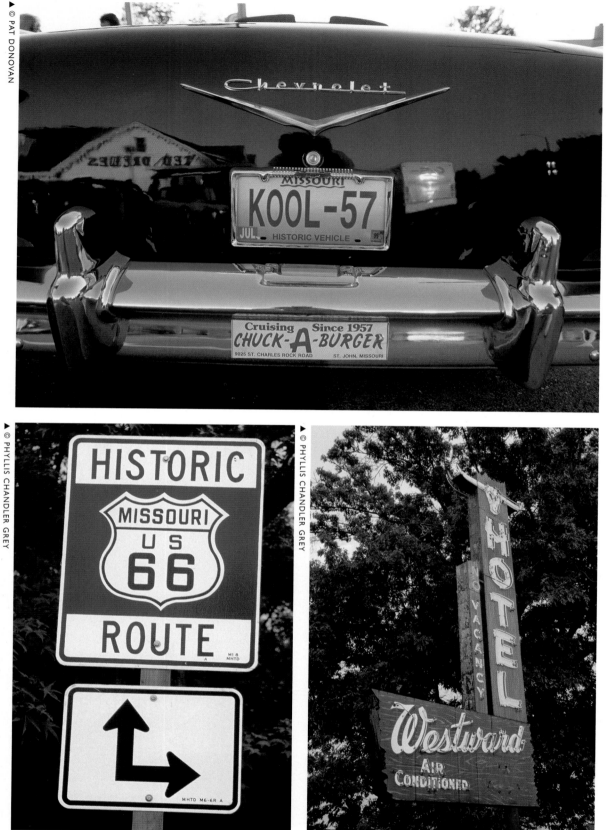

WORLD-FAMOUS ROUTE 66 once went from Chicago to L.A., with 600 of its miles crossing Missouri and Illinois— right through the heart of St. Louis. Before interstate highways efficiently whisked travelers from place to place, the Mother Road, which opened in 1926, wound its way through small towns, sparking America's love affair with the car. Small cottage hotels and other roadside attractions still beckon nostalgic cruisers who take to the road on sentimental journeys.

St. Louis

TEN BRIDGES CROSS THE Mississippi near St. Louis, the newest being the Clark Bridge (OPPOSITE), linking St. Charles County to Alton. Its 170-foot-tall towers connect to epoxy-coated steel cables, which in turn support the four-lane span. The Martin Luther King Jr. Memorial Bridge joins the heart of the city to its neighbor across the Mississippi River, East St. Louis.

THE GREAT RIVER ROAD ROLLS past limestone bluffs along the Illinois River between Alton and Pere Marquette State Park. In 1998, it became part of a 50-mile stretch designated as a National Scenic Byway. French explorers paddling up the river in the 17th century were said to have seen a painting of a mysterious creature—the legendary *piasa* bird—on its cliffs. Perhaps more the product of a literary imagination than Native American myth, it continues as a symbol of the region.

278

THE LONG, FLAT STRETCHES OF rich bottomland along the Illinois side of the Mississippi are rich in corn, soybeans, flax, and sunflowers.

THE METRO AREA'S BACKYARDS and parks teem with wild-life. Bird-watchers are kept busy year-round since St. Louis, long a pass-through point for human travelers, is also at the heart of many north-south migration routes (PAGES 286-289).

FATHER JACQUES MARQUETTE, a French missionary, explored the upper reaches of the Illinois River in 1673 under the leadership of Louis Jolliet, making Marquette one of the first Europeans to enter Illinois. Pere Marquette State Park, along the Great River Road, is named for him. Hiking trails take visitors through the 8,000-acre park to prime eagle-watching spots.

304 ST. LOUIS

Today, Pierre Laclede and Auguste Chouteau might not recognize the little town they laid out more than 200 years ago. But they would find that their vision of a thriving city on the banks of the Mississippi had come to pass as, over the years, St. Louis has grown into one of America's great cities.

A.G. EDWARDS, INC. ❧ AMDOCS, INC. ❧ ANGELICA CORPORATION ❧ ANHEUSER-BUSCH COMPANIES, INC. ❧ ARCH COAL, INC. ❧ BANK OF AMERICA ❧ BJC HEALTH SYSTEM ❧ THE BOEING COMPANY ❧ BRIDGE INFORMATION SYSTEMS ❧ BROWN SHOE ❧ BRYAN CAVE LLP ❧ BUILDING & CONSTRUCTION TRADES COUNCIL OF ST. LOUIS ❧ CDM FANTASY SPORTS/PRIMARY NETWORK ❧ CITIBANK MORTGAGE ❧ CITY OF ST. LOUIS PORT AUTHORITY ❧ CLAYCO CONSTRUCTION COMPANY ❧ CLAYTON CORPORATION ❧ COIN ACCEPTORS, INC. ❧ COMMERCE BANCSHARES, INC. ❧ DAVE SINCLAIR FORD, INC. ❧ DELTA DENTAL OF MISSOURI ❧ DEMAND MANAGEMENT, INC. ❧ DIMAC CORPORATION ❧ THE EARTHGRAINS COMPANY ❧ EDWARD JONES ❧ EMBASSY SUITES ❧ EMERSON ELECTRIC CO. ❧ ENVISION ❧ ESSE HEALTH ❧ FORD MOTOR COMPANY ❧ FURNITURE BRANDS INTERNATIONAL, INC. ❧ GENAMERICA CORPORATION ❧ GRAYBAR ELECTRIC COMPANY, INC. ❧ GUARANTEE ELECTRICAL COMPANY ❧ HAGER HINGE COMPANY ❧ HAMPTON CORPORATE SUITES ❧ HARRIS-STOWE STATE COLLEGE ❧ HASCO INTERNATIONAL INC. ❧ HEARTLAND BANK ❧ HELLMUTH, OBATA + KASSABAUM, INC. ❧ HUSSMANN CORPORATION ❧ IMO'S PIZZA ❧ INSITUFORM TECHNOLOGIES, INC. ❧ INTERIM SERVICES INC. ❧ JCPENNEY ❧ JEWISH FEDERATION OF ST. LOUIS ❧ KELLWOOD COMPANY ❧ KMOX NEWS/TALK 1120 ❧ THE KOMAN GROUP/ KOMAN PROPERTIES, INC. ❧ KRANSON INDUSTRIES ❧ KSDK-NEWSCHANNEL 5 ❧ LABARGE, INC. ❧ MALLINCKRODT INC. ❧ MARKETING DIRECT, INC. ❧ MARRIOTT PAVILION— HOTEL ❧ MARY INSTITUTE AND SAINT LOUIS COUNTRY DAY SCHOOL ❧ McCORMACK BARON & ASSOCIATES ❧ MERCANTILE BANCORPORATION INC. ❧ METROPOLITAN ST. LOUIS SEWER DISTRICT ❧ MILLS & PARTNERS, INC. ❧ MONSANTO COMPANY ❧ NOOTER CORPORATION ❧ NU-CHEM, INC. ❧ PLAZA MOTORS ❧ PPC INTERNATIONAL, L.L.C. ❧ RALSTON PURINA COMPANY ❧ R.G. BRINKMANN CONSTRUCTION COMPANY ❧ SACRED HEART SCHOOLS ❧ ST. ELIZABETH'S HOSPITAL ❧ THE ST. LOUIS AMERICAN ❧ ST. LOUIS COMMUNITY COLLEGE'S CENTER FOR BUSINESS, INDUSTRY & LABOR ❧ ST. LOUIS RAMS ❧ THE ST. LOUIS REGIONAL CHAMBER & GROWTH ASSOCIATION ❧ ST. LOUIS UNION STATION ❧ SAINT LOUIS UNIVERSITY ❧ SCHNUCK MARKETS, INC. ❧ SINCLAIR BROADCAST GROUP ❧ SOLUTIA INC. ❧ SOUTH SIDE NATIONAL BANK IN ST. LOUIS ❧ SOUTHERN ILLINOIS UNIVERSITY EDWARDSVILLE ❧ SOUTHWESTERN BELL ❧ SPARTECH CORPORATION ❧ SRHD ❧ SSM HEALTH CARE ❧ SUNNEN PRODUCTS COMPANY ❧ SUTTLE MINDLIN ❧ SYKES ENTERPRISES, INCORPORATED ❧ SYLLOGISTEKS ❧ TELCON ASSOCIATES OF ST. LOUIS, INC. ❧ TENET HEALTHCARE SAINT LOUIS ❧ THOMAS ROOF, INC. ARCHITEKTS ❧ TONY'S, INC. ❧ TOWERS PERRIN ❧ TRIAD MANUFACTURING, INC. ❧ UNIGRAPHICS SOLUTIONS INC. ❧ UNIGROUP, INC. ❧ U.S. TITLE GUARANTY COMPANY, INC. ❧ VATTEROTT COLLEGE AND CEDAR CREEK CONFERENCE CENTER ❧ WEHRENBERG THEATRES ❧ WIEGMANN & ASSOCIATES INC. ❧ WILLIS ❧ WORLD WIDE TECHNOLOGY, INC. ❧

A LOOK AT THE CORPORATIONS, BUSINESSES, PROFESSIONAL GROUPS, AND COMMUNITY SERVICE ORGANIZATIONS THAT HAVE MADE THIS BOOK POSSIBLE. THEIR STORIES—OFFERING AN INFORMAL CHRONICLE OF THE LOCAL BUSINESS COMMUNITY—ARE ARRANGED ACCORDING TO THE DATE THEY WERE ESTABLISHED IN ST. LOUIS.

[1818]   Sacred Heart Schools

[1818]   Saint Louis University

[1823]   City of St. Louis Port Authority

[1836]   The St. Louis Regional Chamber & Growth Association

[1847]   Bank of America

[1849]   Hager Hinge Company

[1852]   Anheuser-Busch Companies, Inc.

[1855]   Mercantile Bancorporation Inc.

[1857]   Harris-Stowe State College

[1859]   Mary Institute and Saint Louis Country Day School

[1867]   Mallinckrodt Inc.

[1871]   Edward Jones

[1872]   SSM Health Care

[1873]   Bryan Cave LLP

[1875]   St. Elizabeth's Hospital

[1878]   Angelica Corporation

[1878]   Brown Shoe

[1878]   Southwestern Bell

[1887]   A.G. Edwards, Inc.

[1887]   Heartland Bank

[1890]   Emerson Electric Co.

[1891]   South Side National Bank in St. Louis

[1894]   Ralston Purina Company

[1894]   St. Louis Union Station

[1896]   Nooter Corporation

SACRED HEART SCHOOLS

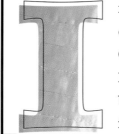

IN 1800, MADELEINE SOPHIE BARAT ESTABLISHED A NEW RELIGIOUS order, the Society of the Sacred Heart, in Paris, France. One of the early members of the order was St. Rose Philippine Duchesne. Born in 1769, she was the first to bring Sacred Heart education to America, introducing it in St. Charles, Missouri in 1818. ¶ Today, there are 139

CLOCKWISE FROM TOP LEFT:
AT THE ACADEMY OF THE SACRED HEART, GRADUATING EIGHTH-GRADE GIRLS DANCE THE MAYPOLE—A MUCH LOVED TRADITION—FOLLOWING MAY CROWNING AND AS PART OF GRADUATION CEREMONIES. SECOND-GRADE GIRLS ALSO TAKE PART IN THIS BEAUTIFUL TRIBUTE TO SPRING AND TO NEW BEGINNINGS.

VILLA DUCHESNE OPENED ITS DOORS IN OCTOBER 1929. THE SCHOOL, WITH ITS FRENCH CHATEAU-STYLE, WAS CONSTRUCTED OF MISSOURI LIMESTONE WITH TWIN NORMAN TOWERS AND WAS DEDICATED TO ST. MADELEINE SOPHIE BARAT, FOUNDRESS OF THE SOCIETY OF THE SACRED HEART.

NOTED ST. LOUIS ARTIST JOHN PILS WAS COMMISSIONED TO CAPTURE THE ACADEMY OF THE SACRED HEART'S CAMPUS, AS VIEWED FROM THE HISTORIC FRONT ENTRANCE ON SECOND STREET.

Sacred Heart schools in 35 countries around the world. Twenty-one of these schools are in the United States, two in the St. Louis area: the Academy of the Sacred Heart in St. Charles, founded by St. Philippine Duchesne; and Villa Duchesne/Oak Hill, located in west St. Louis County.

All the Sacred Heart schools in the United States are united in one philosophy. In 1975, the system formally outlined five goals that shape the framework for a Sacred Heart education. With these goals, the Sacred Heart schools commit to educating students to an active faith in God, a deep respect for intellectual values, social awareness that impels to action, the building of community as a Christian value, and personal growth in an atmosphere of wise freedom.

The two St. Louis-area schools share these values, along with the heritage of St. Philippine Duchesne, who was beatified on May 12, 1940, and canonized on July 3, 1988—one of only four American saints. These Sacred Heart schools exemplify their commitment to glorifying—and radiating—the love of the heart of Jesus.

ACADEMY OF THE SACRED HEART

St. Philippine Duchesne established a boarding school and day school in a cramped log house in St. Charles in 1818. Moving to Florissant for a few years, the religious returned to the site in 1828, and, in 1835, built a three-story brick convent and school, the Academy of the Sacred Heart. After St. Philippine Duchesne died in 1852, she was buried on

the school grounds, where her shrine still stands today.

Her small school, much enlarged over time, is now the largest independent, private elementary school in the St. Louis area, with nearly 700 children from pre-kindergarten through eighth grade. Originally, the school was an all-girl institution that included a high school and boarding school. In 1972, the secondary school was closed, but that fall saw the first classes of boys enrolled in elementary grades. Today, students attend classes on a 10-acre campus that includes 32 classrooms, two computer labs (Macintosh and PC), a fine arts building, and a newly renovated science wing with two state-of-the-art laboratories. Emphasis on science and math, foreign language (French study begins in the primary grades; Spanish is offered in fifth through eighth grades), and computer skills ensures that Academy graduates are well prepared for challenging high school curricula.

An important value of the Academy is living out the Sacred Heart goal of social awareness. From oldest to youngest, children learn the importance of social justice through various long-standing activities: the Christmas Basket Mass and Mission Day; clothing, toy, and food drives; bake sales; and new efforts such as the First Friday of Prayer and monthly visits to a nearby soup kitchen. Moneys raised throughout the year are donated to more than 50 agencies locally, nationally, and worldwide.

Children also enjoy maintaining long-cherished Academy traditions, such as the Feasts of St. Madeleine Sophie Barat and St. Philippine Duchesne, the Lily Procession, the Maypole Dance

spring, and the May Crowning Ceremony.

VILLA DUCHESNE/OAK HILL

Villa Duchesne, a Catholic independent elementary and secondary school located in west St. Louis County, was established in 1929. The school was dedicated to St. Madeleine Sophie Barat, foundress of the Society of the Sacred Heart. In keeping with her vision, Villa Duchesne/Oak Hill school educates the individual to find meaning in his or her life and to be an active influence in building a world of peace and justice.

In 1958, a magnificent chapel was added where students could worship, and a student activities building followed several years later. In 1971, the Oak Hill buildings were constructed on the Villa Duchesne campus and boys were admitted. The school became known as Villa Duchesne/Oak Hill. In the late '80s the Duchesne Building, which was named in honor of St. Philippine Duchesne, was added to

the lower campus, along with a 400-meter track and the state-of-the-art Fleming Science Center. Presently, the Learning and Resource Center is being constructed for students in junior kindergarten (JK) through sixth grade as part of the existing Duchesne Building.

Villa Duchesne/Oak Hill is part of the network of 21 Sacred Heart Schools in the United States that teach the common goals of faith development, intellectual values, social action, building community, and personal growth.

First established as a boarding school and day school for girls, today Villa Duchesne/Oak Hill enrolls 395 boys and girls in the lower school (JK-6) and 376 girls in grades seven through twelve. The school has a strong college preparatory curriculum and students consistently win top academic awards. The Villa Duchesne Service Learning Program provides opportunity for students to serve the community, to apply

skills and understanding developed in the classroom to experiences in their community, and to develop leadership, respectability, and maturity.

Villa Duchesne/Oak Hill treasures its past through the continuation of annual ceremonies and traditions such as First Holy Communion for second graders; feast days, with their delightful *goûters*; the May ceremony; and occasional *congés*.

With a history as rich as the city itself, Sacred Heart Schools will continue to play an important role in the education of children in the St. Louis area for many years to come.

SAINT LOUIS UNIVERSITY

ESTABLISHED IN 1818, SAINT LOUIS UNIVERSITY WAS THE FIRST institution of higher education west of the Mississippi River. From the beginning, this Catholic Jesuit school—the second oldest of all Jesuit institutions in the United States—dedicated itself to excellence. Today, the university continues this tradition with fine undergraduate, graduate, and professional degree programs, which it offers to more than 11,000 students on its three campuses.

Over the years, Saint Louis University has trained national and world leaders. University alumni have served as the U.S. surgeon general, U.S. attorney general, and members of Congress, and more than 95,000 alumni live in all 50 states and in 134 countries. The university has also been an integral part of the St. Louis community, training generations of local leaders. More than 40 percent of all attorneys and 25 percent of all physicians in the Greater St. Louis area are Saint Louis University graduates.

"My vision is to establish and maintain Saint Louis University as the finest Catholic university in the United States, while fulfilling the university's corporate purposes of teaching, research, and community service," says the Reverend Lawrence Biondi, S.J., who has served as university president since September 1987.

PROMISE FOR THE FUTURE

The university is composed of 13 colleges and schools and 19 centers and institutes that educate undergraduates and graduates in the arts and sciences, medicine, law, philosophy and letters, business and administration, engineering and aviation, nursing, social service, allied health professions, public health, professional studies, and public service. Altogether, the university offers some 80 programs of study.

Saint Louis University has three campuses, including the Frost campus, located on Grand Boulevard in the midtown area of St. Louis, which has been the university's home since 1888. A mile down Grand is the Health Sciences Center. And the university also has a campus in Madrid, Spain, which has been recognized by Spain as an official foreign university, the first U.S. institution ever recognized in this way.

Through all of its programs, the university strongly supports effective teaching. On its faculty are 1,192 full-time and 1,851 part-time members, with 30 endowed chairs and nine professorships. More than 100 Jesuits also live, teach, and minister at Saint Louis University.

To facilitate teaching, the university maintains a small class size; the average undergraduate class has only 22 students, and the student-to-teacher ratio is 16-to-1. And to make it possible for all qualified students to attend, the university offers generous scholarship assistance. In 1998-1999, 83 percent of students received financial aid.

Many programs offered by the university have won national recognition. According to *U.S. News & World Report*, the School of Law's health law program ranks second in the United States, and Parks College of Engineering and Aviation ranks in the top 15 engineering schools in the country.

CONTINUING THE TRADITION OF EXCELLENCE THAT BEGAN AT THE INSTITUTION NEARLY 200 YEARS AGO, SAINT LOUIS UNIVERSITY WILL BE HELPING TO TRAIN THE LEADERS OF TOMORROW FOR MANY YEARS TO COME.

BOTH BARRON'S *Best Buys in College Education* AND *U.S. News & World Report's America's Best Colleges* GUIDE FOR 1999 LIST THE UNIVERSITY AMONG THE INSTITUTIONS NATIONALLY THAT GIVE PARENTS AND STUDENTS THE BEST EDUCATIONAL VALUE. IN ADDITION, THEY GET A TRUELY UNIQUE UNIVERSITY MASCOT, THE BILLIKEN.

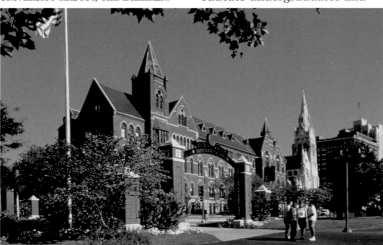

SUPPORTING INNOVATIVE SCHOLARSHIP

As part of its fundamental mission, Saint Louis University also values its faculty's active research efforts. In 1998, research grant and contract research revenue reached an all-time high of $19.1 million. The university is one of only three Catholic universities to receive the Carnegie Foundation's Research II classification.

University researchers have been on the cutting edge of important scientific issues. At the School of Medicine, scientists have teamed up with NASA in studies that will improve the understanding of osteoporosis. Researchers in the Vaccine Evaluation Unit have been working to find an AIDS vaccine. On the clinical side, faculty members are pioneers in organ transplantation, having performed the Midwest's first heart transplant in 1972, the first heart and lung transplant in 1994, and the first split-liver transplant in 1995.

In the university's department of earth and atmospheric sciences, researchers are conducting studies to understand earthquakes and their causes. And the Health Sciences Center is a leading center for research in such areas as chronic disease prevention, the neurosciences, and geriatrics.

IN THE JESUIT TRADITION

In keeping with its Catholic Jesuit identity, Saint Louis University prepares its students to contribute to society and to lead efforts for social change. During 1998-1999, students, faculty, and staff performed more than 240,000 hours of community service. Some 6,000 members of the university community participated in outreach programs that included free legal clinics, open-door health clinics, and neighborhood education programs.

Also in 1998-1999, the Community Outreach Center provided service opportunities to some 700 students. These

programs included Bigs and Littles, a program in which university students paired with at-risk children; tutoring services for children ages 5 to 14 through the Blumeyer Community Program; and Morro House, which offered tutoring to children in the St. Louis public schools.

OTHER IMPORTANT ASSETS

Along with its core strengths, Saint Louis University has other important assets. Both Barron's *Best Buys in College Education* and *U.S. News & World Report*'s *America's Best Colleges* guide for 1999 list the university among the institutions nationally that give parents and students the best educational value. Thanks in part to the 1998 sale of Saint Louis University Hospital to Tenet Healthcare Corp., the university has the 35th-largest endowment among U.S. universities and the second largest among Catholic universities.

The university is still growing, with new buildings such as

the state-of-the-art McDonnell Douglas Hall, home of Parks College of Engineering and Aviation. The university also has added a host of new amenities, including parks, parking garages, clock towers, signage, and statuary.

Continuing the tradition of excellence that began at the institution nearly 200 years ago, Saint Louis University will be helping to train the leaders of tomorrow for many years to come.

CITY OF ST. LOUIS PORT AUTHORITY

EVER SINCE PIERRE LACLÈDE AND AUGUSTE CHOUTEAU founded St. Louis on the Mississippi River bluffs in 1764, riverfront commerce has played a vital role in the city's growth and prosperity. Over the years, early modes of transport—rafts, cargo-carrying keelboats, and similar flatboats of shallow draft—gave way to newer forms

of river transit, such as steam packets.

In 1822, the first steamboat docked at St. Louis; that same year, St. Louis became incorporated. In those days, all activities at the port were supervised by a harbormaster or wharfmaster. One of the first regulations passed in the newly incorporated city was Ordinance #20, which made the position of wharfmaster official.

Early on, the Mississippi River was the object of study and the target of many attempts at remedial action. Due to the hazards of unknown depths and shifting channels, navigation was left to the adventurous, who braved these dangers before the development of present-day navigation equipment.

THE MID-CONTINENT SWITCHYARD
Today, St. Louis functions as the mid-continent switchyard for the national waterways. The Port of St. Louis lies at the center of a 7,000-mile, inland waterway system, which connects the city with industrial centers in 20 states. The Port of St. Louis is also at the head of year-round, open-water navigation on the Mississippi.

The St. Louis Port District serves the general public primarily as a distribution facility, where products are brought in by rail and truck, loaded onto barges, and shipped to points both inside and outside the United States. These shipments include grain, coal, petroleum products, and chemicals. Much of the harbor's activity includes warehousing and manufacturing, around-the-clock switching and fleeting services, and barge cleaning and repair services.

Altogether, St. Louis is home to the second-largest inland port for tonnage in the United States. More than 31 million tons of cargo were shipped through the port's facilities in 1997, and every year some 90 million tons of cargo move through the port.

PROMOTING WELFARE AND DEVELOPMENT
The City of St. Louis Port Authority—managed by the St. Louis Development Corporation, which is under the leadership of Michael Jones, deputy mayor for development of the City of St. Louis, in cooperation with a seven-member port committee—works directly with federal, state, and local agencies to promote general welfare and industrial development and to increase the volume of commerce within the Port District.

The Port Authority staff stands ready to answer questions from members of the public who need information about port-related matters, such as moving products, finding a towing company, or arranging for the use of heavy equipment. Operations Manager Nick Nichols frequently hears stories about people who had no idea how to secure the use of a crane or a dock until they contacted the Port Authority.

Nichols also points to the use of the port for recreational activity. The levee on the Mississippi River is paved with granite stones and houses a riverfront promenade. Paddle wheel steamboats tie up at the levee, ready to take St. Louis' many visitors for a ride on the mighty Mississippi.

CLOCKWISE FROM TOP:
THE CITY OF ST. LOUIS MUNICIPAL TERMINAL IS OPERATED BY BEELMAN RIVER TERMINALS, AND IS THE LARGEST GENERAL CARGO DOCK IN THE AREA.

VISITING PASSENGER VESSELS, PRESIDENT CASINO ON THE ADMIRAL, MCDONALD'S RESTAURANT, ROBERT E. LEE RESTAURANT, AND GATEWAY RIVERBOAT CRUISES ARE ATTRACTIONS AT THE CITY OF ST. LOUIS CENTRAL RIVERFRONT PROMENADE AND LEVEE.

LOUISIANA DOCK CO. HANDLES BULK COMMODITIES, SUCH AS COAL. THE TERMINAL IS DESIGNED TO UNLOAD APPROXIMATELY THREE UNIT TRAINS AND LOAD ONE 15-BARGE TOW PER DAY. STORAGE CAPACITY AT THE TERMINAL IS 500,000 TONS.

314

ILLIAM GREENLEAF ELIOT, A PROMINENT Unitarian minister in St. Louis, was also an educational pioneer who founded Washington University in 1853. In 1859, he took another bold step. Believing that a young woman was "a rational being, who has a mind to think

KEVIN GRACE

with," he established the first girls' school west of the Appalachians: Mary Institute, named for his daughter, Mary, who had died at age 17.

From the start, the school prospered, moving in 1878 from its Lucas Place location to a larger building on Locust Street. In 1902, the school moved west again, this time to Lake and Waterman avenues. Then, in 1928, an alumna donated 22 acres, Washington University added 18 more, and Mary Institute soon had a new campus in the country at Ladue and Warson roads.

Meanwhile in 1854, a school for men had also settled in the country. Smith Academy—an earlier boys' school also founded by Eliot—had closed because of concern over the city's polluted air. Since 1917, Smith's successor school—Saint Louis Country Day School (CDS)—had been operating in an old North County estate under a new guiding philosophy: fresh air, open space, and freedom from city noise. But, by the late 1940s, noise from the jets at nearby Lambert Field was shaking the CDS buildings. This problem was corrected in 1958, when CDS moved to a new campus—also in the country—on a large parcel of land adjacent to Mary Institute. Steps toward curricular coordination between the two institutions came early, and most senior classes were fully coordinated by the late 1970s. Finally, a full-scale alliance was formed in 1992 with the creation of a single school—Mary Institute and Saint Louis Country Day School (MICDS)—that had one board, administration, and faculty, along with a common curriculum.

Today, MICDS is a coeducational school for students from junior kindergarten through grade 12, with a coordinate model for grades five through eight. The Lower School of MICDS—the Ronald S. Beasley School—has been coeducational since 1969. Total enrollment for the 1998-1999 school year was 1,215, with 155 faculty members, small class size, and an 8-to-1 student-to-teacher ratio.

MICDS offers a challenging, liberal-arts-based academic program designed to prepare young men and women for college. For several years, MICDS has been the most active participant in the Advanced Placement program in the Midwest Region of the College Board. Students are also encouraged to pursue interests in the visual and performing arts, athletics, and other activities that will help them develop their talents and leadership skills.

Over the years, Mary Institute and Saint Louis Country Day School have produced outstanding graduates, including former U.S. Senators John Danforth and Thomas Eagleton, former Washington University Chancellor William Danforth, Governor Pete Wilson of California, Olympic gold medalist

Harriet Bland Green, author Marion Rombauer Becker, and Dorothy Walker Bush, mother of former President George Bush.

Today, MICDS is shaping a new generation of stellar graduates. The school's mission is to prepare responsible men and women—who can think critically and stand for what is right—to meet challenges confidently, embrace all people with compassion, and live lives of purpose and service. Says Head of School Matthew Gossage, "Our vision at MICDS rests on the philosophy that academic and personal growth can go hand in hand in the education of young people."

KRISTEN PETERSON

CLOCKWISE FROM TOP:
TODAY, MARY INSTITUTE AND SAINT LOUIS COUNTRY DAY SCHOOL (MICDS) IS A COEDUCATIONAL SCHOOL FOR STUDENTS FROM JUNIOR KINDERGARTEN THROUGH GRADE 12, WITH A COORDINATE MODEL FOR GRADES FIVE THROUGH EIGHT.

THE SCHOOL'S MISSION IS TO PREPARE RESPONSIBLE MEN AND WOMEN—WHO CAN THINK CRITICALLY AND STAND FOR WHAT IS RIGHT—TO MEET CHALLENGES CONFIDENTLY, EMBRACE ALL PEOPLE WITH COMPASSION, AND LIVE LIVES OF PURPOSE AND SERVICE.

MICDS OFFERS A CHALLENGING, LIBERAL-ARTS-BASED ACADEMIC PROGRAM DESIGNED TO PREPARE YOUNG MEN AND WOMEN FOR COLLEGE.

The St. Louis Regional Chamber & Growth Association

CLOCKWISE FROM TOP:

THE CERVANTES CONVENTION CENTER AT AMERICA'S CENTER HAS 502,000 SQUARE FEET OF CONTIGUOUS EXHIBIT SPACE, WHICH CAN BE DIVIDED INTO SIX SEPARATE EXHIBIT HALLS, INCLUDING THE 162,313-SQUARE-FOOT DOMED STADIUM/EXHIBIT HALL.

THE LIVING WORLD IS A MAJOR ANIMAL EXHIBIT AT THE SAINT LOUIS ZOO. THE ZOO IS RECOGNIZED AS ONE OF THE TOP ZOOS IN THE WORLD, AND ONE OF THE FEW FREE ZOOS IN THE NATION.

THE 70,000-SEAT TRANS WORLD DOME, HOME TO THE ST. LOUIS RAMS, IS TREMENDOUSLY FLEXIBLE, AND CAN BE DIVIDED IN HALF THROUGH A FLOOR-TO-CEILING, ACOUSTICALLY SOUND CURTAIN.

WHEN MARK MCGWIRE MADE HOME RUN HISTORY in 1998, the whole world took notice of St. Louis. In critical but less visible ways, the St. Louis Regional Chamber & Growth Association (RCGA) is also putting St. Louis on the national and international map through a host of innovative programs, regional initiatives, and civic improvement ventures.

The mission of the St. Louis RCGA is to unite the region's business community and to engage dynamic business and civic leadership to develop and sustain a world-class economy and community. The RCGA's overall purpose is to provide an inclusive voice for the region's business community, and to leverage the business community's resources to achieve constructive change in the region.

In carrying out this agenda, the RCGA is working to fulfill the needs of its 4,000 members— businesses, hospitals, universities, and nonprofit organizations— which account for some 40 percent of the local workforce. The RCGA serves a 12-county, bistate area, with a total population of 2.5 million.

"The RCGA achieves its mission through the dedicated efforts of a wide range of volunteers," says Richard C.D. Fleming, president and chief executive officer. "In addition to our board of directors, nearly 2,000 volunteers help the RCGA carry out the programs that members request by serving on numerous councils and committees. It is the dedication of our members to the region that makes this organization a success."

◀ A LONG HISTORY IN ST. LOUIS

In 1836, the original St. Louis Chamber of Commerce was established in downtown St. Louis to promote the city as an early national center of commerce, coordinate business growth, and regulate trade. Over the years, the name of the organization changed to the Chamber of Commerce of Metropolitan St. Louis, but the focus remained the same.

Then in 1973, the Chamber merged with the St. Louis Regional Industrial Development Corporation and the St. Louis Research Council; three years later, the new RCGA also affiliated with Illinois Metro East, an Illinois-based industrial development organization.

Today, the RCGA is located in One Metropolitan Square in downtown St. Louis. Its staff of more than 50 employees is split across four major functional areas: the Office of the President; Public Policy and Technology; Economic Development; and Regional Business Services.

A HOST OF RECENT ACHIEVEMENTS

Over the past decade, the RCGA has been instrumental in a number of major developments that have benefited the bistate area. In 1989, for example, the RCGA helped to raise funds and foster community support for the highly successful, $150 million MetroLink light-rail system, which has far exceeded ridership projections. Five years later, the RCGA helped to bring to fruition two crucial Illinois projects: the new, $118 million Clark Bridge

ST. LOUIS CONVENTION & VISITORS COMMISSION

◀▼ BARLOW PRODUCTION

BARLOW PRODUCTION

at Alton, and the $300 million Alton Lock and Dam replacement project.

In January 1995, the RCGA launched the Campaign for a Greater St. Louis, which raised $14 million from more than 200 investors to retain and expand existing businesses, as well as attract new ones to the region. At the time, this campaign was the most successful regional economic development funding program ever undertaken in the nation. To date, more than 81,100 net new jobs have been added—well ahead of the employment goals set by the campaign committee in partnership with the Greater St. Louis Economic Development Council. The target of the program is to create 100,000 net new jobs by the end of 2000.

In 1997, the RCGA actively supported the Missouri State Historic Preservation Tax Credit legislation, providing a tax credit against state income tax equal to 25 percent of the cost of rehabilitation of historic properties. This tax credit constitutes the most aggressive incentive in the nation for private investment in historic properties.

Recently, the RCGA has also targeted infrastructure improvements as a major priority, and has seen some critical accomplishments in this area. Recently, the FAA approved a $2.6 billion expansion and modernization of Lambert-St. Louis International Airport. And in November

1998, the RCGA spearheaded the civic campaign leading to overwhelming voter approval for the Page Avenue extension to Highway 94.

PROGRAMS FOR CONTINUED GROWTH

The St. Louis RCGA has also established programs to support growing industry clusters in the region. One of these is the Technology Gateway Alliance, formed to grow and support St. Louis-area high-technology firms. The Technology Gateway Alliance followed the RCGA's sponsorship—with Deloitte & Touche—of the annual RCGA Fast 50 Technology Awards, which recognize the top 50 fastest-growing technology companies in the region, and a series of in-depth studies by Celeste & Sabety of the area's high-technology potential and needs.

Through its Environmental Council, the RCGA has also been active in making the St. Louis region a better place to live and work through improved regional environmental quality. In 1996, the EPA presented its top regional award to the St. Louis Regional Clean Air Partnership, which was established in 1995 by the RCGA, the American Lung Association, and other regional partners. In 1998, the RCGA successfully led the civic community in supporting passage of a bill in the Missouri legislature allowing the sale of re-formulated gasoline in St. Louis.

The RCGA also works to improve community life through a number of other efforts: Forward St. Louis, a program which advances legislative initiatives dealing with regional issues; Build Up Greater St. Louis, an outgrowth of the RCGA's Infrastructure Council, which marshals regional business resources and advocates infrastructure improvements; and the RCGA's Regional Leadership Exchange, which builds a St. Louis regional community through shared examinations of other regions of the country by means of an annual leadership trip and a local leadership retreat.

"The St. Louis RCGA and its membership are at the heart of a private/public partnership to position the St. Louis region to compete for brainpower and distinction as a place on its way up—combining a vibrant, new economic orientation with our unique historic headquarters role," says Fleming.

CLOCKWISE FROM TOP LEFT: FOUNDED IN 1818, SAINT LOUIS UNIVERSITY IS THE OLDEST INSTITUTION OF HIGHER LEARNING WEST OF THE MISSISSIPPI RIVER. YEAR AFTER YEAR, THE ST. LOUIS REGION'S BROAD RANGE OF EXCELLENT COLLEGES, UNIVERSITIES, TWO-YEAR COLLEGES, AND PROFESSIONAL AND VOCATIONAL SCHOOLS ENHANCES THE QUALITY AND SKILLS OF THE REGION'S WORKFORCE.

LAMBERT-ST. LOUIS INTERNATIONAL AIRPORT IS THE WORLD'S SECOND-FASTEST-GROWING MAJOR AIRPORT. THE AIRPORT WILL SOON UNDERGO A $2.6-BILLION EXPANSION ADDING A NEW THIRD PARALLEL RUNWAY.

THE 630-FT. GATEWAY ARCH IS THE WORLD'S TALLEST MANMADE MONUMENT. DEDICATED IN 1965, THE ARCH SYMBOLIZES ST. LOUIS TO THE WORLD, AND IS THE CENTERPIECE OF THE JEFFERSON NATIONAL EXPANSION MEMORIAL, A 91-ACRE NATIONAL PARK.

BANK OF AMERICA

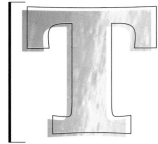

THE NEW BANK OF AMERICA MAY BE THE LARGEST BANK IN the United States, but its heritage is rooted in hundreds of communities across the country. In St. Louis, those roots go back to 1847, when the bank opened its doors to serve the bustling river town that was quickly emerging as a center of commerce in the region. ¶ As a result of its strong local ties, Bank of America works hard to bring the strength of its global capabilities home to each of the communities in which it operates, helping to make lives better and easier for all who live there.

"Our size, breadth, resources, and capabilities give us a challenge, an opportunity, and a responsibility to help build stronger communities in every town, city, and country in which we do business," says David Darnell, president of Bank of America in the Midwest.

REDEFINING CONVENIENCE
Created by the merger of NationsBank and Bank of America in 1998, the new Bank of America serves 30 million households in the United States and more than 2 million businesses through a network of nearly 5,000 banking centers in 21 states and the District of Columbia.

WITH FUNDING BY BANK OF AMERICA AND ITS SMALL BUSINESS INVESTMENT COMPANY, ST. LOUIS ENTREPRENEUR LEROY WRIGHT ACQUIRED HIS LARGEST COMPETITOR, MAKING HIS COMPANY, TLC NEXT GENERATION, THE AREA'S LARGEST CELLULAR PHONE RETAILER (TOP).

AS PART OF ITS $100 MILLION COMMITMENT TO DOWNTOWN ST. LOUIS, BANK OF AMERICA ACQUIRED THE HISTORIC CUPPLES STATION COMPLEX (FOREGROUND) WITH PARTNER MCCORMACK BARON. THE BANK IS DEVELOPING THE WESTERN HALF OF THE COMPLEX INTO UPSCALE OFFICE AND RETAIL SPACE (BOTTOM).

The bank also has international offices in 38 foreign countries, and serves business customers in 190 countries around the world. With more than 14,000 ATMs and the most advanced access to products and services through computer and telephone technology, Bank of America is committed to

redefining convenience for its customers.

Bank of America is a national leader in virtually every consumer financial service business, including card services, mortgage, investing, and wealth management. The bank loans more money—and makes more loans—to small businesses than any other bank in the country and is number one in corporate banking relationships.

UNMATCHED CAPABILITIES
What that means for St. Louis consumers, businesses, and communities is more resources to help them realize their dreams. For businesses, Bank of America provides a continuum of products and services to fuel every stage of their growth, whether they are just starting out, preparing for a major expansion, considering an acquisition, or taking the company public.

Bank of America has brought new capabilities to business and corporate customers in the form of access to public markets (equity and capital markets) and investment banking services. As a result, large corporations that used to have to go to East Coast investment banks for complex financial transactions can now obtain those services in St. Louis.

Small business also is big business at Bank of America. In St. Louis, Bank of America is the top-producing SBA lender in the region. It also operates the only bank-owned Small Business Investment Company that invests venture capital in small and minority-owned companies.

Individual consumers also benefit from unprecedented access and convenience, with 246 ATMs and 68 banking

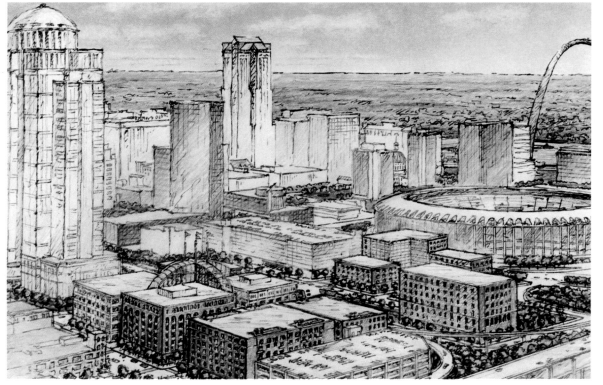

centers, including 18 banking centers located inside Schnuck Markets, Inc. stores. In-store banking centers are staffed seven days a week and have extended evening hours. Telephone banking and on-line banking give retail and commercial customers access to the bank and their accounts at any time of the day or night.

"We want to be there for our customers no matter when or where they may need us," Darnell says.

COMMUNITY INVESTMENT

Bank of America has a long-standing tradition of community investment through financial support of organizations and institutions that promote education, community investment, and the arts and culture.

"Support of our communities is part of our corporate culture; it is the heart and soul of our company," says Darnell. "We recognize that our company is only as strong as our communities, and we understand that the reason a bank exists in the first place is to help make communities stronger."

Bank of America partners with hundreds of local organizations and agencies in St. Louis to build affordable housing and develop small businesses—key ingredients for strong, stable neighborhoods.

Since 1997, the bank has made more than $100 million in loans and investments to stimulate the creation of affordable housing, economic development, and small-business development in St. Louis.

In late 1998, Bank of America joined a partnership of community groups, banks, and government agencies to revitalize nine St. Louis-area neighborhoods. The bank pledged an additional $150 million in loans and investments toward this unprecedented initiative to create sustainable neighborhoods.

The bank has also committed an additional $100 million in capital to jump-start the revitalization of downtown St. Louis.

As part of that investment, Bank of America has acquired three buildings on Washington Avenue, which it is developing into loft apartments. The bank also is the co-owner of the historic Cupples Station complex, along with McCormack Baron & Associates, and will develop the buildings into upscale office and retail space, creating an exciting new doorway to the city from the south.

ADVOCATE FOR EDUCATION

Bank of America also is a strong supporter and advocate for quality education. In St. Louis, the bank has presented substantial grants to Washington University, Harris-Stowe State College, and the University of Missouri-St. Louis. As part of its commitment to education, Bank of America allows its associates to volunteer in the schools up to two hours a week—on company time.

"We believe education is the single most important issue facing all of our communities," says Darnell. "As the largest bank in America, we bear the responsibility to address the educational challenge facing children and families in our communities. As we see it, there is no better investment than in the education of our youth."

N 1849, CHARLES HAGER LEFT GERMANY TO START A NEW LIFE IN America. After settling in St. Louis, he founded a small blacksmithing business that quickly became an American success story. Hager Hinge Company, now celebrating its 150th anniversary, has grown into a major international manufacturer of door-related hardware products. And it remains a

family-owned company, run by the fifth generation of Hagers.

Business is stronger than ever and growing. Since the mid-1980s, sales of Hager products have tripled, with particular strength in eastern Europe and the Middle East. The company attributes this success to three critical factors: the diligent efforts of its workforce of more than 1,000 people at facilities around the world, the loyalty of its customers, and the commitment of its own close-knit family to the business and to each other.

Hager has developed a broad product line that includes commercial and residential hinges,

threshold and weather stripping products, kick plates, pulls, door guards, and door trim products. In all, the company sells 20,000 different products for residential and commercial buildings. "We work hard to serve our customers and to try to understand what the end user in our business wants," says August W. Hager III, chairman of the board, president, and CEO. "We can't be all things to all people, so we focus on what we do best."

THE SCOPE OF THE BUSINESS TODAY

Since the early 1900s, the Hager headquarters has been housed in a complex of 19th-century

buildings in downtown St. Louis, near the Mississippi River. During the 1980s, the company remodeled the space, which now combines a sense of history with an efficient, up-to-date office environment that is listed on the National Register of Historic Places. Some 110 Hager employees work at the St. Louis location.

Other facilities, originally based in St. Louis, have moved elsewhere in the United States and abroad. The company has manufacturing plants in three places: a residential products plant in Greenville, Mississippi; a consumer products plant in Oxford, Alabama; and an architectural division in Montgomery. In addition, Hager has seven distribution centers: a main facility in Montgomery and others in Cincinnati, Los Angeles, Kitchener, Monterrey, Hong Kong, and the United Arab Emirates.

The focus of the three manufacturing plants corresponds to the company's three basic markets. In Hager's consumer business, the company sells packaged hardware to wholesalers who, in turn, market it to retail hardware stores. In its residential business, Hager sells door-related products to customers who prehang doors and frames in single and multifamily housing. The bulk of the company's business is in the third area, the architectural market, in which Hager sells to distributors who specify and bid on supplying commercial hardware for new and existing construction.

A MAJOR MANUFACTURING CHANGE

In 1994, with an increasing amount of imported hardware coming into the United States,

HAGER HINGE COMPANY PRODUCES A VARIETY OF DOOR TRIM PRODUCTS.

Hager took a hard look at its manufacturing processes to see how it could reduce costs. The company decided to make a sweeping change, from a traditional department-based system to a brand-new, cellular approach aimed at turning out high-quality finished products as efficiently as possible. This new method, adapted from Japanese business practices, involves giving responsibility to a group of employees for an entire business unit—from receipt of the steel through packaging. Occasionally, this cell holds a *kaizen* event, in which team members discuss eliminating roadblocks in the system and maximizing efficiency. The company offers incentives based on cell productivity.

"This system has worked very well," says Hager. "Our net operating earnings are up by about 100 percent, and employees absolutely love this new system. Not only do they have more responsibility for their specific job, but they also have more ownership of what their team does."

A History of Progress

The company has come a long way since its early days, when much of its success depended on sales to the growing numbers of farmers. Gradually, its market expanded. When the Panama Canal was built, Hager Hinge supplied custom hinges for the project; World War I also boosted sales. Even during the lean days of the Great Depression, the company managed to stay open and provide jobs for its employees.

Afterwards, sales began to rise again as Hager expanded its market area throughout the United States and Canada. In the early 1960s, the company mounted a highly successful publicity campaign with the slogan "Everything Hinges on Hager." Moving into the commercial market, adopting new technologies, and expanding into Europe and Asia also broadened the company's presence in the global marketplace.

Throughout its history, Hager Hinge has been run by Hager family members, and today, six family members still participate in the firm's daily operations. In addition to August Hager III, family executives include Charles C. Hager Jr., executive vice president and chief operating officer; Ralph J. Hager II, group vice president, sales and marketing; Archer L. Hager II, group vice president, distribution and procurement; Warren Hager, group vice president, architectural sales; and Alice B. Wiegand, group vice president, account services.

In the future, the company will continue to work on its longtime strength of customer service, as it grows its core business. "Obviously, we want to produce a quality product on time and at a competitive price," says August Hager. "That's a great thing to say, but to do that, you have to work on the fundamentals, which means continuous improvement. That is what will keep us competitive past the year 2000."

ANHEUSER-BUSCH COMPANIES, INC.

SINCE ITS FOUNDING IN ST. LOUIS IN 1852, ANHEUSER-BUSCH Companies, Inc. has been marked by a constant, intense focus on one concept: quality. From the company's choice of the finest quality, freshest brewing ingredients, to its marketing efforts, to its environmental policies, Anheuser-Busch has always insisted on the highest standards. This tradition has enabled the firm to grow to become the world's largest brewer, and to be a leader in the container manufacturing, recycling, and family entertainment industries.

A HISTORY OF QUALITY

Anheuser-Busch traces its roots in St. Louis to the Bavarian Brewery, which in its first year of operation produced fewer than 200 barrels of beer. In 1860, the struggling brewery was taken over by Eberhard Anheuser, who, a few years later, brought his son-in-law, Adolphus Busch, into the business. It was Adolphus who began transforming the company into an industry powerhouse, and who is considered its founder.

A brilliant visionary and innovator, Adolphus dreamed of a national beer market and a national beer. As a first step in making that dream come true, he launched the industry's first fleet of refrigerated freight cars. It was also under Adolphus in 1876 that Budweiser was first brewed, using traditional brewing methods and only the finest barley malt, hops, and rice. Twenty years later, still under Adolphus' leadership, the company developed Michelob, which soon became the preeminent American superpremium beer.

Adolphus' son, August A. Busch Sr., led the company during the turbulent eras of World War I and Prohibition. During Prohibition, the company survived and protected the jobs of its employees by making such products as baker's yeast, soft drinks, and Bevo, a non-alcohol, malt-based beverage. One of Adolphus' two grandsons, Adolphus Busch III, guided the company through the end of the Great Depression and World War II. The other grandson, August A. Busch Jr., then led the firm through the postwar era, during which the company first began establishing breweries outside of the St. Louis area.

THE KING OF BEERS

Today, Anheuser-Busch is led by Adolphus' great-grandson, August A. Busch III. Under his guidance, the company has widened its dominance of the beer industry, with a market share approximately twice that of its nearest competitor, while also becoming a growing force in international brewing. In addition, the company has major interests in the packaging and entertainment industries.

Anheuser-Busch now operates 12 breweries, including its original brew site in St. Louis. Budweiser is not only the best-selling brand in the nation, but the best-selling brand in the world. Besides Budweiser, Anheuser-Busch now produces more than 30 brands, including Bud Light, the world's second-leading beer.

Budweiser is brewed in 11 countries, and Anheuser-Busch brands are sold in more than 80 countries worldwide. New links are being forged abroad at a rapid rate, with recent investments and joint ventures in Mexico, China, the United Kingdom, Brazil, Argentina, the Philippines, and Japan.

Over the years, Anheuser-Busch has established several subsidiaries related to its beer operations. Metal Container Corporation, for example, supplies 60 percent of the cans used by Anheuser-Busch and is a significant supplier to the soft drink market as well. In 1978, Anheuser-Busch set up a re-

HARRIS-STOWE STATE COLLEGE HAS
BEEN LOCATED IN MIDTOWN ST. LOUIS
SINCE 1857.

In 1979, by action of the Missouri General Assembly, Harris-Stowe became a state college. Then in 1987, in recognition of the school's African-American heritage, the U.S. Department of Education named it to an elite group: the 120 U.S. institutions designated as Historically Black Colleges and Universities. Over the next 15 years, the college improved its financial condition, expanded its teacher education program to include all levels of pre-secondary teacher education, and added a bachelor's degree program to prepare nonteaching urban specialists. With state support, Harris-Stowe also upgraded its physical plant: a building constructed in 1927 that previously housed Vashon High School.

In 1992, the college commissioned a special study to consider its future mission. This study revealed that there were "significant unmet needs for higher education" in metropolitan St. Louis. Harris-Stowe prepared its Mission Expansion Proposal, which was enacted into law by the Missouri General Assembly and led to the addition of new degree programs.

A NEW BEGINNING

With new programs in place and increasing enrollment, the space constraints on campus became acute. However, room for expansion was severely limited by other educational institutions to the east and west, and a busy thoroughfare to the south. When the federal government announced plans to raze the 53-acre LaClede Town development, just north of Harris-Stowe, and turn the site over to the city, the city agreed to give a 17.5-acre portion of this parcel to Harris-Stowe for $10.

Following the land acquisition, Harris-Stowe developed plans to use the site for a new, $30 million campus. With initial funding provided by a state bond issue, the college dedicated its first new building in the fall of 1998, an 18,000-square-foot library equipped with the latest in computer technology. Five more buildings—an early childhood education and parenting center, a gymnasium and performing arts center, a business administration/classroom building, a student center, and a classroom building for elementary and secondary education programs—will be added by 2004, with the help of generous donations from local businesses.

A BRIGHT FUTURE

Over the years, graduates of Harris-Stowe have gone on to prominence throughout the St. Louis area, including well-known alumnus Julius Hunter, KMOV-TV news anchor. Today, the school's student body consists of some 1,700 students—75 percent of whom are African-American—with an average age of 27. When the new construction is completed, the demographics will probably remain the same, but the campus will be able to accommodate some 4,000 to 5,000 students.

"We are no longer worrying about whether we will be around in the future," Givens says. "Instead, Harris-Stowe State College is focused on positioning itself for the next millennium."

MALLINCKRODT INC.

CONSUMERS WHO STILL THINK OF MALLINCKRODT AS A chemical company need to take another look. Today, Mallinckrodt and its 13,000 employees worldwide are sharply focused on the field of health care. The company had earnings of $2.4 billion in fiscal year 1998 and now supplies medical professionals with the products they need in three critical health care areas: respiratory care, diagnostic imaging, and analgesic pharmaceuticals.

In each of the markets it serves, Mallinckrodt holds a strong leading position, with excellent opportunities for growth. The company ranks number one in respiratory care, with better than one-third of market share. Its endotracheal tubes are used in seven out of 10 general surgeries performed in the United States. It is also the world's largest manufacturer of acetaminophen and the top U.S. supplier of X-ray contrast media.

"Through our dedication to innovation in all of our critically important product areas, Mallinckrodt is well positioned

to accomplish our corporate mission of improving the quality of health care for patients worldwide by providing superior products that sustain breathing, diagnose disease, and relieve pain," says C. Ray Holman, chairman and CEO of Mallinckrodt Inc.

While the focus of the company may have changed in recent years, its corporate philosophy has remained the same since its founding in 1867. The philosophy has at its foundation four core values—integrity, service, achievement, and teamwork. It serves as a guiding principle for the way in which employees deal with their customers and colleagues.

A HISTORY OF PROGRESS

Mallinckrodt, founded by three brothers, began in St. Louis under the name G. Mallinckrodt & Company, Manufacturing Chemists as a manufacturer of fine chemicals used in the production of pharmaceuticals. Upon the death of his two brothers, Edward Mallinckrodt took over the firm and expanded its product line to include anhydrous ammonia for commercial ice plants and chemicals for the brand-new field of photography.

By the 1904 World's Fair, the company was one of the nation's premier chemical producers, making such staple chemicals as chloroform and carbolic acid. When Edward Mallinckrodt, Jr. took over the helm from his father, he broadened the business and instilled in his employees an abiding commitment to quality.

Over the decades, the company continued to develop. During World War II, it produced highly purified uranium compounds for use in the first atomic bomb under a U.S. government contract. In the 1960s, under the leadership of Harold E. Thayer, Mallinckrodt grew from a small, family-run operation into an international company, with a strong role in develop-

At the core of SSMHC-St. Louis are its 8,800 employees and more than 2,000 physicians who serve at SSM's health care facilities conveniently located throughout the St. Louis area. These include SSM Cardinal Glennon Children's Hospital, SSM DePaul Health Center, SSM St. Joseph Health Center in St. Charles, SSM St. Joseph Hospital West in Lake St. Louis, SSM St. Joseph Hospital of Kirkwood, SSM St. Mary's Health Center, SSM Rehab, and SSM Health & Wellness. SSMHC-St. Louis also includes three medical groups—SSM Medical Group, SSM St. Charles Clinic Medical Group, and SSM DePaul Medical Group.

With locations in virtually every part of the St. Louis area, SSMHC-St. Louis and its physicians provide a full continuum of health services to meet every health need, including maternity care expertise to manage high-risk pregnancies and normal deliveries with special care and attention; centers of excellence for innovative knee and hip surgery; expertise to perform intricate heart surgeries of all kinds; advanced cancer treatment programs; specialized neonatal care to give premature infants a chance to grow up healthy; mental health services, including an adolescent residential treatment program; complete rehab services to help people to live again following debilitating injuries; drug or

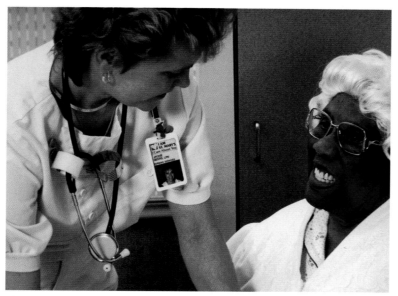

alcohol abuse treatment, including the area's only rapid narcotic detoxification program to cleanse patients' bodies of narcotics quickly while they sleep; and comprehensive home care.

A consistent focus on partnership and innovation has become a hallmark of SSM Health Care-St. Louis. SSM St. Mary's Health Center, for instance, is the home of the St. Louis University School of Medicine's Department of Obstetrics and Gynecology. This relationship enables St. Mary's to provide an unmatched array of advanced OB and women's services, including a neonatal nursery staffed around the clock by newborn specialists from SSM Cardinal Glennon Children's Hospital. Partnership is also the foundation of the Sarah Community, a new

concept in retirement living that offers independent living, skilled nursing, and assisted living facilities in a modern environment on SSM DePaul Health Center's campus. The unique project is sponsored by the Franciscan Sisters of Mary and four other orders of Catholic sisters.

SSM Health Care-St. Louis also strives to care for people in the most convenient and appropriate setting. For example, the superior pediatric care for which SSM Cardinal Glennon Children's Hospital is known nationally is available in communities across St. Louis through SSM Glennon Care for Kids sites at SSMHC's hospitals. Or, if rehab is necessary, SSM Rehab is Missouri's largest provider of comprehensive medical rehab services with 14 convenient outpatient locations in Missouri and Illinois. Another example of keeping SSMHC's patients' needs in the forefront is the new Health Resource Center at SSM St. Joseph Hospital of Kirkwood. Homebound adults and residents of longterm care and assisted living facilities requiring outpatient care can be assessed, diagnosed, and treated in this convenient outpatient setting.

In St. Charles County, the fastest-growing county in Missouri, SSM St. Joseph Health Center in St. Charles, SSM St. Joseph Hospital West in Lake

AT SSM ST. MARY'S HEALTH CENTER, PROVIDERS OF CARE STRIVE TO TREAT PATIENTS WITH DIGNITY AND RESPECT. SSM HEALTH CARE ST. LOUIS OFFERS A FULL RANGE OF HEALTH SERVICES TO MEET THE HEALTH NEEDS OF THE ST. LOUIS REGION.

SSM CARDINAL GLENNON CHILDREN'S HOSPITAL BELIEVES THAT CARING HAS A HEALING EFFECT ON CHILDREN AND THEIR LOVED ONES.

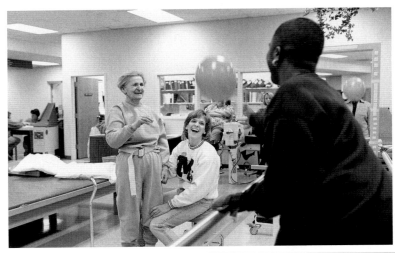

SSM Rehab, SSM St. Joseph Hospital of Kirkwood, and SSM St. Joseph's Health Center in St. Charles provide a spectrum of quality services to meet the needs of the St. Louis community.

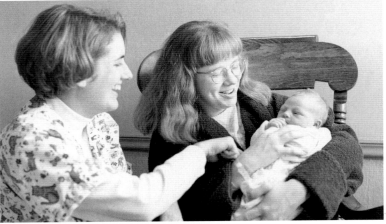

St. Louis, and SSM St. Charles Clinic Medical Group are the area's premier health care providers. The new, 4,000-square-foot Harmon Institute for Heart and Lung Rehabilitation, the unique Chest Pain Emergency Center in the health center's emergency department, and the fastest-growing OB program in Missouri at Hospital West are all part of SSM's expanded health ministry in this area.

As a health partner, SSM Health Care views its role as twofold—helping people stay healthy, and partnering with communities to help make them healthier places to live. It is for these reasons that SSMHC-St. Louis created SSM Health & Wellness, a division devoted entirely to proactive wellness and community health enrichment. More than 1,000 wellness programs are offered annually. Area residents also can call the SSM Health & Wellness line 24 hours a day for a physician referral to get answers to their health questions or to register

for a wellness program. Personal wellness and healthy communities go hand in hand at SSM, which encourages people to attend a women's health forum or a stopsmoking program, join an exercise program at one of SSM's unique WellBridge health and fitness centers, or get a flu shot at an SSM-sponsored health clinic.

"We are very contemporary in our contribution and approach to health care, but we are deeply rooted in the tradition of the Franciscan Sisters of Mary to provide compassionate care and service to people," says Stephanie S. McCutcheon, president/CEO of SSMHC-St. Louis. "We believe it is truly a privilege to work in health care today because it offers the opportunity to touch people, to make a difference in people's lives every day."

Long-Term Commitment to Quality

In 1990, SSM Health Care embarked on a process that has had a major impact on its

quest to deliver quality health services in its many communities. Continuous quality improvement (CQI) was introduced throughout the system with the goal of continuously examining processes, improving health services, and transforming the culture. Today, it is simply the way work is managed at SSMHC.

"CQI is based on the values of SSM Health Care," says Sr. Mary Jean. "CQI offers us several basic principles: our patients and customers are our first priority; quality is achieved through people; work is a part of a process; decisions should be based on facts; and quality is achieved through continuous improvement."

SSM Health Care entities have achieved nationally acclaimed successes using CQI. SSM St. Mary's Health Center in Richmond Heights, Missouri, for example, cut waiting time in its emergency room by more than half. SSM St. Mary's also instituted a pain management process that has increased patient satisfaction by more than 60 percent.

In the nearly 10 years that CQI has been SSM Health Care's culture, its facilities have implemented scores of improvements. In St. Louis, eight hospitals have decreased their rates of cesarean section births. Hospitals in all four states where SSMHC has a presence have received state quality awards, and the system is known nationally as a leader in the quality movement.

"The nice thing about using

CQI as a system," says Sr. Mary Jean, "is that when one hospital improves a process, we have 20 others that can learn from what they did. Then each facility can implement its own improvement processes, with a portion of the knowledge already in place."

Sr. Mary Jean continues, "SSM Health Care is working to deliver health care breathtakingly better than anyone else. Such an achievement requires that we listen closely to our customers, collect and then carefully analyze the data, and develop processes to improve what we do. We try to tap into the ideas of everyone in the organizations to ensure that we are the best that we can be."

Sr. Mary Jean is coauthor of the book *CQI and the Renovation of an American Health Care System*, now in its second printing.

Honors and Awards

In keeping with its commitment to quality, SSM Health Care has set its sights on the highest quality award in the land: the Malcolm Baldrige National Quality Award. In June 1999, the system became one of the first health care systems in America to apply for the award.

SSMHC facilities have also won many state and quality awards. In 1997, three SSMHC entities—SSM St. Mary's Health Center, St. Louis; St. Mary's Health Center, Jefferson City; and St. Francis Hospital & Health Services, Maryville, Missouri—

were selected as regional Missouri Team Quality Award finalists by the Excellence in Missouri Foundation. Sr. Mary Jean was honored with the 1997 Governor's Quality Leadership Award by the same foundation. Two SSMHC hospitals received state quality awards in 1998.

As SSM Health Care begins its second 125 years of meeting the needs of the times, it will focus on women's health, providing compassionate care at the end of life, improving the overall health of its communities, and addressing social problems that result in violence or poor health.

"It takes an ounce of prevention to provide a wealth of cure," says Sr. Mary Jean. "The more we can educate people about intervention, the more likely we will be to keep them out of hospitals."

SSMHC has become one of the first organizations in the nation to form a separate corporation to address health-related public policy in the four states where it operates. The SSM Health Policy Institute will analyze and monitor various state and federal initiatives, such as Medicare and Medicaid reform and child health legislation, as well as research and social welfare legislation.

SSM Health Care recently recommitted itself to increasing diversity throughout the organization. Currently, nearly half of its top executives are women.

Leadership is committed to creating an organization that more truly reflects the make-up of the community. Sr. Mary Jean has promised that SSM Health Care hospitals will keep the needs of diverse populations in mind, as they focus on meeting the needs of their communities.

Just as Mary Odilia Berger boldly and creatively met the needs of her times by building hospitals and orphanages and by taking care of the very sick in their own homes, SSM Health Care today strives to meet the needs of the communities it serves. The commitment to caring for people with kindness and compassion that began in 1872 still flourishes to this day. The same values that guided Mother Odilia and her four companion sisters remain vibrant throughout all of SSM Health Care.

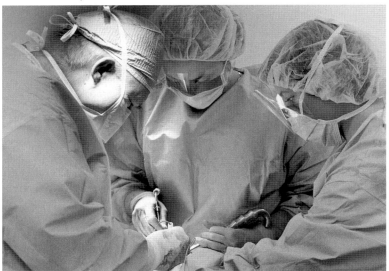

A focus on partnership and innovation characterizes the caring professionals at SSM DePaul Health Center, SSM St. Joseph's Hospital West, and SSM St. Mary's Health Center. SSM Health Care is working to deliver health care "breathtakingly better" than anyone else, according to President and CEO Sr. Mary Jean Ryan, a Franciscan Sister of Mary.

BRYAN CAVE LLP

BRYAN CAVE IS DEEPLY ROOTED IN ST. LOUIS' HISTORY AND ITS links to the past are a source of great pride. Founded in 1873, the Firm recently celebrated 125 years of outstanding service to its clients. From Bryan Cave's origin in a one-room office of three lawyers, the Firm has grown to be the largest law firm in Missouri, one

of the 25 largest in the United States, and among the 50 largest in the world. From 16 offices from the eastern United States to California and from London to the Middle East to Asia, Bryan Cave represents clients worldwide. From the beginning, Bryan Cave has attracted attorneys with world-class legal skills and a dedication to aggressively representing their clients.

Bryan Cave has made substantial investments in innovative and advanced communications and technology systems so the Firm's lawyers have immediate access both to their clients and to their colleagues worldwide. Computer network systems of more than 1,500 personal computers, nationwide videoconferencing abilities, comprehensive Internet/intranet connectivity, and extensive mobile and remote access capabilities allow the Firm's lawyers to meet clients' needs promptly and efficiently.

Bryan Cave has always focused on fostering long-term client relationships based on the concept of working as allies to common ends. The Firm's clients are diverse geographically and by their business structures, and they are in a wide array of businesses: high-tech/biotech, finance, manufacturing, government entities, and not-for-profit organizations. Rather than basing their practice organization along the Firm's internal disciplines, Bryan Cave lawyers work and practice in 30 Client Service Groups. Some, like the health care group, are specific to an industry; others, such as the class action defense group, are dedicated to a particular practice area of law. This unique system makes Bryan Cave's lawyers more accessible to their clients and ensures that the Firm's size is used to the advantage of its clients.

"We find the lawyer with the expertise that best fits the problem, and we present that lawyer immediately to the client," says Walter L. Metcalfe, Jr.,

Chairman of Bryan Cave. "The velocity of the practice is such that we can't sit down with a client and say, 'We will have the contract for you in the next week or so,' because they expect it within 25 minutes. Likewise, we know our clients' goals and objectives, so we can come to a result that is not only legally sound, but also most in line with their business requirements. Bryan Cave operates as One Firm—our Client Service Groups and offices are not profit centers. This means there are no internal economic or political boundaries between offices, practice areas, or lawyers. As a result, there are no barriers to serving our clients' needs and clients are free to develop close working relations with every lawyer who serves them."

GROWTH AND CHANGE

From the Firm's beginnings in St. Louis to its global presence today, positive change has always been Bryan Cave's hallmark. In 1973, the Firm's centennial, Bryan Cave had one office, St. Louis, and 52 lawyers. Since then, demand for the Firm's services has grown rapidly, and Bryan Cave has expanded in such areas as antitrust, securities, corporate finance, product liability, municipal finance, international trade, environmental and technology law, and has opened 15 other offices. "An important thread in our business has been the acceptance of change, and the recognition that such change can be and should be good," says Metcalfe.

Amid this growth and change, Bryan Cave has remained deeply involved in civic and philanthropic activities. Individually, the Partners in St. Louis are on the boards of more than

tive aimed at improving the quality of life in St. Louis.

"Bryan Cave is a global firm in all respects, with a client base consisting of industry leaders," says Metcalfe. "The Firm has had the vision, will-power, and stamina to build well beyond St. Louis, yet the source of our energy, humanity, and culture is here. As we go into the future, St. Louis is a place where we can do business on a global basis effectively and efficiently."

40 nonprofit organizations. The Firm has a deep commitment to providing legal services to charitable and nonprofit organizations at no cost. For example, Bryan Cave represents the Jackie Joyner-Kersee Youth Center Foundation in East St. Louis, as well as representing National Public Radio in a lawsuit filed by the Ku Klux Klan. Also, the Firm was the mediator in the resolution of the 30-year-old St. Louis school desegregation cases. In 1998,

this pro bono work amounted to more than 20,000 hours, which is equivalent to the time of more than 10 full-time lawyers and worth more than $3.2 million.

Bryan Cave is also committed to enhancing life in St. Louis, particularly through the revitalization of the downtown area. The Firm wholeheartedly supports its Partner and former U.S. Senator Jack Danforth in his responsibilities as chair of St. Louis 2004™, a major initia-

ST. ELIZABETH'S HOSPITAL

T. ELIZABETH OF HUNGARY WAS KNOWN FOR HER CHARITY WORK and love of the poor. Her namesake in Belleville—St. Elizabeth's Hospital—has followed in her footsteps, providing the sick and poor with compassionate, high-quality health care since 1875. Even after more than a century of service, St. Elizabeth's is still committed to

the values it has held since its founding.

The facility first saw life when the Hospital Sisters of the Third Order of St. Francis began caring for the sick and needy at a small Belleville-area schoolhouse. Through the years, the hospital has grown and changed. Five years after the sisters began their work, construction started on the first permanent building, a three-story site with a 22-patient capacity.

Today, the hospital is housed in a modern facility equipped with state-of-the-art technology and is affiliated with Hospital Sisters Health System, a 13-hospital system owned by the Hospital Sisters of the Third Order of St. Francis. It is also a member of a seven-hospital provider network—Unity Health Network. The oldest and one of the largest health care providers in its area, St. Elizabeth's offers inpatient care in its 400-plus licensed bed general acute care hospital, as well as outpatient services in surrounding communities.

But, through all these changes, the underlying mission has never changed, and the guiding

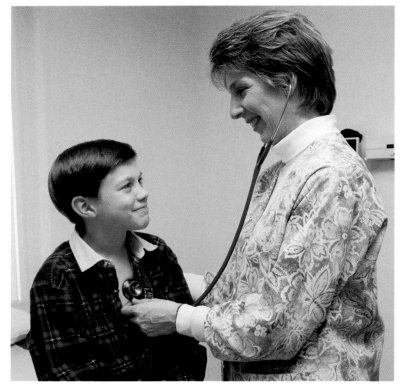

philosophy of St. Elizabeth's Hospital remains its anchor and conscience.

A LEADING CARDIAC CENTER IN THE REGION

Among the hospital's key features is an extensive program of cardiac care. St. Elizabeth's has long had one of the most advanced cardiac catheterization labs in the region, offering some of technology's newest equipment and procedures to treat coronary artery blockages. For example, the lab recently introduced an easier approach to catheterization, using the transradial artery in the wrist instead of the femoral artery in the groin area.

In 1997, the hospital joined forces with Cardiology Consultants Ltd., the largest cardiology physician group in southern Illinois, to form the Southern Illinois Heart Institute (SIHI). Its goal is to offer patients

simplified access to a comprehensive array of cardiovascular services. During its first year of operation, SIHI sponsored a free community walking program that attracted more than 3,000 members. Now, a major construction project is under way to give SIHI a new home: an addition to the hospital with cardiac diagnostics and rehabilitation conveniently located in a single place.

St. Elizabeth's also has a dedicated Cardiac Observation Center, in which patients with chest pain can be evaluated quickly and efficiently by specially trained staff members. Specific protocols are in place so that when patients with signs of cardiac distress come to the hospital's emergency room, the medical team of doctors and nurses quickly respond to those symptoms in an effort to diagnose the cause of distress and begin appropriate treatment.

ST. ELIZABETH'S HOSPITAL'S MEDICAL PARK IS A CONVENIENT OUTPATIENT OPTION FOR RESIDENTS OF O'FALLON, ILLINOIS, AND THE SURROUNDING COMMUNITIES (TOP).

THE MOTHER CHILD CENTER ALLOWS MOTHERS AND THEIR FAMILIES TO STAY IN THE SAME COMFORTABLE ROOM THROUGH LABOR, DELIVERY, AND RECOVERY—THE LDR (BOTTOM).

OTHER IMPORTANT PATIENT SERVICES

Along with cardiac care, the hospital has a full range of other fine programs. Mothers give birth in the homelike Mother Child Center, which also offers education programs and support groups. For premature babies, the center has a Level II+ Neonatal Intensive Care Unit (NICU), affiliated with Cardinal Glennon Children's Hospital in St. Louis. St. Elizabeth's Hospital is the only hospital in southwestern Illinois with a Level II with exceptions designation permitting the care of special care neonates. Following discharge, neonatologists continue to do follow-up checkups on these special care babies through the NICU's high-risk clinic.

St. Elizabeth's has developed the only Voice Clinic in southern Illinois—an interdisciplinary program that diagnoses and treats patients with voice disorders. Those with sleep problems, such as sleep apnea, find help in the Southern Illinois Sleep Disorders Center, the largest such program in this part of the state.

In the Arthritis Care Center, physicians conduct various types of screenings throughout the year. The Physical Therapy Department was the first in southern Illinois to provide treatment for lymphedema, the abnormal collection of lymph fluid in the body. An upgraded magnetic resonance imaging (MRI) unit offers some of the latest in MRI technology.

A successful new partnership with Scott Air Force Base Family Practice Residency and Saint Louis University Medical School has been formed. This links the resources of St. Elizabeth's with the educational expertise of one of the nation's leading medical schools and a major military installation located in the Midwest. Together, they operate the Saint Louis University Family Practice Residency Program, one of the larger programs of its kind in the

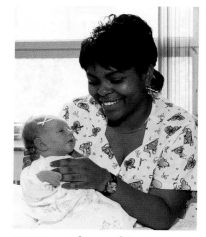

country and one of the top two family practice training programs in Illinois and Missouri.

OUTREACH TO NEARBY COMMUNITIES

St. Elizabeth's works in its own community to help the needy. Each weekday, volunteers from local church groups and civic organizations travel through the Belleville area delivering nutritious meals to homebound residents through the St. Elizabeth's Meals on Wheels program. Since 1974, this program has delivered more than 14,000 meals to people in the area. The hospital also works closely with Belleville Area College to provide a geriatric nurse for the community.

As part of its mission, the hospital reaches out to surrounding areas, increasing people's access to health care. It currently offers outpatient physical therapy treatments in

four locations: west Belleville, downtown Belleville, O'Fallon, and Mascoutah. In addition to physical therapy, the new St. Elizabeth's Medical Park in O'Fallon, a 21,000-square-foot facility, offers an urgent care center, imaging services, lab testing, X rays and mammograms, and physician offices. The newest addition of outpatient services is the St. Elizabeth's Medical Plaza in Mascoutah.

St. Elizabeth's will continue to grow, with expanding outpatient services and health care improvements. But its underlying commitment to service will remain its motivation, just as it inspired the founding sisters more than a century ago.

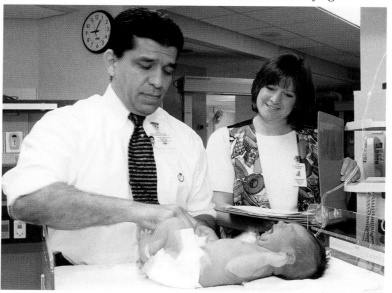

CLOCKWISE FROM TOP LEFT: PARENTS WHO CHOOSE ST. ELIZABETH'S FOR THE BIRTH OF THEIR CHILD CAN COUNT ON THE BEST OF BOTH WORLDS— A LARGE HOSPITAL FEATURING THE TECHNOLOGY AND RESOURCES TO CARE FOR A NEWBORN WITH SPECIAL NEEDS, AS WELL AS A STAFF THAT FOCUSES ON INDIVIDUALIZED CARE AND PERSONAL ATTENTION FOR BOTH MOTHER AND BABY.

OUTPATIENT PHYSICAL THERAPY IS OFFERED BY ST. ELIZABETH'S HOSPITAL AT FOUR LOCATIONS.

DR. FAROUK SADIQ, MEDICAL DIRECTOR OF ST. ELIZABETH'S LEVEL II+ SPECIAL CARE NURSERY, EXAMINES A NEWBORN WHILE DONNA STEPHENS, DIRECTOR OF THE HOSPITAL'S MATERNAL CHILD SERVICES, CHECKS THE BABY'S MEDICAL RECORD.

BROWN SHOE

IN 1878, GEORGE WARREN BROWN FOUNDED THE FIRST ST. LOUIS shoe company—and with it a new industry in the city. Within 25 years, St. Louis had become the leading shoe manufacturing center in the United States. ¶ Yet among the many shoe businesses of the time, Brown Shoe was special. St. Louisans came to know it for its highly visible head-

quarters building in the White House at 1600 Washington Avenue and for its popular brands—especially Buster Brown shoes, whose trademark was little Buster Brown himself and his faithful dog, Tige.

Today, Brown Shoe is headquartered in Clayton, a St. Louis suburb, and the company still sells Buster Brown shoes. But otherwise, much has changed. That small local firm has become a footwear giant—with annual sales of $1.5 billion, major footwear retail chains, and a large portfolio of footwear brands for men, women, and children.

The company's business changed dramatically in the 1970s and 1980s when a number of forces put pressure on Brown's businesses. The flood of imported footwear into the U. S. market during this time forced Brown to close domestic factories and move to a worldwide sourcing structure. After a period of diversification into non-footwear businesses and a name change to Brown Group in 1972, consolidation in the retail industry called for big changes in Brown's other businesses. Brown Shoe was one of the few footwear companies that survived this time of dramatic changes in the industry. Today, it is still considered one of the leading footwear companies, and in early 1999, Brown Group changed its name back to Brown Shoe to reflect its strong position in the shoe industry.

STRUCTURING RETAIL SUCCESS
Brown Shoe, which employs 11,000 people worldwide, 700 of them in St. Louis, today has six primary operating divisions. The first is Famous Footwear, the largest national chain of value-

priced, fashionable, branded family footwear. This division, headquartered in Madison, Wisconsin, was founded in 1960. When Brown Shoe acquired it in 1981, Famous had only 32 stores. The chain currently includes 827 stores located in about 25 major markets, with locations in both strip centers and malls. These stores feature a wide range of athletic, casual, and dress shoes priced at 10 to 50 percent below manufacturers' suggested retail prices. In the St. Louis area, Famous Footwear operates as Supermarket of Shoes stores, with about 30 locations.

Another retail chain operated by Brown Shoe is Naturalizer, with approximately 450 stores throughout the United States and Canada. The company's Naturalizer stores offer a large selection of casual and dress footwear that appeals to the active woman's lifestyle. Naturalizer specialty stores are destination shopping points for loyal Naturalizer brand consumers, who want the highest level of service, selection, and

sizes. In addition to these stores, the Naturalizer brand is sold in about 75 independently operated Naturalizer stores in the United States and some 40 in other countries, building the brand's worldwide recognition.

POWERFUL FOOTWEAR BRANDS
Brown Shoe's wholesale divisions include the Brown Branded, Brown Pagoda, Brown Canada, and Brown Sourcing businesses, all supporting Brown Shoe's powerful presence in today's footwear marketplace. The Brown Branded division is among the nation's leading

FAMOUS FOOTWEAR, WITH 827 STORES, IS BROWN SHOE'S LARGEST DIVISION (TOP).

RONALD A. FROMM WAS NAMED CHAIRMAN, PRESIDENT, AND CHIEF EXECUTIVE OFFICER OF BROWN SHOE IN EARLY 1999 (BOTTOM).

A FORTUNE 1,000 COMPANY, A.G. EDWARDS RANKS FIFTH AMONG BROKERAGE FIRMS NATIONWIDE IN THE NUMBER OF LOCATIONS, AND FIFTH IN THE NUMBER OF FINANCIAL CONSULTANTS AND TOTAL NUMBER OF EMPLOYEES.

A FULL RANGE OF SERVICES

The company offers its clients a comprehensive range of products and services. A.G. Edwards is a holding company whose subsidiaries provide securities and commodities brokerage, investment banking, trust, asset management, and insurance services. Its principal subsidiary, A.G. Edwards & Sons, Inc., is a financial services company that provides financial products and services to individual and institutional investors. The firm also offers investment banking services to corporate, governmental, and municipal clients.

Even though the firm is one of the largest sellers of mutual funds in the United States, it doesn't have its own family of funds. This removes the potential of internal pressure to sell a more profitable in-house fund in place of independent funds that might give the client better diversification, quality of management, and returns. A broad range of services, competitive fees and commissions, and a superior stock-picking track record have helped the firm win a number of national accolades, including *Smart-Money*'s number one ranking in its annual survey of full-service investment firms.

LIVING UP TO ITS HISTORY

A.G. Edwards has been providing financial services since 1887, when it was founded by General Albert Gallatin Edwards, retired assistant secretary of the Sub-Treasury Bank in St. Louis, and his son Benjamin F. Edwards. In 1890, another of the general's sons—George Lane Edwards—joined the firm, which he took over in 1891. In 1898, George Edwards bought the company's first seat on the New York Stock Exchange. In 1919, a third son of the general, Albert Ninian Edwards, became the firm's managing partner. He remained with the firm until 1958.

The third generation of the Edwards family has also played an integral role in the continued development of the firm.

Presley W. Edwards served as managing partner from 1935 to 1966, moving the company toward building its network of branch locations and using computer technology in its business. Today, Benjamin Edwards III, son of Presley Edwards, represents the family's fourth generation, having taken the helm in 1966 and having shaped the firm's customer-friendly corporate culture ever since.

"We still have no size or financial goals, and we try never to forget that our clients pay all our bills," says Edwards. "Serving their interests is what brings us all together, uniting our efforts and giving us a common purpose. We try to live the Golden Rule. It makes work a lot of fun."

LT. A.G. EDWARDS, A MEMBER OF THE 1ST MOUNTED DRAGONS (1835), WAS A GRADUATE OF WEST POINT IN 1831 (LEFT).

ALBERT GALLATIN EDWARDS, THE FIRM'S FOUNDER, SERVED AS A MEMBER OF PRESIDENT ABRAHAM LINCOLN'S SECOND ADMINISTRATION (RIGHT).

HEARTLAND BANK

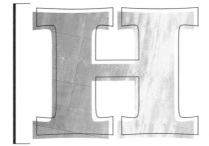

EARTLAND BANK, ONE OF THE OLDEST FINANCIAL INSTITUTIONS in Missouri, has served the St. Louis region since 1887. Throughout its history, Heartland has been an independent bank—and it has no plans to change. In an era of banking consolidations, this St. Louis mainstay intends to remain independent,

locally owned, and committed to growth while providing quality personal service.

With this commitment to quality service in mind and building on the bank's solid foundation, Heartland has transitioned from a traditional savings institution to a full-service bank providing a wide range of products and services. In addition to the more traditional products, Heartland has also demonstrated an entrepreneurial flair by establishing a very active Merchant Banking Division.

Working together, these strategies have proved very successful. From 1993 to 1998, the bank doubled its assets to $509 million, with a strong $39 million in capital, and now serves more than 45,000 customers. The bank currently has 17 locations throughout the St. Louis metropolitan area and surrounding counties, including a new regional office in St. Charles. In addition, Heartland has recently doubled the size of its ATM network to include more than 50 units throughout the region, and through its 50 percent ownership interest in Heartland Cash Network, the bank participates

CLOCKWISE FROM TOP RIGHT: THE EMERGENCE OF HEARTLAND MORTGAGE, A DIVISION OF HEARTLAND BANK, INTO ONE OF THE AREA'S LEADING MORTGAGE LOAN PROVIDERS REQUIRED A MOVE TO SPACIOUS NEW HEADQUARTERS IN CHESTERFIELD.

HEARTLAND BANK PLACES A PREMIUM ON CUSTOMER SERVICE AND SATISFACTION. ITS ANNUAL CUSTOMER APPRECIATION DAY IS ONE WAY HEARTLAND PUTS THIS PHILOSOPHY INTO PRACTICE.

HEARTLAND BANK, UNDER THE LEADERSHIP OF (FROM LEFT) LAURENCE A. SCHIFFER, CHAIRMAN; ANDREW S. LOVE JR., SECRETARY; AND JOHN J. WUEST, VICE CHAIRMAN, PRESIDENT, AND CEO, HAS DOUBLED ITS ASSETS IN THE PAST FIVE YEARS.

in a nationwide ATM network of more than 260 machines. "Heartland has strong, long-standing ties to St. Louis," says President and CEO John J. Wuest. "Building on that history, we hope to expand our business with entrepreneurial vision and energy, while serving the individual needs of our customers."

A HISTORY IN THE HEARTLAND

In 1887, 13 community leaders came together raising $600,000 to found a financial institution, then called Economy Building and Loan Association. Its mission was to make loans to home buyers and to provide friendly, personal attention with each loan they made. Even in the difficult days of the Great Depression, the bank managed to see that no depositor suffered a loss.

Beginning in the 1950s, the postwar housing boom fueled Economy's rapid growth. But with the hyperinflation of the 1970s and 1980s, an infusion of capital became necessary. A new group of investors—John and James McDonnell, Andrew S. Love Jr., and Laurence A. Schiffer came forward and formed the Love Savings Holding Company, which owns 100 percent of the shares of Heartland Bank.

The new investors quickly embarked on an active program

of growth. By stressing single-family mortgage and commercial real estate loans, they began to build assets. During the bank's 100th anniversary year, Wuest—newly hired as president and CEO—spearheaded a name change to Heartland Savings Bank, which was shortened to Heartland Bank in 1995.

A WIDE RANGE OF PRODUCTS AND SERVICES

Today, Heartland offers a full assortment of services, including private banking services; commercial loans to small and middle market companies; commercial real estate loans; checking products including Free as Free Can Be checking, named the area's best by *Money* magazine (May 1997); savings options such as IRAs, CDs, and

money market accounts; and consumer loans including home equity credit lines, auto loans, and home improvement loans. Among Heartland's additional services are a 24-hour bank-by-phone service, credit and debit cards, and Internet banking.

As it has since its founding, the bank still provides mortgage loans to home buyers. Today, those loans are originated by its Heartland Mortgage Division, the area's fifth-largest provider of single-family mortgage loans. While Heartland Mortgage actively engages in traditional mortgage banking activities, it does maintain a policy of retaining all servicing of single-family loans, and currently is servicing more than a billion dollars of residential and commercial loans. Heartland Mortgage is also proud to offer PROLOAN, a special initiative with the local labor union to provide attractive construction and permanent loans to assist consumers in the financing of union-built homes.

Heartland also maintains an active Commercial Real Estate Lending Division, which offers fixed-interest-rate and long-term loans, as well as specialized cash management services, for developers of multifamily housing, office buildings, retail centers, medical buildings and nursing homes, hotels, and industrial buildings. Heartland has also become very active in making commercial loans available to the region's small and middle market companies. These products include working capital lines, term loans, and acquisition financing and cash management products.

Heartland has established a Merchant Banking Division, and, as a result, the bank currently owns 50 percent of four companies: New Jersey-based Heartland Payment Systems, the 11th-largest U.S. processor of merchant credit card business; Heartland Cash Network, a Florida-based company that owns a nationwide network of ATMs; Motorcar Acceptance Corporation of Chicago, which originates sub-prime automobile loans; and Credit America Corporation-San Francisco, which specializes in the acquisition and collection of consumer loans and credit card portfolios.

HAVING A HEART IN THE COMMUNITY
Anchored in St. Louis, Heartland is interested in meeting the needs of the broader community, including low- to moderate-income clients who need special help with loan programs and services. The bank participates actively in programs offered by the Missouri Housing Development Commission, Fannie Mae, FHA and VA, and St. Louis County. Heartland has even created its own community investment initiative known as the Building Neighborhoods Program.

The bank is also involved in a variety of community service activities. Through its support of the Children's Miracle Network, Heartland raised more than $90,000 over a recent four-year period. In addition, employees join in the Neighborhood Housing Services' Block-Aid, an annual hands-on revitalization program for selected area neighborhoods.

Still at the heart of the community after more than 112 years, Heartland Bank prides itself on being accessible and responsive to all its customers, and providing fast, customized solutions to their many diverse needs.

WHILE OWNING THE DEEPEST ROOTS OF ANY LOCAL BANK, HEARTLAND REMAINS AN INNOVATOR, AS WITNESSED BY ITS BECOMING THE FIRST BANK IN THE AREA TO PLACE ATMS IN MOVIE THEATERS.

EVER SINCE ITS FOUNDING IN 1887, HEARTLAND BANK HAS BEEN A STRONG SUPPORTER OF THE LOCAL COMMUNITY. FOR EXAMPLE, HEARTLAND IS A MAJOR ANNUAL CONTRIBUTOR TO THE CHILDREN'S MIRACLE NETWORK AND A HANDS-ON PARTICIPANT IN BLOCK-AID, IN WHICH BANK EMPLOYEES HELP REVITALIZE DISADVANTAGED NEIGHBORHOODS.

EMERSON ELECTRIC CO.

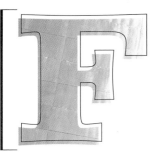

FOUNDED IN ST. LOUIS IN 1890 AS AN EARLY PRODUCER OF electric motors, Emerson Electric Co. today is one of America's best-managed corporations, distinguished by a record of financial consistency equaled by only a handful of other companies. ¶ Emerson is a global manufacturer of a broad range of electronic, electrical, and

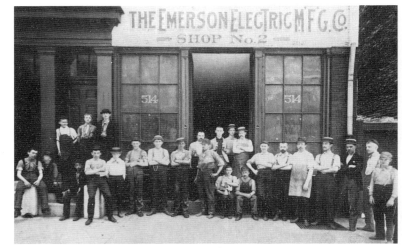

related products and systems for industrial, commercial, and consumer markets. Emerson's businesses include process controls; heating, ventilating, and air-conditioning components; motors and drives; industrial components and equipment; tools; electronic and computer support products; and fractional motors and appliance components.

Emerson consists of more than 60 divisions whose brand names are recognized around the world. Premier Emerson brands include Fisher controls, Rosemount instruments, Copeland compressors, USEM and Emerson motors, White-Rodgers thermostats, Alco regulators, Sears Craftsman™ hand tools, RoboGrip pliers, In-Sink-Erator waste disposers, and Intellution software. Consumers often benefit from Emerson products when they buy an air-conditioning system, washer, dryer, dishwasher, or ceiling fan; install a gas furnace and thermostat; fill their vehicles

with gasoline; or eat and drink many foods and beverages.

Although global in scope, Emerson remains committed to St. Louis, just as it is committed to all the communities in which its employees live and work. Emerson's worldwide charitable and community contributions have grown to more than $13 million a year, with particular emphasis on youth and educational programs.

In St. Louis, company employees are active volunteers in a wide range of community activities. The company has provided substantial funding for Forest Park Forever, an effort to rejuvenate the urban park that is the city's legacy from the 1904 World's Fair. In addition to underwriting renovation of the Grand Basin waterway, Emerson provided major support for two of the park's premier institutions—a new wing for the Missouri History Museum, and the St. Louis Zoo's new Emerson Electric Children's Zoo, replacing a popular but aging attraction. In addition, a major company challenge grant benefited executive education programs at Washington University's John M. Olin School of Business.

A CENTURY OF MANUFACTURING

The people of St. Louis in 1890, like most Americans, were skeptical of electricity, which seemed a dangerous and unreliable energy source. But two Scottish-born brothers, Charles and Alexander Meston, who viewed electricity as a business opportunity, developed and patented a reliable alternating current motor and persuaded John Wesley Emerson, a former Union army colonel, judge, and lawyer, to be the principal investor in their business.

As the company grew, it expanded its product line by attaching electric motors to new products such as sewing

CLOCKWISE FROM TOP:
EMPLOYEES STAND IN FRONT OF AN EARLY EMERSON FACTORY ON ELM STREET IN ST. LOUIS (CIRCA 1891).

THIS COMPRESSOR IS MADE BY EMERSON'S COPELAND DIVISION, THE WORLD LEADER IN THE DESIGN AND MANUFACTURE OF COMPRESSORS FOR COMMERCIAL REFRIGERATION AND COMMERCIAL AND RESIDENTIAL AIR CONDITIONING.

THE MOTOR TECHNOLOGY CENTER IN ST. LOUIS IS AMONG THE EMERSON RESEARCH FACILITIES THAT LEVERAGE THE COMPANY'S TECHNOLOGICAL EXPERTISE TO MEET CUSTOMER DEMANDS.

machines, dental drills, player pianos, and hair dryers. In 1892, Emerson sold the first electric fans in America—a product for which the company soon became renowned.

During World War II, as a supplier to the U.S. Army Air Force, Emerson became the world's largest manufacturer of aircraft gun turrets. In the postwar era, the company faced the dual challenges of rationalizing its highly seasonal fan product lines and responding to heightened competition from much larger electrical motor manufacturers.

Those issues were addressed head-on in 1954 when the company's new chief executive, W.R. "Buck" Persons, retooled and decentralized Emerson's manufacturing base, and began a continuing process of diversification. The company rapidly targeted high-growth markets and then made acquisitions to position Emerson favorably within those markets. Persons reaffirmed a long-standing company policy of manufacturing components rather than end products, and also instituted a strong focus on cost reductions, quality improvements, and formal planning.

When Persons retired as CEO in 1973, Emerson had signifi-cantly expanded its operations from 4,000 employees in two plants in 1954, to 31,000 employees in 82 facilities. Product lines had grown from five basic products to hundreds, and in the process, Emerson had become a diversified corporation with nearly $1 billion in sales.

EMERSON TODAY

Under Charles F. Knight, who was named CEO in 1973, Emerson has become a global market leader in each of the businesses in which it competes, and in 1998 sales were $13.4 billion. International sales accounted for more than 40 percent of the total, and 33 percent of sales came from products introduced in the previous five years. Emerson's record of consistency is evident in uninterrupted increases in earnings and dividends over the last four decades, a record equaled by no other U.S. manufacturing firm.

The key to Emerson's continued profitability is its widely recognized Best Cost Producer strategy, developed and refined over a 15-year period in response to the pressure of expanding global competition. The strategy, which concentrates on improving gross profit margins in Emerson's base company, enables Emerson to fund growth initiatives and protect profit margins as it continues to add acquisitions and joint ventures.

Today, Emerson is specifically focusing on growth initiatives companywide through several means, including integration of products and services to respond to customers' needs for solutions. Growth is also being accelerated through outstanding sales support and delivery performance, after-sales service, infrastructure expansion in the world's developing regions, rapid technological development, investment in fast-expanding markets to improve the company's growth mix, fostering risk acceptance and "out of the box" thinking, budgetary protection of major growth efforts, and instilling a passion for growth that rivals Emerson's commitment to continuous profit improvement.

Though its roots reach deep into St. Louis soil, Emerson is now a leader in serving its customers throughout the world.

SOUTH SIDE NATIONAL BANK IN ST. LOUIS

I N 1932, SOUTH SIDE NATIONAL BANK WAS IN TROUBLE. AS ONE OF the banks closed by President Franklin D. Roosevelt at the height of the depression, the future of this St. Louis institution looked uncertain. But the community stepped in to help. Customers took shares of stock in exchange for their deposits—and the bank was able to reopen. ❡ Throughout its history,

South Side has been a community bank, and that role continues today. At the bank's 10 locations, its 190 dedicated employees offer their customers expert, personalized service. The bank's slogan, in fact, reflects this emphasis: "Service you can count on."

For the convenience of its customers, South Side provides a comprehensive range of banking products and services: checking and savings accounts, consumer and home loans, business lending, trust services, and even passbook savings accounts for children. A large population of Asian-Americans now live near its headquarters located on Gravois and Grand avenues. In order to overcome the language barrier and provide quality service, the bank has hired employees who speak a variety of foreign languages, including Chinese and Vietnamese.

"We want our customers to know that they can come to us today and talk about their personal financial needs, and we will provide the planning help they need at no cost," says

THROUGHOUT ITS HISTORY, SOUTH SIDE NATIONAL BANK IN ST. LOUIS HAS BEEN A COMMUNITY BANK, AND THAT ROLE CONTINUES TODAY.

SOUTH SIDE'S MANAGEMENT TEAM INCLUDES (FROM LEFT) STEVEN R. RAY, SENIOR VICE PRESIDENT AND SENIOR TRUST OFFICER; THOMAS M. TESCHNER, PRESIDENT AND CEO; LAURIE A. PENNYCOOK, SENIOR VICE PRESIDENT AND OPERATIONS OFFICER; AND JOSEPH W. POPE, SENIOR VICE PRESIDENT.

STEPHEN R. DOLAN

Thomas Teschner, president and CEO. "That is an important niche that we, as community bankers, can fill."

MORE THAN A CENTURY IN ST. LOUIS

The history of the bank dates from 1891, when Adolphus Busch, founder of Anheuser-Busch Companies, Inc., opened South Side Bank at the corner of Broadway and Pestalozzi Street. In 1928, this predecessor organization—now South Side Trust Company—merged with Farmers Merchant and Trust Company to form South Side National Bank. The following year, the new organization built its current home: a landmark, nine-story structure with marble floors, high ceilings, and old-fashioned iron teller cages.

In recent years, South Side has expanded to meet the changing demographic needs of its depositors. In 1982, a holding company, Southside Bancshares Corporation, was formed to purchase the Bank of St. Genevieve. Subsequent acquisitions have included the State Bank of Jefferson County, the Bank of St. Charles County, and, most

recently, Public Service Bank. This newest acquisition brought with it South Side's first West County location. The bank has also expanded into South County with a brand-new branch at Telegraph Road and I-255.

A WEALTH OF COMMUNITY ACTIVITIES

An important effort of the bank today is its service to the community. Each year, South Side employees participate in Christmas in April, a program in which they volunteer to spend a weekend day fixing up a home that needs repair. They also teach the Basics of Banking to local schoolchildren, and work through churches and civic groups to help stabilize nearby neighborhoods.

"What most independent banks have to offer today is service," says Teschner. "With our history, and the community's involvement in saving this institution in 1932, South Side is particularly involved in our community. I hope we can continue to carry that message through to our existing customers, our new employees, and the new generations that we serve."

ON SEPTEMBER 1, 1894, A HUGE CROWD GATHERED AT 18TH and Market streets to celebrate the grand opening of St. Louis Union Station, designed by architect Theodore Link in the Richardsonian Romanesque style. Awed by its beauty—especially its stenciled and gilded Grand Hall—one speaker called Union Station

"a magnificent architectural concept . . . the most completely equipped railroad station in the world."

In those days, Union Station was the world's largest rail terminus, with 22 railroads and 30 tracks converging on its 10-acre train shed. During the station's heyday in the mid-1940s, more than 100,000 passengers from all over the country passed through its midway each day. After World War II, the public began choosing other forms of transportation, and in 1978, the last train pulled out of Union Station.

A NEW LIFE

In 1979, Oppenheimer Properties bought the deteriorating complex—which had been declared a National Historic Landmark—and chose the Rouse Company of Baltimore to undertake its rehabilitation. St. Louis Union Station reopened in August 1985 after a massive, $150 million restoration and reuse project, the largest ever in the United States.

During the renovation of St. Louis Union Station, the Memories Program was initiated to make the story of the railroad station approachable and available to all. "Through historic displays, storyboards, and personal letters," says Donna K. Laidlaw, vice president of St. Louis Station Associates, "anyone coming to the Station can become immersed in the soul of the Station while enjoying a thoroughly up-to-date hotel/retail/entertainment experience."

Today, St. Louis Union Station has a successful new life as one of the city's major attractions for tourists and residents alike. More than 5 million visitors a

year enjoy the 44-acre mix of dining, shopping, and entertainment. Many combine this experience with a stay in the deluxe hotel accommodations of the Hyatt Regency St. Louis—also part of Union Station—with its 550 luxurious rooms and suites, plus more than 35,000 square feet of flexible meeting space.

The old midway and the train shed concourse are now home to more than 80 nationally known or one-of-a-kind shops featuring men's and women's clothing, accessories, gifts, and St. Louis- or train-related items. Colorful carts are set up to sell specialty items. Some 20 restaurants, specialty food stores, and picnic express eating establishments offer places to enjoy elegant meals or just a quick bite while shopping.

In 1998, there were some exciting new arrivals at the Station. A 10-screen movie theater opened at the rear of the complex. Also new to the Station are the Bacchus Brewing Company, the popular Hard Rock Café, and the Have a Nice Day Café.

Located on the MetroLink light-rail system, St. Louis

Union Station has a variety of special features, such as the Grand Hall, now meticulously restored to its 1894 grandeur, and the stained glass Allegorical Window, which is framed by the famous whispering arch. Concerts, festivals, and other special events take place year-round, and both children and adults enjoy the carousel and Ferris wheel rides, as well as the small lake with paddleboats, turtles, fish, and beautifully restored train cars located on the remaining station tracks. All these attractions allow St. Louis Union Station to remain one of the top tourist destinations in St. Louis.

CLOCKWISE FROM TOP: ST. LOUIS UNION STATION'S OLD MIDWAY AND TRAIN SHED CONCOURSE ARE NOW HOME TO MORE THAN 80 NATIONALLY KNOWN OR ONE-OF-A-KIND SHOPS FEATURING MEN'S AND WOMEN'S CLOTHING, ACCESSORIES, GIFTS, AND ST. LOUIS- OR TRAIN-RELATED ITEMS.

LOCATED ON THE METROLINK LIGHT-RAIL SYSTEM, ST. LOUIS UNION STATION HAS A VARIETY OF SPECIAL FEATURES, SUCH AS THE GRAND HALL, NOW METICULOUSLY RESTORED TO ITS 1894 GRANDEUR, AND THE STAINED GLASS ALLEGORICAL WINDOW, WHICH IS FRAMED BY THE FAMOUS WHISPERING ARCH.

ST. LOUIS UNION STATION REOPENED IN AUGUST 1985 AFTER A MASSIVE, $150 MILLION RESTORATION AND REUSE PROJECT, THE LARGEST EVER IN THE UNITED STATES.

RALSTON PURINA COMPANY

C HISELED INTO THE BASE OF THE STATUE OF A FARM BOY THAT stands on the Ralston Purina Company campus are four slogans from the company's founder, William H. Danforth. They reflect his belief in high standards, hard work, and personal integrity as the basis for his business. But one slogan, What Next? also speaks to the initiative

that his company has shown since 1894—in meeting challenges, seizing opportunities, and sharpening its focus—to become the corporate giant that it is today.

Ralston Purina is a leader in two global growth businesses: Ralston Purina Pet Products, the world's largest producer of dry dog and dry and soft-moist cat foods; and Eveready, the world's largest manufacturer of dry cell batteries and flashlights. The company also is a leading manufacturer and marketer of cat box filler, sold primarily under the Tidy Cats label in the United States and Canada. Altogether, these operations employ about 8,500 people in the United States and 14,000 more internationally. For the fiscal year that ended September 30, 1998, Ralston had sales of $4.7 billion and earnings of $394 million, before unusual items.

Heading the companies are W. Patrick McGinnis, chief executive officer and president of Ralston Purina Company, and J. Patrick Mulcahy, chairman and chief executive officer of Eveready Battery Company. William P. Stiritz, who retired

after 16 years as CEO, continues as Ralston's chairman of the board.

MEETING CHALLENGES
Ralston Purina's roots extend back to 1894, when William H. Danforth founded a small horse and mule feed business on the St. Louis riverfront. He faced his first major challenge only two years later, when a tornado leveled his mill. Undaunted, Danforth borrowed the money to rebuild—and even began expanding into the burgeoning breakfast cereal market. He adopted the highly visible checkerboard logo as his promise of quality and purity.

Ralston Purina continued to expand, even during the Great Depression, decentralizing its operation by opening mills in other states. Over the years, the company also introduced a steady stream of new products, including Chex cereals and Dog Chow pet food, an extruded product sold in grocery stores that revolutionized the pet food business and became the number one brand virtually overnight.

Beginning in the late 1960s, Ralston worked to diversify, investing in a number of businesses, including floriculture,

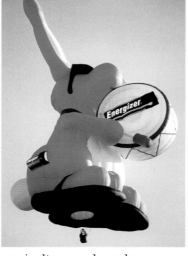

mariculture, and mushroom farming. But by 1980, the company's focus had shifted. It sold off many operations—including Purina Mills, its original domestic animal feed business—and bought Continental Baking Company, the largest wholesale producer of fresh bakery products in the United States. In 1986, the company also acquired Eveready Battery Company and its flagship Energizer alkaline battery brand from Union Carbide Corporation.

SHARPENING ITS FOCUS
In recent years, Ralston has sharpened its focus through a series of strategic acquisitions,

CLOCKWISE FROM TOP: CHIEF EXECUTIVE OFFICER AND PRESIDENT OF RALSTON PURINA COMPANY W. PATRICK MCGINNIS (LEFT) AND EVEREADY BATTERY COMPANY CHAIRMAN AND CHIEF EXECUTIVE OFFICER J. PATRICK MULCAHY STAND OUTSIDE RALSTON PURINA COMPANY'S WORLD HEADQUARTERS AT CHECKERBOARD SQUARE IN ST. LOUIS—NOT FAR FROM WHERE WILLIAM H. DANFORTH, THE COMPANY'S FOUNDER, BEGAN SELLING HORSE AND MULE FEED ON THE BANKS OF THE MISSISSIPPI RIVER IN 1894.

THE ENERGIZER BUNNY HOT "HARE" BALLOON LEADS AN ARRAY OF COLORFUL BALLOONS THROUGH THE SKIES OVER ST. LOUIS DURING THE ANNUAL GREAT FOREST PARK BALLOON RACE. ATTRACTING APPROXIMATELY 130,000 SPECTATORS, THE EVENT IS THE MOST WELL ATTENDED SINGLE-DAY BALLOON RACE IN THE UNITED STATES.

THIS ST. LOUIS MILL, PICTURED HERE IN THE 1930S, SUFFERED FROM A DUST EXPLOSION AND FIRE IN 1962, ENDING PRODUCTION. THAT SAME DAY, THE COLDEST DAY OF THE YEAR, RALSTON PURINA STOCK WAS LISTED ON THE NEW YORK STOCK EXCHANGE.

352

ST. LOUIS

MIKE BIZELLI

The Growth of the Federation

Organized Jewish life in St. Louis began in the 1850s with the formation of congregations, auxiliaries, and burial associations. With these groups came the first efforts to provide a joint philanthropic response to community needs. As new waves of Jewish immigrants arrived, it became clear that these efforts needed stronger coordination.

In 1901, a group of organizations came together and formed the federation under an umbrella group of Jewish community leaders called the Committee of 100. At first, they simply raised money and distributed it by formula to the organizations they supported—a model later adopted by the United Way. In 1902, the federation also acted as a coordinating body to launch the Jewish Hospital.

Over the years, the organization expanded its efforts to provide aid to Jews overseas, and it took on a new thrust—community planning—to devise more coordinated ways of spending contributed funds. But the most dramatic change came in the late 1940s with support for the new nation of Israel. Working through the Jewish Agency for Israel, the federation helped to resettle millions of Jews displaced by World War II, as well as those from lands of distress.

The Jewish Federation Today

The Jewish Federation of St. Louis and its partnership group of 185 other federations around the United States continue to provide many forms of support today. When the government of Israel was negotiating the release of 15,000 Ethiopian Jews, each federation paid a share of the $40 million it cost to rescue them and bring them to Israel.

"Although we are all independent organizations, there is unanimity of purpose," says Rosenberg. "If a fax came in

WILLIAM GREENBLATT

today that said, 'We need to airlift 100,000 Jews out of the Moldovan Republic because of unrest. Please advance your share of the money,' there would be a meeting tomorrow and the money would go out."

The federation, which is located on the Millstone campus in St. Louis County, also takes care of Jews and non-Jews in St. Louis who are in need through its many social service agencies and programs. These include the Metropolitan Employment & Rehabilitation Service, Jewish Food Pantry, Jewish Center for Aged, Jewish Information Service, Jewish Community Center (JCC) child care program, JCC Adult Day Services, Covenant House/ CHAI Apartments, and Jewish Family & Children's Service programs.

A vital role of the federation lies in its efforts to create a strong Jewish community in which families feel supported and connected, and in which children are closely involved. At the Millstone campus, activities for every age group take place from 6 a.m. to 10 p.m. daily. Recognizing that some Jewish families were moving farther west of the St. Louis area, the federation established a west area office in the new Jewish Community Center facility in Chesterfield.

None of the federation's programs would be possible without the generous support of the community and the work of many volunteers who

provide hundreds of needed hours working on committees for fund-raising and planning. Affinity groups for young professionals, physicians, and others also help the community.

"Taking care of Jews in need, from the cradle to the grave, and providing basic human services for them, wherever they are in the world—that was the challenge 100 years ago, and it continues to be our challenge today," Rosenberg says.

CLOCKWISE FROM TOP:
THE FEDERATION'S ANNUAL FUND-RAISING CAMPAIGN IS THE BACKBONE OF A WELL-ORGANIZED AND EFFICIENT SYSTEM THAT THE JEWISH COMMUNITY DEPENDS ON TO MEET ITS NEEDS.

THE JEWISH FEDERATION IS PART OF A WORLDWIDE NETWORK ABLE TO RESPOND TO EMERGENCY SITUATIONS WHEN THEY ARISE. A 1991 AIRLIFT BROUGHT 15,000 ETHIOPIAN REFUGEES TO ISRAEL IN 36 HOURS.

THE FEDERATION'S HOLOCAUST MUSEUM AND LEARNING CENTER IN MEMORY OF GLORIA M. GOLDSTEIN IS A VALUABLE RESOURCE TO THE COMMUNITY. THE MUSEUM ATTRACTS MORE THAN 20,000 INDIVIDUALS FROM THROUGHOUT THE REGION EACH YEAR.

MONSANTO COMPANY

WHEN THE MONSANTO COMPANY NAME IS NOW printed, the trademark red of old is gone, replaced by a warm green. Next to it is the symbol of a vine, enclosed in an earth gold box and growing vigorously. Beneath the name, the tag line reads: "Food. Health. Hope."

This is Monsanto's new logo, a symbol of its new strategic direction. In the 1997 spin-off of its chemical businesses to create Solutia Inc., Monsanto abandoned its longtime heritage as a chemical company. The business has now become a global life-sciences company, committed to developing breakthrough products that help people everywhere live longer, healthier lives through improved food, health, and nutrition. By providing environmentally sustainable solutions to these problems, the company is also helping to make for a healthier planet.

Today, Monsanto—which has annual net sales of some

CLOCKWISE FROM TOP:
AT MONSANTO'S CAMPUS IN CREVE COUER, MISSOURI, PASSERSBY ARE REMINDED THAT THE 21ST CENTURY WILL BE DEFINED BY EXPANDING DEMAND FOR BETTER FOOD AND BETTER HEALTH.

MONSANTO FOCUSES ITS GRANT-MAKING EFFORTS ON SCIENCE EDUCATION.

MONSANTO'S CORN SEED BUSINESS CONSISTS OF WELL-KNOWN BRANDS, INCLUDING DEKALB AND ASGROW.

$8.6 billion and employs 31,000 people around the world—is composed of three core sectors: agriculture, pharmaceuticals, and nutrition and consumer products. Each division manufactures a host of well-known products, including Roundup herbicide, NutraSweet-brand sweetener, and pharmaceutical treatments for arthritis and high blood pressure. At least 60 other products are in the company's active near-term research pipeline, including pharmaceutical compounds designed to treat infections and certain cancers or to prevent blood clots, as well as agricultural products

that will allow growers to raise crops that require fewer pesticide applications or that yield more desirable oils or proteins for consumers and livestock.

For the future, Monsanto is committed to continued growth, fueled by the ongoing revolution in biotechnology. This growth will take place in a variety of ways, including the development of a larger pharmaceutical sales force; partnerships in agriculture, food, and pharmaceuticals; and investments in information technology and genomics. This will help to increase the rate at which Monsanto launches its products around the globe.

GROUNDED IN THE COMMUNITY

Amid all this change at Monsanto, there is also stability. Established in 1901 as a manufacturer of saccharin, the company is committed to being a responsible corporate citizen. From its large, suburban St. Louis campus, Monsanto maintains strong ties to local academic institutions and makes grants worth nearly $6 million a year throughout the St. Louis region to support academic and community priorities.

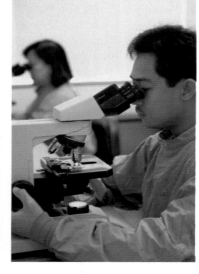

362

Monsanto's founder was John F. Queeny, who named the new company for his wife, Olga Monsanto Queeny. During the early years, it branched out into products such as caffeine and aspirin while expanding internationally. Next, the company moved into new areas, such as plastics and synthetic fibers. In 1960, Monsanto created the Agriculture Division, which soon developed the well-known herbicides Lasso and Roundup.

During the 1980s, Monsanto began a gradual shift into the life-sciences area, which culminated in the 1997 Solutia spin-off. In 1982, researchers genetically modified a plant cell and later grew plants with genetically engineered traits. The company purchased G.D. Searle & Co. in 1985, and moved into pharmaceuticals and sweeteners, including the well-known NutraSweet brand. More recently, Monsanto has acquired a number of life-sciences companies, among them DEKALB Genetics, the second-largest seed company in the United States.

In fall 1998, the company announced an exciting new initiative: the Nidus Center for Scientific Enterprise. The Nidus Center is an $8.5 million life-sciences incubator, located near the Monsanto campus, which will promote the development and commercialization of plant and life-sciences technology by assisting entrepreneurs with business expertise and capital.

Work done there will tie in with another project, also supported by the Monsanto Fund and Monsanto: the Donald Danforth Plant Science Center, due to open in 2000. Together, these projects are aimed at making the St. Louis region the Silicon Valley for biotechnology research and development.

A Partner in Education
Throughout its history, Monsanto and its charitable foundation, the Monsanto Fund, have forged strong ties with local educational institutions, thanks to coopera-

tive ventures, and corporate and foundation funding. In 1982, the company embarked on a historic collaborative agreement with Washington University in St. Louis to pursue biomedical research. Currently, the Monsanto Fund sponsors a scholarship program for minority MD/PhD students at the Washington University School of Medicine.

Monsanto and its foundation have long supported programs designed to attract students, especially underrepresented groups such as women and minorities, to science careers. Along with Maryville University and St. Louis Public Schools, the Monsanto Fund has created a pilot program for young students in science education curriculum. In conjunction with the *St. Louis Post-Dispatch*, Monsanto supports the annual Greater St. Louis Science Fair, one of the largest in the country. In addition, Monsanto has made leading contributions to museums, including the Hall of Biodiversity at the American Museum of Natural History in New York, *Underground Adventure* at the Field Museum in Chicago, and the DNA Zone at the St. Louis Science Center.

The company also funds projects that enhance students' enjoyment of science. Recently, the Monsanto Fund has committed $3 million to the St. Louis Zoo for construction of an insectarium, a leading-edge facility and one of only three in the United States. Additionally, the Monsanto Fund backs educational efforts beyond the realm of science, including the St. Louis Symphony's outreach program and a collaborative program with Opera Theatre of St. Louis to identify artistic talent in urban education venues.

Planning for the Future
As it has for the past nine decades, Monsanto Company continues to act as a community leader while planning for its own future. Much of its development may come through

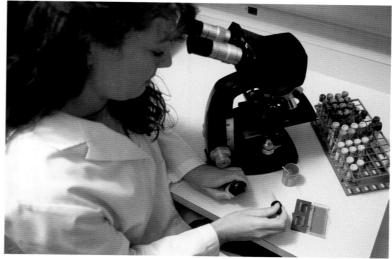

PAULA GAGE

innovative products that lie at the intersections of agriculture, food, and health. Someday soon, for example, it may be possible to engineer health-enhancement compounds—such as a cholesterol-lowering substance—into food crops. The company will also promote sustainable development through the promises of biotechnology.

Monsanto is determined to play a large role in all this groundbreaking research. The company believes that, through food, health, and hope, a strong and successful company can help create a better future.

AT MONSANTO'S LIFE SCIENCES RESEARCH CENTER LOCATED IN SUBURBAN ST. LOUIS, RESEARCHERS ARE DEVELOPING PLANTS THAT PRODUCE HEALTHIER PROPERTIES FOR MARGARINES AND SHORTENINGS.

GUARANTEE ELECTRICAL COMPANY

WHEN VISITORS CONVERGED ON ST. LOUIS FOR THE 1904 World's Fair, they found many exciting attractions: glorious cascades, a giant Ferris wheel, beautiful buildings, even the newly invented ice-cream cone. And at night, they were awestruck by the brightly lit exhibit

halls, electrified by a group of young construction entrepreneurs that later became Guarantee Electrical Company.

Just a few years away from its own centennial, Guarantee is still lighting up St. Louis as one of the city's oldest electrical contractors. Today, Guarantee is also powering the nation, as one of the top 25 electrical contractors in the United States. The company is working in 16 states, from New York to California, for a range of customers: general contractors, industrial and commercial firms, and institutional clients.

In St. Louis alone, Guarantee has performed electrical design, installation, and maintenance work for some of the region's largest companies in the following markets: aerospace, chemical, automotive, medical, brewing, and data and information, among many others. Guarantee has helped build every medical center in the area. The company has recently completed a major project: Boeing's new Learning Center at the old Vouziers estate on the bluffs of the Mississippi River. Also for Boeing, Guarantee is engaged in building a 1 million-square-foot Delta IV rocket fabrication plant in Decatur, Alabama.

Many aspects of Guarantee's business have changed since its founding in 1902. The once fledgling electrical firm has grown into a $100 million business that employs some 600 people. Long ago, Guarantee outgrew its original locations in downtown St. Louis. Today, the company is headquartered in a 150,000-square-foot facility in south St. Louis, where it is a bulwark of its city neighborhood.

But one thing that has not changed—and has only improved with the years—is the company's own guarantee of quality. In fact, its founders chose the name Guarantee to assure World's Fair organizers of the quality of their installation. The company was the first electrical contractor to offer what is now provided as a common, industry-wide practice: a one-year warranty for its work.

"We are taking our guarantee to a higher level than ever with a preventive program we call GEM, or Guarantee Electrical Maintenance," says Charles Oertli, chairman of the board and CEO. "On our large Design-Build projects, we audit the entire installation with an

independent, specially trained and equipped crew. We give the owner a very thorough study on the backbone of the electrical distribution: every cable or panel board—anything that carries the main power to the panels that feed the receptacle.

"We will also check to make sure the circuits are not overloaded, that they are properly balanced, and that there are no code violations, vibrations, or hot spots," Oertli adds. "We give the client a report—which may be up to 400 pages long—

completely free of charge. And if there are violations to our design or the building codes, we will make those corrections during the warranty period at our own expense."

THREE FACETS OF GUARANTEE'S BUSINESS

The bulk of Guarantee's business—perhaps 60 percent—takes place through its Construction Division, which handles medium- to large-sized projects in the industrial, commercial, and institutional markets. A national division oversees projects outside the St. Louis area, while a Granite City office handles all the work in southern Illinois.

A second piece of Guarantee's business, representing some 30 percent, is its service operation. The company has a fleet of 48 service trucks that travel to small repair and maintenance jobs. In addition, the firm also has maintenance crews permanently assigned to clients as part of the electrical arm of its operation. For special systems, such as data cable, temperature control, fire alarm, or security, Guarantee has a team of specially trained engineering and installation personnel.

While the construction and service divisions both fall under Guarantee Electrical Company, a third area—GECO Engineering Corporation—is a wholly owned subsidiary of the com-

pany, providing engineering services for clients, often in conjunction with the Construction Division.

Guarantee's Design-Build business also takes place through GECO Engineering. In 1956, Guarantee became the first company in St. Louis, and probably one of the first in the nation, to provide a full-service, Design-Build function. Today, the company is a member of the Design-Build Institute of America (DBIA), and this area constitutes a large, rapidly growing business focus for the company. Recently, Guarantee won DBIA awards for three projects: the St. Louis Rams Corporate Headquarters and Training Facility, the Clayco Construction Company's headquarters, and the Scott Air Force Base Officers' Club.

EXCEEDING CUSTOMERS' EXPECTATIONS

For many years, Guarantee has been a family-centered business. When Oertli himself was a young boy, he used to work unloading trucks and making deliveries for the firm his father had bought in 1945. Today, other members of the Oertli family are involved, along with fathers, sons, siblings, and relations from other families—all drawn to Guarantee by the warm atmosphere, as well as by the opportunities for education and advancement.

The company prides itself on its willingness to explore new ideas. Guarantee was the first in the Midwest, for example, to use a computer-aided design system. Today, the company regularly sends employees to training sessions so they can learn and apply the latest technology developments in the industry.

"We are known for our workmanship and for our competitive pricing. It would be hard to come up with a company in St. Louis that we haven't worked for," says Oertli. "We have been blessed, but it is mostly because of the follow-through and commitment of our people. A company is only as good as its people and the quality of its performance."

CLOCKWISE FROM TOP LEFT: OVER THE YEARS, GUARANTEE HAS PERFORMED NUMEROUS ELECTRICAL CONSTRUCTION PROJECTS FOR WASHINGTON UNIVERSITY. SHOWN HERE IS THE WASHINGTON UNIVERSITY SCHOOL OF LAW BUILDING.

GUARANTEE HAS PERFORMED ELECTRICAL CONSTRUCTION SERVICES FOR ST. LOUIS COUNTY JUSTICE CENTER. IN ADDITION, GUARANTEE ASSISTED IN THE DESIGN AND INSTALLATION OF THE FACILITY'S HIGH LEVEL SURVEILLANCE/SECURITY SYSTEM.

GUARANTEE'S MOST RECENT ELECTRICAL CONSTRUCTION PROJECT AT SIGMA WAS TO RENOVATE BUILDING N'S CHEMICAL LABORATORIES.

KRANSON INDUSTRIES

V IALS OF PERFUME, BOTTLES OF WINE, JARS OF SPAGHETTI sauce, and spray dispensers of cleaning fluid— nearly any household item that comes in a bottle, jar, tube, sprayer, or other container may well be the product of Kranson Industries. This St. Louis-based firm, founded in 1902, is the world's only

superdistributor of glass and plastic bottles, closures, and dispensing devices.

With annual sales in excess of $300 million, Kranson holds a 25 percent share of its market— more than twice that of the second-largest distributor and five to 10 times as much as other competitors. The company, which has 28 locations throughout the United States and Canada, also has the largest sales and support force in the business. It sells to some of the biggest U.S. corporations, such as Polaroid, Amway, and Lipton.

To provide the best service for its customers, Kranson works with every major container and component manufacturer in the United States, and maintains several strategic supplier partnerships in Europe, Latin America, and the Pacific Rim. These supplier-partners are the designers and manufacturers of the highest-quality packaging components and secondary processes in the world.

In addition, Kranson has its own custom library of 10,000 designs and the largest library of proprietary molds—some 2,500 shapes in all—among its competitors. With these resources and Kranson's proprietary

Kranson Industries • TricorBraun • Clinton Packaging • r/d design • Neveeti Industries

Componetics™ technology, the company can combine stock containers of different shapes and colors to create distinctive packages quickly, without mold lead time.

Kranson has won industry-wide recognition for its products. At the 1998 meeting of the National Association of Container Distributors, Kranson won the Best of the Show award for top overall achievement. The company also received gold medals for its designs in three out of seven packaging categories.

A FAST-GROWING FIRM
In recent years, under the leadership of its officers— Kenneth Kranzberg, chairman of the board, and Richard Glassman and Jeffrey Segar, co-chief-executive-officers— Kranson has been growing quickly. In 1995, as an $80 million company, Kranson began carrying out plans to expand through acquisition, as well as internal growth. In 1996, the company bought Texas-based Texberry Containers. Then, in 1997, Kranson acquired a financial partner, Bain Capital, a Boston-based firm with investments in 60 companies that have

aggregate annual sales of more than $10 billion.

Just a few months later, Kranson made a major acquisition when it bought Caliber Packaging of Los Angeles, which has supplied the U.S. wine industry with top-quality wine bottles and related products since 1982. The company carries traditional and new imported and domestic bottle styles, as well as specialty antique green and cobalt blue colors, plus a variety of popular neck finishes.

In 1998, Kranson acquired W. Braun Co. of Chicago, a leading supplier of containers to the personal care and cosmetics industries. Its customers manufacture products such as

366

Gillette's Oral-B mouth rinse and Procter & Gamble's Ivory Hand Soap.

Today, Kranson consists of four divisions: TricorBraun, the packaging design and distribution organization; Neveeti Industries, a manufacturer of rayon, cotton, and polyester coil for the nutraceutical, health, over-the-counter, and pharmaceutical industries; Clinton Packaging, an importer of unique glass containers from sources in Europe and the Pacific Rim; and r/d design, a full-service marketing design firm.

Roots in the Bottle Business

When the company, then called Western Bottle Company, was established in 1902, one of

the founders was Kenneth Kranzberg's grandfather, Samuel Kranzberg. In those days, it was a used-bottle business; the company purchased empty glass milk, beverage, and patent medicine bottles from men who collected them in pushcarts. Western then washed and resold them to manufacturers who needed to bottle their products.

Soon after its founding, the company—located in the northwest section of downtown St. Louis—underwent a name change. Kranzberg discovered that a Cincinnati firm was already called Western Bottle, so he revised his to Northwestern Bottle.

The Great Depression was hard on the company, but Kranzberg sensed that repeal of Prohibition was in the air. He bought the Schlitz beer distributorship and had two railroad cars of beer waiting on the day that repeal took effect. The rush of customers helped to save Northwestern.

After World War II, the company got into the plastic bottle business. In 1967, Northwestern opened its first location outside of St. Louis—a small distribution center in Memphis.

Focused on Growth

Today, Kranson has its corporate headquarters in St. Louis, along with a warehouse, the St.

Louis sales office, and Clinton Packaging. The firm employs some 60 people in St. Louis and 300 overall.

One goal for the future is to continue integrating the newest acquisitions into Kranson's corporate culture, relying on the company's strong management team for careful planning and strong follow-through.

Already the largest company in its industry, Kranson also plans on still more growth. In coming years, the company hopes to continue expanding at a rapid pace through internal growth and acquisition.

VIALS OF PERFUME, BOTTLES OF WINE, JARS OF SPAGHETTI SAUCE, AND SPRAY DISPENSERS OF CLEANING FLUID— NEARLY ANY HOUSEHOLD ITEM THAT COMES IN A BOTTLE, JAR, TUBE, SPRAYER, OR OTHER CONTAINER MAY WELL BE THE PRODUCT OF KRANSON INDUSTRIES. THIS ST. LOUIS-BASED FIRM, FOUNDED IN 1902, IS THE WORLD'S ONLY SUPERDISTRIBUTOR OF GLASS AND PLASTIC BOTTLES, CLOSURES, AND DISPENSING DEVICES.

HUSSMANN CORPORATION

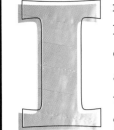

N 1906, WHILE SELLING SUPPLIES TO ST. LOUIS BUTCHERS, HARRY L. Hussmann saw the need for a safe, attractive way to display cuts of meat in clear view of shoppers. In 1917, he developed a glass-front refrigeration case, cooled by salt and ice. With that product, a new company—and industry leader—was born. ❡ Today, Hussmann Corporation is the world's largest manu-

facturer and marketer of food store equipment and commercial refrigeration products. The company—whose 1998 sales and revenues totaled $1.2 billion—has the leading market share position in the United States, Canada, the United Kingdom, Spain, Portugal, Mexico, and China. In most of these markets, its share is close to double that of its closest competitor.

On January 30, 1998, Hussmann reached an important milestone: It spun off from its parent company, the Whitman Corporation, and became an independent company. The new public company, Hussmann International, Inc., parent to Hussmann Corporation, is now

traded on the New York Stock Exchange.

This is only the latest step forward for a company that already has a solid record of achievement. Its 8,700 employees—one-third of them based outside the United States—design, manufacture, sell, install, and service Hussmann's merchandising and refrigeration systems for the world's food industry. Hussmann's global manufacturing capabilities include 26 plants located in 10 countries. The company also staffs a distribution and service network that reaches 80 countries in North America, Latin America, Europe, the Middle East, Africa, and the Asia Pacific region.

Through sophisticated research and development, strategic acquisitions, and a strong global expansion strategy, Hussmann intends to build on its record of growth.

"We believe our responsiveness to our customers and to industry trends, such as the emergence of home meal replacement, positions us for future success," says J. Larry Vowell, Hussmann's president and chief executive officer. "Our core North American operations are

experiencing strong demand, international business is expanding, and our product line leads the industry in quality and operating efficiency."

QUALITY, VALUE, AND SERVICE FOR EVERY CUSTOMER

Hussmann's core business, and 70 percent of its market, is in providing supermarkets with merchandising and refrigeration equipment for fresh and frozen foods. The company manufactures more than 550 types of merchandisers, which can be customized to display a variety of items. The majority of Hussmann's merchandiser sales are in its North American region; the United Kingdom; Mexico; and, to a lesser extent, Brazil and Asia.

Other customers include convenience and specialty stores, which constitute about 20 percent of the company's business. From sandwich merchandisers and salad bars to refrigerated cases for bakeries, florist shops, and ice-cream parlors, Hussmann serves the market with a wide range of products.

Refrigeration system sales account for just under 10 percent of Hussmann's business.

CLOCKWISE FROM TOP:
SINCE 1906, HUSSMANN CORPORATION HAS LED THE INDUSTRY WITH NEW PRODUCT INNOVATIONS.

HUSSMANN'S IMPACT MERCHANDISERS PROVIDE ENERGY EFFICIENCY AND STABLE PRODUCT TEMPERATURES.

HUSSMANN'S STATE-OF-THE-ART MANUFACTURING PROCESSES HAVE RESULTED IN IMPROVED OPERATING EFFICIENCIES.

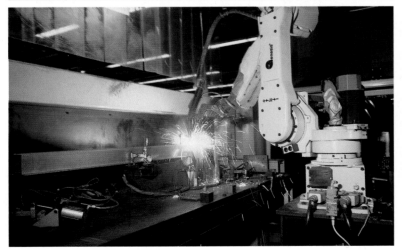

Hussmann coils, condensers, and refrigeration systems are custom engineered for cold storage warehouses, large food processing plants, bottling companies, and other applications.

DOING BUSINESS AROUND THE WORLD

Hussmann's North American market is the company's largest business unit. The supermarket business in this area is flourishing as well, and Hussmann supplies 19 of North America's top 20 food retailers with its products.

Outside of North America, Latin America is Hussmann's largest and most rapidly growing international business segment. In 1998, the region generated approximately $150 million in sales. Mexico is one of Hussmann's most active growth markets, particularly in the beverage industry, where the company supplies coolers for soft drink and brewery merchandisers.

BUILDING FOR THE FUTURE

Over its 93-year history, Hussmann has grown through a series of key acquisitions. One of the company's most recent acquisitions is Koxka, the leading commercial refrigeration company in Spain and Portugal. "The addition of Koxka will contribute significantly to Hussmann's worldwide industry-leading position," says Vowell. "It establishes a prominent market position for Hussmann in continental Europe and ensures a platform for future growth in the European marketplace."

The company has also expanded through innovation. By 1930, Hussmann had patented the first refrigerated display case and helped to develop the industry's first frozen food case. More recently, Hussmann introduced the environmentally friendly PROTOCOL Refrigeration System. PROTOCOL is Hussmann's proprietary product that was designed to perform quietly and efficiently in the merchandising area of a store, thus eliminating the requirement for the costly back room area. And in 1995, the company introduced its most energy-efficient line of merchandisers, the IMPACT line. The line already accounts for more than 80 percent of Hussmann's supermarket display case sales.

Today, the company continues to actively develop new products—46 of them in 1997 alone—in its $14 million research and development laboratory located at Hussmann's corporate headquarters in Bridgeton, Missouri. With 50,000 square feet of space, it is the largest facility of its kind in the industry, and allows Hussmann to simulate a variety of climates, test the durability of cases on over-the-road truck trips, and measure the cases' noise levels. Hussmann also conducts in-store testing of its products at customer locations and partners with vendors to test supplied components.

Hussmann plans to continue its tradition of growth. From 1994 to 1999, the company invested more than $50 million in its Bridgeton plant in order

to expand its production of refrigerated display cases to meet the growing demand. And the company is investing $33 million in a global information system that covers all major business processes, including global purchasing, financial controls, working capital management, engineering, design, and more.

Throughout its history, Hussmann has remained committed to continuing its overall support for the communities where its employees live and work. The company lends its support through a variety of means, including monetary contributions, employee volunteers, and donations such as food supplies and operating equipment.

"We have built a reputation as a leader in our industry and in the communities in which we work," says Vowell. "Now we intend to bring that same level of achievement to our performance as an independent company."

CLOCKWISE FROM TOP LEFT: HUSSMANN R&D CENTERS ENSURE QUALITY THROUGH STRINGENT PRODUCT TESTING.

LATIN AMERICA IS ONE OF HUSSMANN'S MOST RAPIDLY GROWING BUSINESS SEGMENTS.

THE IMPACT LINE ACCOUNTS FOR MORE THAN 80 PERCENT OF HUSSMANN'S SUPERMARKET DISPLAY CASE SALES.

IN 1906, FRED WEHRENBERG OPENED HIS FIRST SMALL THEATER IN St. Louis at the corner of Cherokee Street and Jefferson Avenue. While silent movies flickered on the screen, his nephew drummed in the background and his wife played piano in the pit. Since then, much has changed. Today, Wehrenberg Theatres has 40 locations in three states—Missouri, Illinois, and Arizona—with a total of 300 movie screens. And the family no longer provides sound effects. Wehrenberg was the first in the region to have THX digital sound systems, and in 1999, the company will install an even more sophisticated, seven-track Dolby system in its theaters.

Amid these improvements, Wehrenberg retains a strong sense of continuity as the oldest family-held theater company in the United States. Ronald Krueger, grandson of the founder, is president and CEO. His son, Ronald Krueger II—the fourth generation—is director of theater operations. In 1998, the company won an award from Southern Illinois University as the top family-held business in St. Louis.

"We are proud to offer the latest in entertainment facilities, and to be a progressive company," says the elder Krueger. Among these facilities are several new locations. Wehrenberg, the first company in St. Louis to create a multiplex theater, has opened 14 screens in Arnold and Jamestown Mall, 20 screens at Ronnies, and a 24-screen multiplex in Chesterfield Valley. Another new theater is coming in Eureka, and an enlarged facility—from six to 15 screens—is coming to Mid Rivers Mall. All are equipped with the latest features, including comfortable stadium seating.

Wehrenberg, the only area company to offer reserved seating in multiplex theaters, is also embarking on innovative ways to sell movie tickets. In the future, Wehrenberg Theatres will inaugurate a frequent moviegoer program in which patrons win prizes, discounts, and admissions for buying tickets and concession foods. The company also plans to offer a way for moviegoers to purchase tickets via the Internet.

During his lifetime in the movie business, Krueger has had many exciting opportunities. As a child, he was photographed with Roy Rogers and Trigger. He has also met an assortment of Hollywood stars, such as Michael Douglas, Clint Eastwood, and Robin Williams. Today, he and his company are busy giving opportunities to others. Krueger has served as head of the 5,200-member Shrine Temple of Eastern Missouri, which supports many charities, including the Shriners Hospital for Children.

Wehrenberg Theatres has a hot-air balloon, minitrain, and calliope that are often visible at civic events. And at holiday time, the company supports the Salvation Army Tree of Lights campaign with its Cans Film Festival, which collected more than 70,000 cans of food in 1998. With a commitment to serving its home community and offering a superior movie experience to its patrons, Wehrenberg Theatres enters the new millennium assured of continued success.

TODAY, WEHRENBERG THEATRES HAS 40 LOCATIONS IN THREE STATES— MISSOURI, ILLINOIS, AND ARIZONA— WITH A TOTAL OF 300 MOVIE SCREENS.

THE EARTHGRAINS COMPANY OPERATES PACKAGED fresh-bakery and refrigerated-dough businesses in the United States and Europe. One of the few international baking companies, Earthgrains is aggressively pursuing acquisitions and is also growing through new-product development; through

THE EARTHGRAINS COMPANY

partnerships with customers, including some of the biggest grocery retailers in the United States; and through innovative use of information technology.

Earthgrains is one of the largest producers of fresh packaged bread and baked goods in the United States, marketing products under leading brands, including Colonial™, Rainbo®, IronKids®, Earth Grains®, Grant's Farm®, San Luis Sourdough®, Sunbeam®, and Break Cake®. Earthgrains bakes bread in more than 40 bakeries across the country. In Europe, Earthgrains is the largest baker of packaged American-style sliced bread in Spain and the second largest in Portugal. Leading European brands include Bimbo®, Silueta®, and Martínez®.

Earthgrains is also one of just two manufacturers of refrigerated-dough products in the United States, making such items as jumbo biscuits, dinner rolls, cinnamon rolls, croissants, and cookie dough that can be found under leading grocery-store brands and the Merico® label. Earthgrains is a major manufacturer of store-brand toaster pastries. In Europe, Earthgrains is the largest refrigerated-dough producer in France—Europe's largest refrigerated-dough market— and the only producer of canned refrigerated dough on the Continent.

Earthgrains, established in 1925, was known as Campbell Taggart, Inc., for many years. The company changed its name to the Earthgrains Company in February 1996, a month before being spun off as an independent public company with its stock trading on the New York Stock Exchange (ticker symbol: EGR). Anheuser-Busch Com-

panies, Inc., owned Earthgrains from 1982 to 1996.

SUCCESS THROUGH QUALITY PRODUCTS, CUSTOMER SERVICE, COST CONTROL, AND ACQUISITIONS

Earthgrains has used focus, flexibility, and rewards to drive rapid, continuous improvement. In the U.S. baking industry, Earthgrains has focused on developing new value-added bread and bakery products, primarily in the emerging premium and superpremium product sectors. Examples of new-product successes include the Earth Grains brand super-premium shelf-stable bagels, premium Grant's Farm Potato Bread, and a new calcium-fortified IronKids Bread for children. These products were developed using Earthgrains' R&D facility located in St. Louis.

Earthgrains has also used its flexibility to react quickly to new opportunities. Among Earthgrains' recent acquisitions are the CooperSmith, Inc., baking system in the southeast United States; San Luis Sourdough, Inc., a specialty baker in California; and Repostería

Martínez Group, a leading baked-sweet-goods producer in Spain.

Earthgrains is using information technology to partner with customers, sharpen its business focus, and enhance efficiencies. The company has consolidated its domestic accounting functions into a St. Louis-based Financial Shared Services Center that employs about 140 professional and office workers. Through specialized teams and automation, the center is increasing efficiency and improving customer service.

More information on Earthgrains is available on the company's Web site at www.earthgrains.com.

EARTHGRAINS COMPANY HEAD-QUARTERS IS LOCATED IN CLAYTON, MISSOURI.

A LEADING MANUFACTURER OF BAKERY PRODUCTS AND REFRIGERATED DOUGH IN THE UNITED STATES AND EUROPE, EARTHGRAINS MAKES FRESH PACKAGED BREAD, BUNS, ROLLS, BAGELS, SNACK CAKES, REFRIGERATED-DOUGH PRODUCTS, AND TOASTER PASTRIES.

LOAVES OF SUNBEAM® BRAND BREAD HEAD FOR THE SLICER AT EARTHGRAINS' BAKERY IN VALDESE, NORTH CAROLINA—ONE OF SEVERAL BAKERIES THAT HAVE BEEN ACQUIRED BY THE COMPANY SINCE IT BECAME INDEPENDENT IN 1996.

FURNITURE BRANDS INTERNATIONAL, INC.

FOUNDED IN ST. LOUIS IN 1911, FURNITURE BRANDS INTERnational, Inc. is today the largest residential furniture manufacturer in the United States. Supported by a highly focused growth strategy and three of the best-known brand names in the industry—Broyhill, Lane, and Thomasville—Furniture Brands continues the tradition of excellence that has been the hallmark of its long history.

INTERNATIONAL SHOE COMPANY

International Shoe Company was formed in St. Louis in 1911 by the merger of Roberts, Johnson & Rand Shoe Company, established in 1899, and Peters Shoe Company, originally formed in 1836. Through the years, International Shoe expanded its operations in St. Louis and around the world, and by 1960, had grown to become the largest footwear manufacturer in the country. Generations of St. Louis children grew up wearing Red Goose, Poll Parrot, and Weatherbird shoes manufactured by this hometown company.

In 1953, International Shoe began acquiring companies in footwear and other industries such as retail merchandising and apparel manufacturing. In recognition of its new identity as a diverse holding company, the corporate name was changed to Interco Incorporated on March 1, 1966.

By the mid-1980s, Interco had 24 major operating subsidiaries and divisions in four operating groups: footwear manufacturing and retailing,

apparel manufacturing, general retail merchandising, and furniture manufacturing. In addition to International Shoe, such well-known St. Louis-based companies as Central Hardware, Golde's, P.N. Hirsch, Biltwell, and International Hat were all a part of Interco.

A FOCUS ON FURNITURE

Beginning in the mid-1980s, Interco initiated an asset redeployment program, which continued through a more accelerated restructuring of the company in 1988 and a reorganization in 1991 and 1992. This process culminated in 1994 with the spin-off to the Interco shareholders of the last of the company's nonfurniture operations.

In 1979, Interco had entered the furniture business with the acquisition of Ethan Allen Inc. This segment of the company's business expanded with the acquisition of Broyhill Furniture Industries, Inc., in 1980 and the Lane Company, Incorporated in 1987. Ethan Allen was sold as part of the restructuring in 1989. With the acquisition of Thomasville Furniture Industries, Inc. in 1995, Interco completed its transformation from the largest footwear manufacturer to the largest residential furniture manufacturer in the United States. On March 1, 1996, in recognition of the new focus of its business, Interco changed its name to Furniture Brands International, Inc.

QUALITY AND STYLE LEADER

Today, the company markets its products under three of the best-known brand names in the industry—Broyhill, Lane, and Thomasville—and is a quality and style leader across a broad spectrum of price categories, from premium home furnishings to lower-priced, ready-to-assemble furniture. The company is organized into three primary

operating subsidiaries of similar size that target particular product and price categories.

Since its founding more than 70 years ago, Broyhill has become one of the most widely recognized residential furniture brands in America. The company manufactures a full line of wood furniture, upholstered products, and occasional pieces designed to appeal to a wide consumer base. Its product strategy is to be a style leader while maintaining the quality and value long associated with the Broyhill brand name.

Lane operates six divisions that specialize in niche markets, including reclining and motion furniture, 18th-century reproductions, wicker and rattan furniture, cedar chests, and finely tailored upholstered furniture. Through its biggest division, Action Industries, Lane is the largest manufacturer of motion furniture in the country and the second-largest manufacturer of recliners. The company's other operating divisions—Hickory Chair, Pearson, Hickory Business Furniture, Lane, and Lane Venture—all service their own markets with finely crafted furniture.

Thomasville, Furniture Brands' most recent acquisition, produces a broad line of wood and upholstered products, and has been rated by consumers as the highest-quality furniture brand. Thomasville's wood division covers the major style categories: American traditional/country, 18th century, European traditional, and casual contemporary. Its upholstery division markets products in three major styles—traditional, American traditional/country, and casual contemporary—targeting the best and premium price categories.

AN ENDURING FORMULA FOR SUCCESS

Since the days of its founding, Furniture Brands has been actively involved as a leader in the St. Louis business community. As a member of Civic Progress, the company is a

strong supporter of activities promoting the development of the local economy. Additionally, through the Interco Charitable Trust, Furniture Brands makes significant contributions each year to charitable, civic, and educational organizations and projects throughout the metropolitan area.

From its home base in St. Louis, Furniture Brands has become the largest and most profitable residential furniture manufacturer in the country. While the nature of its business has changed, the company remains focused on the same competitive strengths that spurred the growth of its founding predecessor: widely recognized brand names; a broad range of product offerings across all price categories; extensive distribution networks, including dedicated galleries located in independently owned retail locations; innovative, high-quality products; highly efficient, low-cost manufacturing capabilities; and experienced management teams.

These proven growth strategies have been the key to the continuing realization of the simple goal established in Furniture Brands' mission statement: To become the industry's undisputed leader as an innovative furniture manufacturer and, in the process, to deliver a significantly improved stockholder value.

SUPPORTED BY A HIGHLY FOCUSED GROWTH STRATEGY AND THREE OF THE BEST-KNOWN BRAND NAMES IN THE INDUSTRY—BROYHILL, LANE, AND THOMASVILLE—FURNITURE BRANDS CONTINUES THE TRADITION OF EXCELLENCE THAT HAS BEEN THE HALLMARK OF ITS LONG HISTORY.

FORD MOTOR COMPANY

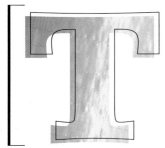

THE FORD EXPLORER IS THE NUMBER-ONE-SELLING sport utility vehicle (SUV) in the world, and it is produced at the Ford Motor Company, St. Louis Assembly Plant, which has been rated in customer satisfaction surveys as the number one Ford plant in the United States. ¶ The St. Louis plant, located in suburban Hazelwood, employs some 2,300 people: 2,100 hourly workers, members of the United Auto Workers (UAW) union, and 200 salaried employees. In 1998, they produced some 221,000 Ford Explorers, working two shifts in production and three in maintenance operations. Only one other Ford plant in the United States—located in Louisville—makes the Explorer.

"Our goal is to provide the highest-quality sport utility vehicle in the world," says Morris Wilson, plant manager. "Through the continuous involvement of hourly and salaried workforce on the floor, we are constantly discussing new ways of improving the quality of our product."

BUILT WITH PRIDE

To maintain the momentum of this quality improvement effort, the St. Louis Assembly Plant has initiated two important programs. One is Ford Total Productive Maintenance (FTPM), which got fully under way in 1996 and has since been extremely successful. Workers clean and inspect equipment, fixing potential defects that could cause a quality issue or production loss. The other is Ford Production System (FPS). This program, begun recently, is aimed at delivering vehicles to customers quicker and reducing inventory.

The plant has also embarked on a major, $22 million expansion to the Hazelwood facility, which is already 2.6 million square feet in size. This new construction will add more room to the back of the plant, so that workers can sequence vehicles more efficiently and get them to the customer sooner.

THE FORD MOTOR COMPANY, ST. LOUIS ASSEMBLY PLANT, LOCATED IN SUBURBAN HAZELWOOD, EMPLOYS SOME 2,300 PEOPLE: 2,100 HOURLY WORKERS, MEMBERS OF THE UNITED AUTO WORKERS (UAW) UNION, AND 200 SALARIED EMPLOYEES.

This expansion is due to be completed in January 2000.

A LONG HISTORY IN ST. LOUIS

In the front lobby of the St. Louis Assembly Plant is a large mural, painted by a Ford employee, which depicts highlights of company history—including the Ford Model T—as well as that of the city. After displaying his cars at the 1904 World's Fair, Henry Ford opened the company's first St. Louis sales office in 1905 at 3667 Olive Street. Business grew quickly, and in 1914, Ford established a new plant nearby on Forest Park Boulevard. Over the years, this plant turned out Ford cars and even tractors. By 1943, when World War II temporarily shut down civilian car production, more than 800,000 vehicles had been produced at the Forest Park facility. But this plant was small and outdated, so in 1946, Ford began construction of its present facility in Hazelwood, which was dedicated in 1948.

This plant was originally intended to produce Fords, but instead it was turned over to

IN 1914, HENRY FORD ESTABLISHED A PLANT ON FOREST PARK BOULEVARD THAT TURNED OUT CARS AND EVEN TRACTORS. BUT THIS PLANT QUICKLY BECAME OUTDATED, SO IN 1946, FORD BEGAN CONSTRUCTION OF ITS PRESENT FACILITY IN HAZELWOOD, WHICH WAS DEDICATED IN 1948.

the Lincoln-Mercury Division. By September 1953, the St. Louis Assembly Plant had assembled 500,000 cars. Then, on January 25, 1984, its mission changed again, when it was turned over to Ford's truck division.

From 1985 through 1997, the St. Louis Assembly Plant was the sole U.S. plant to build the popular Aerostar minivan. To meet demand, the company often had to schedule two 10-hour shifts, which collectively produced 1,000 vans daily. In August 1992, the St. Louis Assembly Plant was awarded Q1 status by Ford—a prestigious certification given for hard work and attention to detail.

In 1995, the plant began producing the Explorer, along with the Aerostar. But by 1997, the market was changing, and Ford decided to cease Aerostar production. On August 22, after more than 2 million had been built, the last of these minivans rolled off the line, and the plant was entirely dedicated to SUV production.

SPIRIT OF ST. LOUIS

More than 85 years after its founding, the St. Louis Assembly Plant continues to have a significant impact on the local community. In 1996, for example, it had a total payroll of $163 million and paid $11.9 million in state and local taxes, in addition to making contribu-

tions to the United Way totaling $155,000.

Plant employees, both hourly and salaried, also work together to help charitable causes throughout the area. Together, they donate scholarships to high school students from disadvantaged backgrounds so they can attend college. Last year, they began a new program called Love Our Children in which they help terminally ill children of plant employees. One boy received a trip to Disney World, and a young girl got a specially equipped computer setup. In some cases, hourly and salaried employees work independently on certain projects. Through the St. Patrick's Center, salaried workers last year took time off the job to help restore homes and work with needy people in the community.

In 2001, the St. Louis Assembly Plant will undergo another change, as a face-lift of the

Explorer requires some major retooling. But as it has in the past, says Wilson, the St. Louis workforce will meet this challenge with hard work, pride, quality workmanship, and excellent cooperation between union and management. He notes, "We have proven that, together, hourly and salaried workforce members can and do produce quality products efficiently."

DIMAC CORPORATION

FOR DIMAC CORPORATION, TOTAL PROGRAM MANAGEMENT™ is more than just a slogan. Offering a wide spectrum of direct marketing services, DIMAC is the largest vertically integrated direct marketing company in the United States, with more than 2,800 employees in 10 cities nationwide. The company's many services include creative development, strategy and planning, research, print production, personalization, lettershop, database management and information services, tracking and fulfillment, and telemarketing.

"The unique position of this corporation is that we are truly an A-to-Z shop when it comes to direct marketing. We are not a general agency that provides direct marketing services, and we're not a production facility that has a creative component. We are truly a vertically integrated direct response marketing organization—really a one-stop shop," says Alex Crohn, senior vice president, sales and marketing.

Since DIMAC was founded in St. Louis in 1921, a significant piece of its business has been located in the area. Within its large facility in suburban Bridgeton is the corporate headquarters of one major DIMAC subsidiary, DIMAC DIRECT, which employs some 750 people.

DIMAC DIRECT

DIMAC DIRECT provides an extensive range of services—strategic/creative, printing, laser, and lettershop; database; and fulfillment—for some of the most prominent U.S. companies: AT&T, American Express, American Banker's Insurance Group, Capital One, NationsBank/Bank of America, Prudential, and Honda Corporation, among many others.

Since 1989, the company has done direct mail nationally for Blockbuster Video, supporting the grand openings of some 4,500 Blockbuster stores. Through DIMAC DIRECT's demographic and research capabilities, the company maps the households within a certain radius of each store, and then works with the stores to bring targeted traffic to that location.

Among DIMAC DIRECT's capabilities is the traditional direct mail letter package, which includes various components, such as a cover letter, business reply card, envelope, and brochure. The company also produces a range of job sizes from small-volume complex programs to 10 million pieces or more, and has everything needed to accommodate programs ranging from single-color to full-color high-quality printed pieces on a wide variety of paper stocks.

In addition to the St. Louis facility, DIMAC DIRECT has another production location employing more than 500 people in Central Islip, Long Island. The two facilities per-

CLOCKWISE FROM TOP: DIMAC DIRECT'S SENIOR MANAGEMENT INCLUDES (STANDING, FROM LEFT) JOHN MENEOUGH, PRESIDENT; MIKE TASCHLER, EXECUTIVE VICE PRESIDENT; GARY VEST, SENIOR VICE PRESIDENT, AT&T ACCOUNT; SHERRY DONAHUE, DIRECTOR OF HUMAN RESOURCES; (SEATED, FROM LEFT) ALEX CROHN, SENIOR VICE PRESIDENT OF SALES AND MARKETING; RON LUEBBERT, VICE PRESIDENT OF ADMINISTRATIVE SERVICES; MIKE SPEICHINGER, VICE PRESIDENT AND CFO; AND CAROL MYERS, ASSISTANT TO THE PRESIDENT.

FROM ONE-COLOR TO SIX-COLOR JOBS AND MORE, DIMAC'S PRODUCTS ARE PRODUCED TO FIT EACH PROGRAM'S GOALS.

HEADQUARTERED IN SUBURBAN ST. LOUIS COUNTY, DIMAC DIRECT OPERATES FROM A 280,000-SQUARE-FOOT FACILITY.

BILL LESLIE

BILL LESLIE

form the same kinds of print and mail functions.

DMW Worldwide and Other Subsidiaries

DMW Worldwide is the strategic/creative arm of DIMAC Corporation, headquartered in Philadelphia with offices in New York and Boston. DMW Worldwide serves a national client base of financial, high-tech, insurance, health care, and business-to-business firms. Its services encompass all direct response media, including broadcast, print, mail, and interactive.

In addition to DMW Worldwide, DIMAC Corporation has a variety of other complementary subsidiaries. Palm Coast Data, headquartered in Palm Coast, Florida, handles subscription renewal programs for many of North America's largest publishers, and MBS Multimode, based on Long Island, is a database marketing company.

In 1998, DIMAC joined forces with AmeriComm, a large direct mail firm with a number of subsidiary companies, to form DIMAC Promotional Graphics. One of the subsidiaries, Convertagraphics, headquartered in Roanoke, specializes in producing in-line formats, such as letters attached to envelopes as part of a continuous-feed process. Another subsidiary is Double Envelope, an envelope manufacturer that die-cuts, folds, and glues a full range of standard and custom envelopes at its three locations.

Total Program Management™

Altogether, DIMAC's acquisitions have created a company with broad-based capabilities and complementary skills. For example, DIMAC DIRECT did not previously have the ability to produce envelopes. Now, most envelope conversion can be done through Double Envelope. This flexibility has many advantages for the firm's clients. For one thing, they can count on DIMAC—which is rarely depen-

▶ BILL LESLIE

dent on the schedules of outside vendors—to deliver on deadline.

"We also approach the market as a kind of chameleon, since we sell all the pieces of our business," says Crohn. "If we go into ABC Corporation and they need subscription renewal work, we can bring in Palm Coast Data. If the client is a major player in direct marketing, they may need a lot of our services, from database work through production. Whatever the client wants, we are able to access it through our nucleus of companies."

In the future, DIMAC intends to become increasingly involved in direct marketing through the Internet, which the company sees as a major area of growth. In addition, DIMAC will continue to help clients achieve higher efficiencies and optimal returns on their marketing investments. "As we head into the 21st century, it is important for us to recognize all the channels that are now opening up to us," says Crohn. "We look forward to aggressively looking at all of these areas, while continuing to expand our capabilities to the business community."

▶ BILL LESLIE

BUILDING & CONSTRUCTION TRADES COUNCIL OF ST. LOUIS

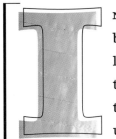 N 1972, CONSTRUCTION INDUSTRY LEADERS IN ST. LOUIS TOOK A bold step toward progress. For decades, conflict had pitted labor against management and union against union. Realizing that the development of the city could not take place amid this kind of antagonism, the leaders signed a memorandum of understanding—a kind of peace treaty—promising teamwork

and mutual respect. The group also formed a groundbreaking organization called PRIDE, the nation's first labor-management organization in the construction trades. Its name—an acronym for Productivity and Responsibility Increase Development and Employment—set the tone for the group.

On the labor side, it was the Building & Construction Trades Council of St. Louis, affiliated with the AFL-CIO, that helped bring this group together. In fact, Richard Mantia, secretary-treasurer of the Council, served as PRIDE's first cochair, along with contractor Al Fleischer, representing the Council of Construction Employers.

Today, PRIDE is still working actively to bring management and labor together. Over the years, it has resolved dozens of disputes through communication and compromise, and it has served as a model for other programs across the United States. PRIDE is still a forum and a mediator, more than 25 years after its founding, thanks in part to the strong role played at the outset by the Building & Construction Trades Council of St. Louis.

ORGANIZED FOR THE FUTURE

The history of the Building & Construction Trades Council of St. Louis dates back to 1922, when the construction trades were flourishing in the area. Between the two world wars, St. Louis was a booming place. The city's older businesses were expanding, while newer industries—brewing, milling, shoe manufacturing, and chemical goods—were going up quickly.

The Building & Construction Trades Council of St. Louis was established to act as the union of unions: a single entity that would help unite and lobby for the individual trade unions then organized throughout the city. Today, the Building & Construction Trades Council of St. Louis is still a vibrant organization composed of 28 AFL-CIO building trades unions, representing thousands of local journeymen and apprentice workers.

"We are a very strong council—one of the strongest in the country—because of the solidarity in the trades," says Gerald T. Feldhaus, executive secretary-treasurer. "The city is heavily unionized, more than 98 percent of them AFL-CIO members, and the home building industry is 85 percent building and construction trades. In the rest of the country, the figure is probably 15 or 20 percent."

TODAY, THE BUILDING & CONSTRUCTION TRADES COUNCIL OF ST. LOUIS IS A VIBRANT ORGANIZATION COMPOSED OF 28 AFL-CIO BUILDING TRADES UNIONS, REPRESENTING THOUSANDS OF LOCAL JOURNEYMEN AND APPRENTICE WORKERS.

production studio, in which commercials and other recorded items are produced. A satellite uplink and downlink system receives foreign broadcasts and sends programs, such as the St. Louis Cardinals play-by-play, around the world.

A New Focus on Innovative Programming

The goal of KMOX has always been the same: to become the best regional radio station in America. But the station is now working in new ways to achieve that goal, especially through partnerships with television stations and newspapers, including the *St. Louis Post-Dispatch*, the *St. Louis American*, the Suburban Journals publications, and the *St. Louis Business Journal*, for example. KMOX has initiated the weekly *Progress Report* to update listeners on regional development. The station also provides extensive information on its Web site.

KMOX is also adding to its news, features, and specialty programming. It is expanding the number of staff members doing on-the-street reporting; it has also added features such as a Saturday morning segment with Martha Stewart and a stock report from Edward D. Jones.

"This is programming that we think today's active person between 35 and 60 years old wants to hear," says Carroll. "We are constantly challenging ourselves to provide new information, and we ask our listeners to tell us what they need and want to know."

Reaching Out to the Community

For years, KMOX has been sponsoring community programs, such as safety seminars, town hall meetings, scholarships, and internships. The station has also supported fund drives, and relief for hospitals and homeless shelters, as well as helping families throughout the St. Louis area.

In the future, KMOX plans to become still more involved in

community efforts. The station now has its own not-for-profit charitable arm called Outreach, a division of CBS Radio St. Louis, that raises funds through special events and custom-designed on-air programming for clients. Its aim is to publicize some of the area's smaller charitable organizations, which are not funded by the United Way, and attract both funding and volunteers to help support them.

The station also endeavors to help build community pride. In fall 1998, KMOX gathered a number of St. Louis organizations—the Regional Commerce and Growth Association (RCGA), Downtown St. Louis, Sports Commission, and Mayor's

Office—and sponsored a huge, highly successful Fanfest event downtown to celebrate Mark McGwire's 62nd home run.

"For a quarter of a century, KMOX has served St. Louis in a positive way," says Carroll. "Most broadcast markets don't have this kind of consistency, whether in print, television, or radio. In today's ever changing world of consolidation, KMOX is a community mainstay."

CLOCKWISE FROM TOP: KMOX RADIO TALK SHOW HOSTS DOUG McELVEIN AND CHARLES BRENNAN PERFORM LIVE ON-AIR AT KMOX'S ANNUAL HOLIDAY RADIO SHOW AT WESTPORT PLAYHOUSE TO BENEFIT LOCAL CHARITIES.

ST. LOUIS CARDINALS OWNER FRED HANSER, KMOX SPORTSCASTER JACK BUCK, AND ST. LOUIS CARDINALS OWNER BILL DeWITT JR. ARE SHOWN IN FRONT OF THE BUST OF BUCK, HONORING HIM FOR HIS LEGENDARY CAREER IN BROADCASTING.

CHARLES BRENNAN OF *The Morning Meeting* IS A HOUSEHOLD NAME IN ST. LOUIS.

JCPENNEY

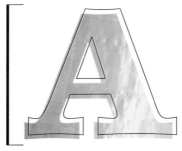

ANY SHOPPER WHO HAS NOT VISITED A JCPENNEY STORE for the past few years needs to take another look. A $30 billion company headquartered in Dallas, with a district office and nine stores in the St. Louis area, JCPenney has adapted to changing American shopping patterns. ❡ Once considered a mainstay for middle America, the company has expanded its range of products to appeal as well to a more affluent customer. While mid-range items still make up 60 to 70 percent of the merchandise, some 15 to 20 percent consists of higher-priced items. The mix has increased substantially, with the addition of a host of well-known labels and such popular private brands as Arizona, St. John's Bay, Hunt Club, and Stafford.

And the company has made other changes as well, expanding its burgeoning catalog business—number one in sales nationwide—with an increasing number of specialty catalogs. It has also opened a new line of home stores—including one in south St. Louis County—that carry only household furnishings and accessories.

JCPenney has also been branching out in new directions. In 1997, the company acquired Eckerd Corporation, one of the nation's largest drugstore chains. JCPenney Insurance, which markets life, accident and health, and credit insurance, has more than 9 million policies across the United States and Canada. And the company has also established an international division.

AN AMERICAN LEGEND
Such ability to size up and meet customer needs has made JCPenney a legend in retail history. The company, which will celebrate its 100th anniversary in 2002, is one of America's largest department store chains, operating more than 1,230 stores in all 50 states, Puerto Rico, Mexico, and Chile. It has more store space—most of it in premier shopping malls— than any other U.S. department store.

While JCPenney's business has changed, its basic business philosophy—based on the Golden Rule—has not varied from the beginning. In fact, the first JCPenney store, opened by 26-year-old James Cash Penney in a small Wyoming mining town in 1902, was even called the Golden Rule Store.

Penney, the son of a Baptist minister, believed firmly in pricing fairly, avoiding credit, and giving customers good products and service. His philosophy— captured in the company's early slogan of Honor, Confidence, Service, and Cooperation— worked. Penney opened more and more stores, gradually replacing the Golden Rule name with his own, and established a corporate headquarters, first in Salt Lake City and later in New York City.

Even during the depression, the company flourished. By the end of the 1930s, JCPenney had grown to 1,586 stores, with annual sales exceeding $300 million. During World War II, the firm produced uniforms for the various service units and participated in countless wartime collection drives.

A ST. LOUIS FIRST
Before the war, JCPenney placed most of its stores on main streets in small towns across America. But following the war, the company responded to the rapid growth of the suburbs by opening

THE JCPENNEY HAMPTON VILLAGE STORE OPENED IN 1949 AS THE COMPANY'S FIRST STORE LOCATED IN A SUBURBAN SHOPPING CENTER.

its first suburban store off Main Street, in the Hampton Village Shopping Center at the corner of Hampton Avenue and Chippewa Street in St. Louis. The store is still open today, the only JCPenney still operating within the city of St. Louis.

During the 1950s, JCPenney began to serve the suburban market with stores that included appliances, sporting goods, and home furnishings, along with apparel. In the 1960s, it added styling salons, restaurants, and automotive and garden centers. The company issued the first JCPenney catalog in 1963.

In the 1980s, the firm inaugurated a dramatic restructuring, placing primary emphasis on higher-scale apparel and soft home furnishings. It also announced plans to spend more than $1 billion to modernize its stores. The corporate headquarters moved to a 125-acre campus in Dallas in 1987.

AMERICA'S NATIONAL DEPARTMENT STORE

By the 1990s, the company was making the shift from mass marketer to become America's national department store. Today, some 41 percent of store

space is devoted to women's clothing, with another 27 percent to men, 16 percent to children's, and 16 percent to home and leisure. Women account for more than 80 percent of clothing purchases in the JCPenney stores.

In addition to Hampton Village, there are eight St. Louis-area JCPenney stores. Five older stores are in the West County Center, South County Center, Fairview Heights, Alton, and Northwest Plaza, while three newer ones are at Jamestown Mall, St. Peters, and Chesterfield. Altogether, they employ some 2,200 associates.

True to its founding spirit, the company also believes in supporting civic and philanthropic causes in the communities it serves. On a national level, JCPenney is involved in activities related to education, minority business development, diversity, women's issues, volunteerism, and the environment. In St. Louis, the local associates strongly support the United Way and the American Red Cross, cosponsoring a major annual fund-raising event called Swing for Relief.

Other evidence of the company's local presence is found on the University of Missouri-

St. Louis (UM-SL) campus, where the expansive JCPenney Building is home to continuing education classes, conference rooms, and a 450-seat auditorium. The school constructed this building in 1971 with funds obtained from the sale of a downtown warehouse, donated to UM-SL by JCPenney.

With this compassion for the community, a history of excellent service, and a dedication to constant improvement in the future, JCPenney is poised to remain a retail leader in its second century of business.

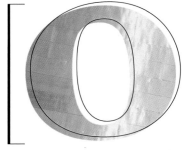

O N THE FRONT PAGE OF A RECENT EDITION OF THE *St. Louis American* was a story about three small children in the area who were adopted by an African-American couple. A heartwarming story, to be sure, but it also embodies the aesthetic behind the influential weekly. "That's the kind of

story we are very concerned about," says Dr. Donald Suggs, the *American*'s president and publisher. "It is not dramatic, but it lets people know that there is a great deal of humanity and concern, as well as negative experiences, out there."

Since the *American* was first published in 1928, the St. Louis-based newspaper has been running a broad range of stories about the city's African-American community of about 450,000. Some are inspirational features that highlight traditional values—hard work, family, self-reliance, and consumer news. Others are hard-hitting reports covering local politics and civil rights.

This rich mix reflects Suggs' view that, despite much progress made over the last few decades, African-Americans still face problems that are rooted in external forces. At the same time, he believes that African-Americans—particularly those in the emerging middle class— have an obligation to be engaged in resolving persistent problems, such as the growth of the black underclass. A newspaper like the *American*, he says, acts as

a kind of gadfly, prompting the entire community to take action and reminding the black community, in particular, of its own responsibility.

ACHIEVING SUCCESS IN A CHALLENGING MARKET

The *St. Louis American* plays a formidable role in its home city; it is the largest African-American newspaper in Missouri and one of the largest in the United States. Each week, from the paper's new headquarters on Lindell Boulevard, the 17-member staff turns out a new edition, sometimes with a special supplement. Then, 65,500 free copies are printed and distributed to some 750 locations, from supermarkets and pharmacies to freestanding boxes, throughout the city.

Certainly, there are challenges to running a "black weekly," as the *American* calls itself. With new and greater opportunities available in mainstream journalism, it is often hard to retain talented African-American staff members. In addition, the black community itself is becoming more geographically dispersed.

Yet, the *American* has still achieved considerable success.

Since Suggs, an oral surgeon, took over the paper a decade ago, revenues have quadrupled and circulation has increased dramatically. The newspaper now reaches an impressive 40 to 45 percent of African-American households in the Greater St. Louis region. It has also amassed numerous awards from the National Newspaper Association and the Missouri Press Association.

Suggs and his staff are also deeply involved in the community. During the Christmas holidays, for example, the *American* collaborates with a grassroots organization, Community Women Against Hardship, to help people in need. Suggs, whose board memberships include the St. Louis Zoo and the St. Louis Science Center, also founded the African-American Leadership Initiative, which in 1998 raised $700,000 for United Way.

"The *St. Louis American* is still a work in progress," says Suggs. "But I am convinced that a black weekly newspaper that is done well—that does a good job for its advertisers and serves its readers' interests—can be successful."

SINCE THE *AMERICAN* WAS FIRST PUBLISHED IN 1928, THE ST. LOUIS-BASED NEWSPAPER HAS BEEN RUNNING A BROAD RANGE OF STORIES ABOUT THE CITY'S AFRICAN-AMERICAN COMMUNITY OF ABOUT 450,000. SOME ARE INSPIRATIONAL FEATURES THAT HIGHLIGHT TRADITIONAL VALUES— HARD WORK, FAMILY, SELF-RELIANCE, AND CONSUMER NEWS. OTHERS ARE HARD-HITTING REPORTS COVERING LOCAL POLITICS AND CIVIL RIGHTS (LEFT).

THE *ST. LOUIS AMERICAN* PLAYS A FORMIDABLE ROLE IN ITS HOME CITY; IT IS THE LARGEST AFRICAN-AMERICAN NEWSPAPER IN MISSOURI AND ONE OF THE LARGEST IN THE UNITED STATES (RIGHT).

**W**HAT DOES IT TAKE TO BECOME THE PREEMINENT human resource consulting firm in St. Louis? Joe Vogl, who heads Towers Perrin's local office, will tell you it takes vision and expertise—the ability to anticipate and appropriately respond to organizations'

complex and ever changing needs. This assessment is especially true today, with human resource departments in the midst of a revolution of sorts.

"For years, an employee would devote his or her career to the firm and in return would receive steady pay increases and a standard set of health and retirement benefits," says Vogl. "But, as any human resource director will tell you, those days are over."

A COMPANY WITH VISION
Human resource departments are changing largely because the needs have changed for employers and employees. But Towers Perrin was prepared for this change. The firm has created a framework it calls Total Rewards, which looks at the big picture of how employee performance is affected by the four major areas of a company's reward program: pay, benefits, learning and development, and work environment. The key is integration.

"Human resource managers used to be able to solve their problems by handling them separately in each of those four areas," says Sherry Tucker, a principal in Towers Perrin's St. Louis office and a leader in the firm's Total Rewards initiative. "But now the areas are too closely interwoven. A broader perspective is required."

A COMPANY WITH EXPERTISE
Breadth is certainly a Towers Perrin strength. Located in the Interco Corporate Tower in Clayton, the office is staffed with 130 employees who are skilled in all areas of human resource management, including retirement plans, health and welfare plans, compensation, perfor-

mance management, change management, employee communications, risk management, and workers' compensation. And through Tillinghast-Towers Perrin, a Towers Perrin consulting company, counsel and actuarial services are provided to life and casualty insurance entities.

Additionally, the office draws from the resources of the rest of the firm, which comprises more than 8,200 employees in more than 80 offices worldwide.

ST. LOUIS SERVICE
SINCE 1945
The St. Louis office is the 11th largest of Towers Perrin's 43 offices in the United States. It established its local presence in 1945 through a predecessor

company, which later became Tillinghast, Nelson & Warren and in 1986 merged with Towers Perrin.

Towers Perrin's local clients include such well-known organizations as AmerenUE, Anheuser-Busch Companies, Inc., Brown Group, Inc., Daughters of Charity National Health System, Emerson Electric Co., Graybar Electric Company, Maritz Inc., Monsanto Company, Ralston Purina Company, and Solutia Inc.

These and many other St. Louis organizations value Towers Perrin's vision and expertise— the vision to help them anticipate the changes that lie ahead and the expertise to convert the changes into opportunities for the organization to improve its bottom line.

TOWERS PERRIN'S SENIOR LEADERSHIP INCLUDES (FROM LEFT) CRAIG KAINTZ, JOE VOGL, SHERRY TUCKER, CRAIG JONES, AND RANDY LYNN.

GenAmerica Corporation

A FAMILY OF PREMIER INSURANCE AND FINANCIAL SERVICES companies, GenAmerica Corporation helps people accumulate and preserve wealth during their productive years and meet the financial needs associated with retirement, illness, and death. A major player in the financial services industry, GenAmerica Corporation is listed as a Fortune 500 company.

GenAmerica Corporation evolved from General American Life Insurance Company, which reorganized in 1997 under a mutual holding company structure. GenAmerica Corporation, is a family of organizations that comprises 12 major subsidiaries, including General American Life and more than 50 affiliated companies. Through these various operating units, GenAmerica Corporation conducts business throughout North America and the world.

"We believe the creation of GenAmerica Corporation and

RICHARD A. LIDDY IS CHAIRMAN, PRESIDENT, AND CHIEF EXECUTIVE OFFICER OF GENAMERICA CORPORATION (RIGHT).

GENERAL AMERICAN LIFE INSURANCE COMPANY BEGAN ITS LIFE IN 1933 IN THIS BUILDING AT THE CORNER OF 15TH AND LOCUST STREETS IN ST. LOUIS (BELOW).

its family of companies is an approach that will serve our customers well," says Richard A. Liddy, chairman, president, and chief executive officer. "With this structure in place, we're confident about meeting the challenges of today's marketplace."

General American Life Insurance Company, which operated successfully as a mutual for more than 50 years, now ranks among the top 1 percent of all U.S. life insurance organizations.

In January 1999, GenAmerica's board of directors approved the development of a plan for the company to demutualize. Then in August 1999, the board authorized a Definitive Agreement with Metropolitan Life Insurance Company whereby MetLife acquires GenAmerica Corporation, including all its divisions and subsidiaries. MetLife is one of the world's largest financial services companies and the leader in life insurance sales in the United States. GenAmerica's headquarters will remain in St. Louis, and MetLife plans to preserve and build upon GenAmerica's franchise and brand names. MetLife has also announced plans to demutualize in 2000.

CREATING A SUCCESSFUL NEW OPERATING STRUCTURE
GenAmerica Corporation's four major business segments are Individual Life Insurance, Group Life and Health, Asset Management and Accumulation, and Reinsurance Group of America, Incorporated (RGA).

Individual Life primarily helps business owners, executives, and professionals with life insurance and related financial services. The company protects more than 350,000 policyholders from coast to coast.

The Group line primarily offers insurance and managed care services to medium-sized and large organizations. Many of them are household names, like Phillips Petroleum and Southwest Airlines. About 2 million employees and their dependents are covered. This line also helps organizations meet their employees' retirement plan needs.

Focusing on the insurance industry, Conning Corporation provides asset management, private equity, and research services to investor organizations. Cova Corporation offers individuals products and services for asset accumulation and retirement income. It markets life insurance and annuities through regional broker-dealers, national wirehouses, and financial institutions.

RGA shares risks with major life insurance companies in the United States and Canada. One of the biggest reinsurance companies in North America, it also offers special risk and financial reinsurance, as well as product development in U.S. and foreign markets. RGA

THE C-17 GLOBEMASTER III CAN CARRY 85-TON PAYLOADS, AND IS THE U.S. AIR FORCE'S MOST ADVANCED AND VERSATILE AIRLIFTER (LEFT).

THE NEW F/A-18 SUPER HORNET WILL BE THE CORNERSTONE OF U.S. NAVAL AVIATION INTO THE NEXT CENTURY (BELOW).

company's fighter aircraft and tactical missile manufacturing operations. The F-15E Eagle, the most able fighter-bomber in the U.S. Air Force, is built at the St. Louis plant, as are F-15 variants for international customers. The U.S. Marines' AV-8B Harrier II—with its unique vertical takeoff and landing capabilities—is assembled alongside the T-45C Goshawk, part of the U.S. Navy's newest aviator-training system.

The new centerpiece of U.S. naval aviation, the F/A-18 Super Hornet strike fighter, is now in low-rate production and will join the fleet in 2001. Designed to perform both air-to-air and air-to-ground missions, the Super Hornet is a more advanced version of its Hornet predecessors, which are the mainstay fighters of the U.S. Navy and Marine Corps and which are used by the air forces of seven other nations. Super Hornet production is expected to continue beyond 2010.

The Harpoon antiship missile and its advanced derivative, the U.S. Navy's SLAM-ER precision-guided standoff missile, are built in St. Charles. The Joint Direct Attack Munition (JDAM), also built in St. Charles, is a low-cost kit that converts conventional bombs into guided "smart"

weapons. More than 87,000 JDAM kits are expected to be produced by 2009.

St. Louis is also home to the Boeing Phantom Works, an advanced research and development operating unit. It pursues breakthrough innovations in design and manufacturing as part of broad, corporatewide initiatives to continuously improve the quality, performance, and affordability of all Boeing products. These initiatives are driven by a commitment to be the world-class leader in the aerospace industry; to achieve total customer satisfaction; to capitalize on the skills and strengths of a diverse workforce; and to be a good corporate citizen.

A GOOD CORPORATE CITIZEN
Boeing takes corporate citizenship seriously. In 1997 (the most recently reported period), the company and employee contributions to chosen causes reached a total of $90.5 million nationally through the Boeing Charitable Trust, the Boeing-McDonnell Foundation, 13 employee community funds, and a national gift-matching program. The company also donates computers and office supplies and furnishings, as well as transportation for community activities and materials for volunteer projects.

In 1997, the St. Louis Boeing Employees Community Fund distributed nearly $2.4 million in grants to more than 125 area organizations serving in the fields of health, human and social services, the environment, education, and arts and culture. And whether they are rehabilitating a house, teaching in a classroom, or participating in a fund-raising event, Boeing employees and retirees volunteer uncounted hours in the community. They are a clear expression of The Boeing Company's integral role in the tapestry of St. Louis.

THE BOEING F-15 EAGLE IS ONE OF FOUR TACTICAL AIRCRAFT BUILT IN ST. LOUIS, INCLUDING THE F/A-18 HORNET, AV-8B HARRIER, AND T-45 GOSHAWK.

SCHNUCK MARKETS, INC.

GIVING BACK TO THE COMMUNITY HAS MULTIPLIED THE positive impact of St. Louis' most successful supermarket company, Schnuck Markets, Inc. The personal involvement of the company's leaders and its 15,000 employees in local community organizations has helped make the difference between surviving and

AS CHAIRMAN OF THE 1996 SAY AMEN BANQUET, SCHNUCK MARKETS, INC. CHAIRMAN CRAIG SCHNUCK (LEFT) PRESENTS AN OVER-SIZED CHECK WITH ANDREW CRAIG (RIGHT) OF BOATMEN'S BANCSHARES (PREDECESSOR TO NATIONSBANK) TO MARTIN MATHEWS, EXECUTIVE DIRECTOR OF THE MATHEWS-DICKEY BOYS CLUB (TOP).

SCHNUCKS WORKS WITH SUCH ORGANIZATIONS AS THE URBAN LEAGUE TO DISTRIBUTE HOLIDAY MEALS TO AREA FAMILIES. PACKAGING BOXES IN 1998 WERE (FROM LEFT) SCHNUCKS DIRECTOR OF COMMUNITY AFFAIRS NANCY DIEMER AND CAROL VERMEIL, WIFE OF ST. LOUIS RAMS COACH DICK VERMEIL. SCHNUCKS ALSO CONTRIBUTES FOOD VALUED AT MORE THAN $4 MILLION ANNUALLY TO OPERATION FOOD SEARCH, THE ST. LOUIS AREA FOOD BANK, AND OTHER COMMUNITY RESOURCES DEVOTED TO FEEDING THE HUNGRY (BOTTOM).

thriving for groups that feed the needy, care for children, support family life, and enhance educational efforts.

The impact of Schnucks' commitment to community service is woven into the tapestry of its rich history, dating back to its start in 1939 as a small, 1,000-square-foot confectionery in north St. Louis. Company cofounders and brothers Edward and Donald Schnuck began the legacy of community service, motivated by a combination of genuine love, care, and concern for their family of customers.

Their commitment reflected a belief: "As a community goes, so goes our business." Schnucks Chairman and CEO Craig Schnuck notes, "We believe our partnerships with effective community organizations contribute greatly to the quality of life in the communities where we do business." Adds President Scott Schnuck, "All the business

success in the world means nothing if we have done nothing to improve life for our customers beyond the doors of our stores."

MAKING A WORLD OF DIFFERENCE

The cofounders' legacy of community service has multiplied through the efforts of the next generation as Craig, Scott, Terry, Mark, Todd, and Nancy—the children of Donald and Doris Schnuck—have become involved in helping such organizations as the United Way, Urban League, Salvation Army, local area food banks, St. Louis Children's Hospital, Boy Scouts, and Junior Achievement.

Their efforts are magnified by the thousands of Schnucks employees who share the family's desire to make a difference in the communities they serve. Since the late 1950s, for instance, Schnucks employees have been generous givers to the United Way. Today, more than 90 percent of Schnucks employees set a model of generosity at all salary levels to those who need United Way's help.

Among the company's strongest advocates for United Way are Craig Schnuck and Chief Financial Officer Todd Schnuck, who both serve on the United Way board of directors and executive committee, along with Director of Community Affairs Nancy Schnuck Diemer, vice chair of a United Way allocations committee. As United Way's communications chairman, Craig has kept alive a tradition begun when his father chaired the 1985-1986 campaign—coordinating all the local television stations in a simultaneous telecast of the fund drive kickoff.

In a similar way, the company's efforts to help the Salvation Army are more successful because of employees' support and involvement. Schnucks employees serve as Salvation Army ambassadors at every checkout register. Miniature Salvation Army kettles, an innovation developed by Ed Schnuck in 1984, stand ready at each checkout to accept donations while customers' wallets are open. The kettles serve another important purpose, reminding others of the important safety

net provided by the Salvation Army. To date, three Schnuck family members have chaired the annual Tree of Lights campaign: Ed in 1984, Don in 1988, and Craig in 1995. Mark Schnuck, vice president of shopping center development for Schnucks and president of The DESCO Group, has chaired the Salvation Army Advisory Board.

Scott Schnuck has given special attention to five long-standing efforts: the St. Louis Variety Club to benefit area children, a tradition at Schnucks since 1976; the Dollar-Help campaign, initiated in 1975 to help local citizens pay their utility bills; St. Louis Children's Hospital, dating to 1971; the Foundation for Special Education, beginning in 1985; and Junior Achievement of Mississippi Valley, for which Scott serves as 1997-1999 chairman of the board. Scott has led the way for hundreds of Schnucks associates to offer hands-on involvement in each program, whether providing fund-raising assistance or volunteer service.

The service and involvement of Terry, Mark, Todd, and Nancy in a wide range of organizations and efforts further extend Schnucks' community impact. Terry combines his retail and legal training to help guide such groups as the Better Business Bureau in promoting consumer-friendly business practices. Mark uses his real estate expertise to help many organizations tend to their facility needs. Todd lends his specialized knowledge to ensuring sound financial futures for such long-standing organizations as the Urban League, as well as helping in the formation of such relative newcomers as the Foster Care Coalition. Nancy uses her organizational skills to manage the allocations of cash and in-kind gifts from Schnucks to more than 2,000 schools, churches, and community organizations helped by Schnucks each year. Community assistance also is provided in the form of Schnucks employees, who

volunteer for a wide array of community events.

GIVING BACK TO THE COMMUNITY

Notes Schnucks General Counsel Terry Schnuck, "We feel a corporate responsibility to support the communities that have fostered our success. As the food retailing industry's pacesetter, we've motivated others to join our efforts and together make an even greater community impact."

The same creativity used by Schnucks to bring innovation, convenience, and service to customers is applied to offering effective promotional, in-store, and advertising support to nonprofit groups. In this way, Schnucks makes a world of difference in the success of countless fund-raising events and awareness campaigns by organizations seeking to build community support for their causes.

The spirit of giving comes full circle at Schnucks. As St. Louis' largest purveyor of food, Schnucks also contributes food valued at more than $4 million each year to Operation Food Search, the St. Louis Area Food

Bank, and other community resources devoted to feeding the hungry.

"Through our years in business, we've come to know the truly generous nature of our employees and our customers," says Craig. "We are proud and pleased to be a channel for so many to give their time, talent, and financial support to those who need it. We will continue to do everything we can to improve and support the quality of life for people in the communities we serve."

THE CITY OF COLLINSVILLE RECENTLY DEDICATED THE DONALD O. & EDWARD J. SCHNUCK MEMORIAL PARK WITH A RIBBON CUTTING FEATURING LOCAL SCHNUCKS ASSOCIATES, AREA CITIZENS, AND SCHNUCK FAMILY MEMBERS (HOLDING GREEN RIBBON, FROM LEFT) TERRY SCHNUCK, NANCY DIEMER, AND TODD SCHNUCK. SCHNUCKS DONATED 9.2 ACRES FOR THE PARK.

TONY'S, INC.

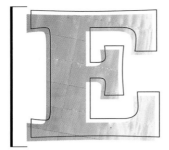

EVERY EVENING, ABOUT 20 MINUTES BEFORE THEIR RESTAURANT opens, Vincent J. Bommarito and his three sons assemble their employees for a meeting. The Bommaritos take nothing for granted. Once again, they stress the importance of quality, service, and careful attention to detail. They then conclude with their staff at the stroke of five

LEGENDARY IN ST. LOUIS, TONY'S, INC. INVENTED THE SUPERLATIVES—THE PERFECT MEALS, THE FINEST WINES, AND THE MOST ELEGANT SERVICE— WHICH TOGETHER CREATE A TRULY UNIQUE DINING EXPERIENCE (TOP).

TODAY, TONY'S IS STILL OWNED AND RUN BY THE BOMMARITO FAMILY, INCLUDING (FROM LEFT) JAMES BOMMARITO, SECRETARY/TREASURER; VINCENT P. BOMMARITO JR., EXECUTIVE CHEF AND PRESIDENT; ANTHONY BOMMARITO, VICE PRESIDENT; AND VINCENT BOMMARITO, OWNER (BOTTOM).

with the very same closing every time, "Show time!"

Legendary in St. Louis, Tony's invented the superlatives—the perfect meals, the finest wines, and the most elegant service— which together create a truly unique dining experience. The many local and national awards hanging on the office walls are testimony to Tony's ranking with the best restaurants anywhere. Yet these honors pale beside "Show time" each evening with yet another opportunity to please both regular and first-time customers.

"We always wanted to be among the best restaurants in the country and we are gratified that our customers tell us that we are," comments Bommarito, owner of Tony's. "We never rest on our reputation because we know we start over with each meal every night. We earn our reputation anew each time a guest is seated."

Tony's is the only restaurant ever to receive the coveted AAA five-diamond award in the state of Missouri. There are only 34 restaurants in North America to receive this recognition.

Bommarito's father, both the namesake and the founder of Tony's, opened the small Italian restaurant in 1946 just north of downtown St. Louis. When he died in 1949, Vincent—just graduated from high school— took over and fell in love with the business. His brother Anthony joined him a year later. By 1955, they had replaced the old storefront. Many other improvements, including a larger kitchen, a new parking lot, and a 10,000-bottle wine cellar, followed over the years.

Along the way, Vincent Bommarito acquired additional help from his three sons: Vincent Jr., executive chef and president; James, secretary/treasurer; and Anthony, vice president. He has also attracted a cadre of loyal employees who have stayed with him for decades.

NEW LOCATION, SAME EXCELLENT SERVICE

In 1992, the city needed Tony's site for the new Transworld Dome. The Bommaritos chose a new space in the heart of downtown on Market Street. The restaurant opened with the same precise procedures, outstanding staff, and familiar artwork.

The restaurant is now serving its fourth generation with the finest ingredients—including fresh seafood from Boston, Dover sole from England, and cheeses and truffles from Italy. The world is truly Tony's marketplace.

Tony's has long held the favored table to close a business deal, to entertain a client, or to celebrate an anniversary, birthday, or engagement. Guests who have long enjoyed Tony's with their parents now bring their children.

"In the old building and now here, we have a big sign in the kitchen that says Pride," remarks Bommarito. "We have an intense pride in what we do. And we truly believe we can satisfy everybody every time they dine at Tony's."

I N 1947, AARON S. LAPIN OF ST. LOUIS BECAME FRUSTRATED WITH THE short shelf life of whipping cream. He would buy a container and put it in the refrigerator, and before long, half of it had spoiled. He decided to come up with a better method of keeping the cream so it would last for several weeks. Lapin came up with an idea that called for new packaging, so he added

an aerosol dispenser. With this breakthrough, Reddi-wip® Whipped Cream was born, and Lapin became the first president of Reddi-wip, Inc.

Today, Lapin is chairman of Clayton Corporation, a company initially developed to manufacture valves for Reddi-wip. Clayton continues to be a major manufacturer of aerosol valves and covers for a range of markets: OEM dairy, food, industrial building materials, and consumer products for the do-it-yourself hardware industry. The company also houses a closures division, which makes injection-molded plastic caps for dairy and juice containers.

EXPANDING THE PRODUCT LINE

Taking this valve technology one step further, Byron Lapin, Aaron's son and president/CEO of Clayton Corporation, launched Convenience Products, a subsidiary, in 1979. His goal was to produce a full line of easy-to-use, insulating, aerosol sealants for the do-it-yourselfer under the Touch 'n Foam® label.

Today, in addition to the Touch 'n Foam line, Convenience Products produces Reddy® Insulation and Touch 'n Stick® Multi-Purpose Spray Adhesive, both of which are internationally known for their quality and value. Convenience Products was also first in its industry with an All-Direction Dispensing System—which allows foam to be dispensed at any angle and in any direction—and an environmentally safe foam product.

In 1985, Convenience Products established its industrial building materials division to

service the needs of residential, commercial, and industrial contractors. This division produces a full line of Touch 'n Seal® foam products for the professional applicator.

EXPANDING THE COMPANY

Due to the success of its various products, Clayton Corporation today has two locations. Its world headquarters and valve manufacturing facility are housed in an 80,000-square-foot building in Fenton, Missouri. It has also recently expanded to a new, 60,000-square-foot plant in Pacific, Missouri, which houses the foam production lines and warehouse facilities. Altogether, the company has more than 200 employees.

Looking ahead to the future, the firm is heavily involved in

developing new products through its consumer and industrial divisions, and in streamlining its operations with state-of-the-art equipment. Innovation is still the hallmark of Clayton Corporation, just as it was back when Lapin first developed Reddi-wip.

CLOCKWISE FROM TOP: CONVENIENCE PRODUCTS' STATE-OF-THE-ART PRODUCTION FACILITY IN PACIFIC OPENED IN 1997.

THIS VALVE ASSEMBLY MACHINE IS LOCATED IN CLAYTON CORPORATION'S FENTON, MISSOURI, PLANT.

CONVENIENCE PRODUCTS, A SUBSIDIARY OF CLAYTON CORPORATION, OFFERS A FULL LINE OF CONSUMER AND INDUSTRIAL PRODUCTS.

KSDK-NewsChannel 5

SINCE GOING ON THE AIR IN 1947 AS ST. LOUIS' FIRST television station, KSDK-NewsChannel 5 has been continuously broadcasting superior programming throughout the area. Today, the NBC affiliate is not only the top-rated station in the St. Louis market, but also routinely ranks among the top three network affiliates nationwide.

CLOCKWISE FROM TOP: NEWSCHANNEL 5'S NUMBER-ONE-RATED MORNING TEAM FROM *Today in St. Louis* INCLUDES (FROM LEFT) ART HOLLIDAY, JENNIFER BLOME, AND METEOROLOGIST SCOTT CONNELL.

NEWSCHANNEL 5 ANCHOR AND *Nightbeat* REPORTER DEANNE LANE AND PHOTOJOURNALIST TONY CHAMBERS ARE PART OF THE TRUSTED TEAM AT NEWSCHANNEL 5.

THE STATION'S NEWS COMES FROM A TEAM THAT INCLUDES SOME OF ST. LOUIS' MOST FAMILIAR AND TRUSTED FACES, INCLUDING ANCHORS KAREN FOSS AND DAN GRAY.

"News is very important to us," says Lynn Beall, president and general manager of NewsChannel 5. "We want to do the best, most credible job so the people who watch our programming will feel that it is time well spent. By giving them solid, concise, accurate information, we can make a difference in their lives."

From late-breaking news to reports on recent medical research, NewsChannel 5 provides coverage of stories that impact the station's 50- to 75-mile viewing area, which includes nearly 2.8 million people. It is also the only local station to have working bureaus, staffed by local reporters and photojournalists, in the fast-growing markets of St. Charles and southwestern Illinois. The station's news comes from a

team that includes some of St. Louis' most familiar and trusted faces. Among them are anchors Karen Foss, Deanne Lane, Dan Gray, Jennifer Blome, and Art Holliday. Complementing them is a talented team of sports reporters, headed by Mike Bush, and an outstanding weather team, headed by Cindy Preszler.

Along with news, NewsChannel 5 has another locally produced program, *Show Me St. Louis*, which debuted in September 1995. Hosted by Debbye Turner and Dan Buck and airing from 3 to 3:30 p.m. Monday through Friday, this popular show features stories

about St. Louis, its people and places. Since April 1998, viewers have been able to watch the show live through the station's Window on St. Louis, modeled after the *Today* program's successful Window on the World.

A LONG HISTORY IN ST. LOUIS

The station signed on the air in 1947 as KSD-TV and became one of only seven television stations in the United States at that time. Joseph Pulitzer II of the Pulitzer Publishing Company recognized the potential of television and brought it to St. Louis. Just days after its

debut, the young station televised the first play-by-play sports event in the Midwest from Kiel Auditorium.

As television grew in popularity, KSD grew with it. Soon, it was producing such popular local programs as *St. Louis Hop* and *To the Ladies*, with Charlotte Peters, Stan Kann, and Marty Bronson. By the 1960s, news operations had taken the forefront with such well-known broadcasters as Chris Condon, Max Robey, Bob Chase, and John Roedel, along with weathercasters Clif St. James and Howard De Mere. During the 1970s, the station's programming expanded to include live St. Louis Cardinals baseball broadcasts.

In 1983, Pulitzer sold the station to Multimedia, Inc., a South Carolina-based communications company, and its name changed to KSDK-TV. Also in the mid-1980s, the station began producing Sally Jessy Raphael's *Sally* program, which later moved to New York City and into national syndication.

Ownership changed again in 1995, when Multimedia sold NewsChannel 5 to Gannett, Inc. Soon afterwards, Ardyth Diercks became the station's general manager—and the first female general manager in the St. Louis market. When Diercks was promoted to senior vice president of the Gannett Broadcast Division in 1998, Lynn Beall took over as general manager, becoming the second female

general manager in the market. Today, the station has some 200 employees, including many native St. Louisans and long-time residents.

SERVING THE ST. LOUIS COMMUNITY

With the encouragement of Gannett, NewsChannel 5 places greater than ever emphasis on serving the community. The station supports a variety of organizations and outreach efforts, such as the AIDS Foundation and the Salvation Army Tree of Lights campaign. In addition, KSDK has urged teens to quit smoking and promoted car-seat and bike-helmet safety.

The station's Volunteer 5 program, started in January 1993, links potential volunteers with organizations that need help. So far, the program has tallied some 2 million volunteer hours and nearly $21 million in service. KSDK also airs an annual Volunteer 5 awards program, in which the station honors outstanding area volunteers.

In cooperation with BJC Health Systems, NewsChannel 5 spearheads a breast cancer awareness program called Friend to Friend. On the fifth of every month, the station airs stories and public service announcements encouraging friends to remind each other to do a breast self-exam. The station also provides a breast cancer hot line and a packet that includes information on the disease.

PLANNING FOR THE FUTURE

Over the years, NewsChannel 5 has won myriad awards, including local Emmys and Gabriel awards, and it has been honored by such organizations as the National Association of Black Journalists and the Associated Press. The station plans to continue doing the kind of quality work that has won such widespread recognition.

"In the future, we look forward to being an important part of St. Louis, as we have been for more than 50 years, working to make the region grow and become a better place to live and work," says Beall. "All of us at NewsChannel 5 are committed both to serving our viewers and to contributing to our community."

CLOCKWISE FROM TOP LEFT: MIKE ROBERTS (LEFT), CINDY PRESZLER, AND JOHN FULLER ARE NEWSCHANNEL 5'S EVENING METEOROLOGISTS.

DAN BUCK AND DEBBYE TURNER ARE HOSTS OF THE POPULAR PROGRAM *Show Me St. Louis*.

KSDK-NEWSCHANNEL 5'S 10 O'CLOCK TEAM, WHICH INCLUDES (FROM LEFT) MIKE BUSH, DAN GRAY, KAREN FOSS, AND CINDY PRESZLER, IS NUMBER ONE IN THE ST. LOUIS MARKET AND ONE OF THE TOP-RATED NEWSCASTS IN THE NATION.

[1953] LaBarge, Inc.

[1954] Metropolitan St. Louis Sewer District

[1955] Hellmuth, Obata + Kassabaum, Inc.

[1957] Southern Illinois University Edwardsville

[1958] Coin Acceptors, Inc.

[1958] Delta Dental of Missouri

[1961] Kellwood Company

[1964] Imo's Pizza

[1966] Dave Sinclair Ford, Inc.

[1968] Spartech Corporation

[1969] Arch Coal, Inc.

[1969] Commerce Bancshares, Inc.

[1969] Vatterott College and Cedar Creek Conference Center

[1972] Citibank Mortgage

[1973] McCormack Baron & Associates

[1974] Bridge Information Systems

[1974] PPC International, L.L.C.

[1976] TelCon Associates of St. Louis, Inc.

[1976] Unigraphics Solutions Inc.

[1977] HASCO International Inc.

[1977] Sykes Enterprises, Incorporated

[1978] Interim Services Inc.

[1979] Marriott Pavilion Hotel

[1979] Willis

to none," says John Sinclair. "I'll bet you could walk into nearly any place of business in the St. Louis area and ask people's opinion of Dave Sinclair, and you'd get a good one. The average blue-collar worker is the person to whom we sell a lot of cars. If you take care of people, they will reward you with their business."

FULL SPEED AHEAD

Together, the four Dave Sinclair dealerships have earned an impressive array of awards. Dave Sinclair himself served as chair of the national Dealer's Council for two terms. He was also cited by the Automotive Hall of Fame, and recently named as Management Man of the Year by local unions. The latest survey from Ford Motor Company shows that Sinclair is in the top 10 percent of dealers nationally for owner loyalty.

Dave Sinclair Ford—the original dealership owned by Sinclair—was number one in sales in the entire United States for three successive years, 1984 through 1986. That statistic is unusual because St. Louis ranks as a B-sized automotive district in population size. Dave Sinclair Ford is the only dealer ever to achieve number one status from a district of that size. Today, it is

still among the top 10 dealers nationally.

In addition, Dave Sinclair Buick-GMC Truck is number one in the region and ninth in the United States; the Lincoln-Mercury dealership also remains first in the region; and Dave Sinclair Oldsmobile, the most recent acquisition, was number one in the region during its first 11 months of Sinclair ownership in 1998.

Just as people are loyal to him, Sinclair is loyal to the St. Louis community. In addition to numerous personal acts of charity, especially to retired police officers, he has funded a program to help St. Louis-area schools. This program, called Dave Sinclair Ford, Inc. Business Partners in Education, provides two public relations

professionals to schools to assist with such things as guest speakers, remedial reading volunteers, refreshments for open houses, and field trips. When a customer buys a car, Dave Sinclair Ford also pays $100 to the school or nonprofit organization of the customer's choice.

To his own employees, Sinclair is also generous, both in salary and benefits. "My philosophy is I lock up thieves, I don't hire them," says Sinclair, the one-time policeman. "I've got good people in every store.

"I've been all over the world on the trips you win in this business, but I would never consider moving," Sinclair says. "I've never been anywhere that I like better than where I started from."

DAVE SINCLAIR FORD HAS THE LARGEST INVENTORY IN THE MIDWEST (TOP).

TODAY, DAVE SINCLAIR'S FOUR SONS AND THREE SONS-IN-LAW RUN HIS VARIOUS DEALERSHIPS: DAN SINCLAIR AT THE OLDSMOBILE STORE, JAMES SINCLAIR AT LINCOLN-MERCURY, JOHN SINCLAIR, WHO RUNS THE FORD DEALERSHIP WITH HIS FATHER, AND DAVID SINCLAIR AND TONY GODFREY AT BUICK-GMC. JOHN WILLETT HANDLES FINANCE FOR ALL THE STORES, AND MIKE DETWILER IS HEAD OF SERVICE OPERATIONS (BOTTOM).

REFRIGERATION LINERS, WINDOW SHUTTERS, TRUCK BUMPERS, children's playground equipment, roofs for pop-up campers, and parts for fire engines have one thing in common: They were all once made from fiberglass, wood, or metal, but are now made from lightweight, durable, and recyclable plastic. These plastics are

SPARTECH CORPORATION ANNUALLY RECOGNIZES THOSE INDIVIDUALS WHO PERFORM AT THE HIGHEST LEVEL OF EXCELLENCE IN THEIR DESIGNATED AREAS OF EXPERTISE.

produced by Spartech Corporation, a Clayton, Missouri-based firm and a leading plastics processor for more than 5,000 manufacturing customers. The company's 40 North American and European facilities, which employ more than 2,900 people, process some 1.2 billion pounds of extruded sheet and rollstock, color and specialty compounds, and molded and profile products each year.

"You normally don't see our name on the items you buy because we're the middleman," says Bradley Buechler, chairman, president, and chief executive officer. "Our plastic is used to create the lining in Sub-Zero refrigerators and the shower surrounds in Jacuzzis, but you see the Sub-Zero and Jacuzzi names because those companies are our customers who actually form the plastic into the end product."

Over the past decade, Spartech's business as a plastics intermediary has been growing steadily. From sales of approxi-

mately $150 million in 1991, the company expects to reach $750 million in sales by 2000. Some of this growth comes from strategic acquisitions, through which the firm has purchased 11 plastics companies since 1999. Most recently, Spartech acquired Lustro Plastics in January 1998 and Alltrista's Plastic Packaging Division in May 1999, both extruded sheet and rollstock manufacturers.

The company's success has earned it a number of awards. For six straight years, the *St. Louis Post-Dispatch* has recognized Spartech as one of the top 50 best-performing local companies. The Regional Commerce and Growth Association (RCGA) also gave Spartech its Fast 50 Technology Award in 1997 and 1998 for the firm's technological advances. Of the 40 Spartech plants, 36 have received ISO or QS 9000 certification.

"There are several reasons for our success, but the one that stands out above the rest is people," says Buechler. "I'm a firm believer in surrounding yourself with good people. If you do that, and if you continue to train your people—while at the same time striving to improve your operations—your business should move forward successfully."

FOUR CORNERSTONES FOR GROWTH

Founded in 1968, Spartech originally manufactured furniture, electronics, plastics, machine parts, and store fixtures. But in 1984, the company decided to focus on plastics. By 1991, it had developed core competencies in extruded sheet and rollstock and engineered thermoplastic compounds.

Also in 1991, Spartech developed a focused growth plan that would allow it to become a leading producer of engineered thermoplastic material and polymeric compounds. The company initiated a comprehensive growth strategy called Four Cornerstones for Growth, which aimed at a balanced revenue expansion program, both through internal means (product transformations and new alloy plastics) and through strategic acquisitions.

The first of the four cornerstones, announced in 1991, was Business Partnerships. Spartech declared its commitment to building business partnerships that provide long-term growth opportunities and enhanced relationships with customers and resin suppliers. These relationships are developing new applications for the firm's products and state-of-the-art solutions for its customers.

In 1993, Spartech announced its second cornerstone— Strategic Expansions. The management team recognized an important demographic fact: A large number of U.S. plastics processing companies, established at the height of the space program and during the worldwide oil shortage in the late '60s and early '70s, had

SUB-ZERO FREEZER COMPANY, INC. HAS USED SPARTECH'S CO-EXTRUDED SHEET IN ITS REFRIGERATORS FOR MORE THAN 15 YEARS.

owners who were ready to retire or were looking for ways to consolidate their businesses. It was a good time for Spartech to begin acquiring firms that would add complementary product lines and increased geographic presence. Since 1993, Spartech has acquired 11 businesses and has become the North American leader in the production of custom extruded sheet and rollstock with a 40 percent-plus share of the market.

Two years later, Spartech presented its third cornerstone, a key element of the company's continued internal growth: Product Transformations. Increasingly, manufacturers in various industries—appliance and electronics, automotive, construction, and packaging—are turning to plastic to replace older wooden, glass, fiberglass, or metal components in their products. By tapping the expertise of its own sales and production personnel, as well as by utilizing its partnerships with suppliers and customers, Spartech can identify and develop new applications for its products. Product Transformations represent the key reason why the plastics market has grown by practically twice the gross domestic product during much of the '90s.

More recently, in 1997, Spartech added its fourth cornerstone: Alloy Plastics. Through an aggressive development effort, the company works toward developing products that combine new proprietary thermoplastic compounds and additives with the latest in manufacturing techniques. In the second half of 1997, Spartech introduced four new products; another five were introduced in 1998; and in April 1999, the company's class of 1999 Alloy Plastics were announced. These new Alloy Plastics are accelerating the firm's ability to provide unique solutions to its customers.

An Emphasis on Quality Improvement

In the years surrounding the cornerstone announcements, Spartech developed programs focused on quality, safety, environmental awareness, training, and total customer satisfaction. Among these programs, the company's Total Transaction Quality initiative was the key. It instills quality into every transaction by implementing various customer, supplier, and employee action programs.

One of the firm's quality-oriented programs is Adopt-a-Customer, in which Spartech production workers and customer service representatives go out in small groups to a customer site and observe—from the customer's viewpoint—Spartech plastic being formed into a product. They also learn more about customer needs and any changes to the product or process that would help the customer's business. This program has been so successful that Spartech recently instituted a variation: the Reverse Adopt-a-Customer program, in which customers come to Spartech sites to walk through the company's manufacturing process and make suggestions for improvement.

In the future, Spartech looks forward to many more years of growth through strategic acquisitions, new product transformations, and continued introductions of new alloy products. "We feel good about the company's future and our overall philosophy—our mission to create value for our customers, shareholders, and employees through continuous improvement in everything we do," says Buechler.

E-One's Daytona fire truck utilizes Spartech's new glass-filled polycarbonate rigid sheet, Millennium III™.

Arch Coal, Inc.

ACH DAY, MILLIONS OF AMERICANS TURN ON THEIR COMPUTERS, televisions, and fax machines, using low-cost electricity to power their high-tech lives. But where does all that electricity come from? Some 57 percent is derived from coal, a fuel source that is crucial to America's modern way of life. ¶ Arch Coal, Inc., headquartered in suburban

St. Louis, is the second-largest coal producer in the United States, with annual production of approximately 110 million tons. The company supplies 10 percent of America's coal needs, and in doing so, provides the fuel for approximately 6 percent of the nation's electricity.

Arch is a national coal producer with mining operations in seven states ranging from West Virginia to Utah. The company ships its products to nearly 150 power plants across the nation, as well as to customers in 12 foreign nations on five different continents.

RAPID GROWTH

The company has grown quickly and dramatically in recent years. During 1997 and 1998, Arch Coal quadrupled its production and more than doubled its reserve base. The bulk of this growth was achieved through two major transactions. The first came on July 1, 1997, when two of the nation's strongest regional coal companies, Ashland Coal, Inc. and Arch Mineral Corporation, combined to create Arch Coal, the largest producer of low-sulfur coal east of the Mississippi River. Then, in June 1998, the company grew again with the acquisition of Atlantic Richfield's domestic coal operations, giving Arch Coal leading positions in the two principal low-sulfur coal basins in the western United States as well.

With these transactions, Arch Coal is now poised to capitalize on America's growing demand for electricity and the low-cost, low-sulfur coal to generate it. Domestic demand for electricity has increased by 25 percent in the past decade and should

ARCH COAL, INC. IS AMERICA'S SECOND-LARGEST COAL PRODUCER (TOP).

COAL IS THE SOURCE FUEL FOR 57 PERCENT OF THE ELECTRICITY GENERATED IN THE UNITED STATES (BOTTOM).

420

continue to climb. With its broad network of mines, Arch Coal can ship coal cost-competitively to the vast majority of U.S. power plants.

Today, Arch Coal controls a 3.7 billion-ton base of high-quality coal reserves, 90 percent of which is low in sulfur and 66 percent of which meets the most stringent requirements of the Clean Air Act. The company operates 17 mining complexes in four major coal-producing basins. Overall, the firm employs some 4,500 people at its mines and administrative offices.

Symbolizing St. Louis

Even after its dramatic expansion, Arch Coal remains strongly rooted in the St. Louis community. Its predecessor company, Arch Mineral, was founded in the city in 1969 by Merle Kelce, who wanted to build a company that would help meet America's growing need for domestic energy. Arch Coal and St. Louis even share the same symbol—the Gateway Arch—and the company's marketing materials carry this St. Louis emblem around the world. In fact, as the home of America's two largest coal companies (the other being Peabody Group), St. Louis might be considered the nation's coal capital.

Arch Coal supports St. Louis through a variety of civic and philanthropic causes, including the Gateway Chapter of the Leukemia Society and the United Way. Arch Coal is also involved in other communities in which it operates. In West Virginia, Arch Coal supports a teacher achievement awards program that each year provides cash awards to 10 of the state's top educators. In Wyoming, it helps fund a major arts and education outreach program for school children in Campbell County.

Environmental Stewardship and Safety

Arch takes its responsibility to its employees, its neighbors, and the environment seriously. Over the past several years, Arch Coal and its subsidiaries have won more than 50 awards for excellence in employee safety and environmental stewardship.

Arch Coal's Hobet 21 mine in southern West Virginia is a past recipient of the nation's highest honor for land reclamation, the prestigious Director's Award from the U.S. Department of the Interior. In 1998, West Virginia honored Arch Coal's Samples mine with that state's highest reclamation award for the second time in three years. Other Arch Coal subsidiaries have garnered numerous awards for reclamation excellence from such organizations as Ducks Unlimited and the National Wild Turkey Federation.

In the safety arena, Arch has repeatedly ranked among the nation's safest coal producers. Recently Arch Coal's Huff Creek mine on the Kentucky-Virginia border earned a Sentinels of Safety Award from the Mine Safety and Health Administration as the industry's safest underground mine.

Former Arch Coal mine sites are used for agriculture, pastureland, recreation, and wildlife habitat. The company integrates the reclamation process into every phase of mining. In the eastern United States, reclaimed mine lands provide excellent habitat for turkeys, deer, foxes, rabbits, hawks, and other native species. In southern Illinois, lakes and ponds are integrated into the landscape to enhance wildlife habitat, increase ecological diversity, and provide recreational opportunities. In the high, semiarid plains of Wyoming, herds of elk, mule deer, and pronghorn antelope thrive on reclaimed lands where water and vegetative cover are generally more plentiful than in the surrounding terrain.

As it continues to grow, Arch Coal will strive to meet America's growing need for energy. In doing so, the company will stress innovation, productivity, safety, and environmental responsibility—qualities that lie at the heart of the Arch Coal culture.

ARTHUR MEYERSON

LAKES AND LUSH VEGETATION COVER THE LANDSCAPE AT THIS RECLAIMED ARCH MINE SITE IN SOUTHERN ILLINOIS.

COMMERCE BANCSHARES, INC.

COMMERCE BANCSHARES, INC., HEADQUARTERED JOINTLY IN St. Louis and Kansas City, is a leading regional banking company, with $11.4 billion in assets. It operates an extensive network of Commerce Banks over a three-state area, in Missouri, Illinois, and Kansas, with 313 locations and more than 320 ATMs. It also provides its

customers with a full line of sophisticated banking services, a range that is usually available only from a national banking company.

Commerce Bank has achieved this business success (including record earnings, 31 consecutive years of increasing dividends, and record sales growth in 1998) through something far less tangible—an emphasis on stronger customer relationships. This focus is reflected in a new company mission statement, developed by employees over a nine-month period of discussion and planning. Simple and to the point, the company's mission is realized through these key action words: Be Accessible. Offer Solutions. Build Relationships.

"This means that we try to be accessible to our customers, both in our personal service and through convenient tech-

nologies," says David W. Kemper, chairman, president, and CEO, Commerce Bancshares, Inc. "We work to offer the best financial solutions at the right time and at the right prices; and to continually build and nurture our relationships with individuals, communities, and businesses."

STRONG CORE COMPETENCIES

Commerce Bank has three primary lines of business: consumer banking, commercial banking, and investment services, including trust, brokerage, and money management. In addition, it has five nonbanking subsidiaries engaged in mortgage banking, credit-related insurance, venture capital, and real estate activities.

For more than 130 years, Commerce has provided commercial banking services to businesses in the communities it serves. These services include credit, cash management, and treasury services; international banking; investment management; 401(k) plans; commercial real estate; and leasing.

In the money management area, total trust assets have been rising steadily, along with new personal and institutional accounts. The proprietary Commerce Funds, a group of nine mutual fund portfolios aimed at individual and institutional customers, netted $1 billion in assets within a three-year period. Many new investors have also found the Commerce Portfolio Manager appealing, with its low minimum investment of $25,000.

The area of consumer banking—consumer and mortgage lending; checking and money market accounts; ATMs; credit cards and Visa check cards; and student loans—is a long-time strength at Commerce, which ranks as one of Missouri's top banks in number of customers. One out of four Missouri households does business with Commerce Bank. And retail account households are growing in number and profitability. Commerce is one of only a few

TOWER GROVE PARK IS ONE OF THE MANY AREAS OF ST. LOUIS THAT HAVE BENEFITED FROM COMMERCE BANCSHARES' COMMUNITY-DRIVEN SPIRIT.

DAVID W. KEMPER IS CHAIRMAN, PRESIDENT, AND CEO OF COMMERCE BANCSHARES, INC.

financial institutions still offering the basic transaction account free to the consumer.

A SUPER-COMMUNITY BANK

Commerce has a consistent strategy for delivering these financial services. Dubbed the Super-Community Bank, this model consists of four key ingredients: competitive products, competitive pricing, superior service, and superior knowledge of the market. This market-driven strategy reflects the bank's determination to develop and enhance the bank's relationships with its customers through a more localized, community-driven approach to doing business.

Through a new tool, Managing Local Markets, Commerce empowers its people in each community that it serves to analyze, plan, and implement an active program of customer service, account retention, and business development. All 41 branches in the St. Louis area actively participate in this program, while commercial lenders have a similar program focusing on market-driven sales management.

A LONG HISTORY OF SUCCESS

Commerce Bank was founded in 1865, when Francis Reid Long came to Kansas City with $10,000 and opened a bank, the Kansas City Savings Association. Its name changed a few years later to reflect the bank's growing involvement with commerce. In 1906, William Kemper joined Commerce as its president.

Through the years, Commerce expanded throughout Missouri communities. Commerce entered the St. Louis market in 1969, with the acquisition of banks in University City, St. Charles, and Kirkwood. In 1972, Commerce established a location in the city of St. Louis at 500 Broadway. A 1978 merger with Manchester Financial Corp. increased Commerce Bank's commercial banking presence in the St. Louis market, where it currently holds

nearly $2 billion in loans and $2.5 billion in deposits.

Over the years, Commerce has earned a number of prestigious awards, such as the E Star Award, from the president of the United States, for the bank's record in promoting export activity. In 1995, *Money* magazine named Commerce the Best Bank in Missouri. For five consecutive years, *U.S. Banker* magazine rated Commerce Bank America's Safest Bank in its annual ranking of the top 100 U.S. banks. Commerce Bank was also ranked among the nation's top 10 banks for technology.

A BUSINESS PHILOSOPHY FOR THE FUTURE

Today, Commerce is continuing to adapt to the changing marketplace through new technology and information-based customer service. A new database management system will help employees better understand and meet customer needs to maximize efficiency and value. Commerce customers are benefiting from advanced banking systems, particularly in Commerce's Telephone Banking Centers, where 80 employees make Commerce more accessible and help with banking solutions.

The bank is expanding through strong internal growth and through careful acquisitions in its market area. Since 1992, Commerce has completed 22 mergers totaling $3 billion in assets.

"Our superior level of service, coupled with sophisticated products, has allowed us to gain market share over the last several years," says Kemper. "We will continue to focus on building relationships and quickly meeting our customers' financial needs as the cornerstone of our business philosophy."

ATTEROTT COLLEGE IS ONE OF THE FASTEST-GROWING AND most innovative private career schools in the Midwest. The college has expanded from a single campus location in downtown St. Louis in 1969 to a network of 14 campus locations, providing instructions to more than 2,500 students in seven midwestern states. Vatterott College operates three St. Louis-area campuses in St. Ann, Missouri; Sunset Hills, Missouri; and Gillespie, Illinois.

During the past 30 years, Vatterott College has trained thousands of highly skilled workers to meet the needs of St. Louis' employers. Vatterott College is a St. Louis-based private career college offering a range of associate degree and diploma programs focused on fast-growing, technology-driven industries, including computers, business operations, and technology trades. AT&T, Boeing, General Motors, Graybar Electric, IBM, Monsanto, Ralston Purina, and Southwestern Bell are just a few of the area employers that regularly hire graduates of Vatterott College.

The college has experienced extraordinary growth during the past five years. Since 1994, Vatterott has added nine campuses and its student population has increased by more than 150 percent. In 1998, Vatterott began offering its courses online through the college's newly created division, Vatterott Global Online. Vatterott is the first private career school in St. Louis to offer programs via the Internet.

TRAINING AT VATTEROTT COLLEGE

The diverse student population at Vatterott College ranges from recent high school graduates to laid-off workers retraining for new careers, as well as employees seeking to update their technical skills in order to become more proficient in their current jobs. Vatterott also offers short-term training programs tailored specifically for employers. The college designs and implements customized programs for such employers as Boeing, Ford Motor Company, Chrysler Motors, the Department of Defense, and the National Park Service. In fall of 1999, Vatterott will begin a Degree Plus program that will offer advanced computer courses to students with undergraduate degrees.

Vatterott is a fully accredited college and offers a range of technology-driven programs, including computer programming and network management; computer-aided drafting technology; computer electronics and networking technology; applied electrical technology; and heating, air-conditioning, and refrigeration technology.

The programs at Vatterott College are designed to accommodate the busy lives of working individuals. New classes begin every 10 weeks, programs can be completed in 50 to 90 weeks, and both day and evening classes are available. Vatterott also offers a variety of financial

aid packages through each campus's Financial Assistance Department to provide funding for a student's education.

Vatterott College has a proven track record in training students who are in high demand by area employers. "A high percentage of our graduates are placed in training-related careers, and often at starting salaries that are higher than many entry-level jobs for a four-year college graduate," says John Vatterott, president of Vatterott College. The college ensures its students are prepared for the real-world workplace by using a hands-on learning style. Students receive ample lab experience using state-of-the-art technology to enforce lecture material.

MEETING AT VATTEROTT'S CORPORATE CONFERENCE CENTER

Vatterott College is the only private career college in St. Louis to operate a corporate meeting facility. Cedar Creek Conference Center, located one hour from St. Louis in New Haven, Missouri, is the premier site for the corporate meetings and retreats of many St. Louis-based organizations. Vatterott College frequently utilizes

Cedar Creek for its customized training for such organizations as the Department of Defense.

Cedar Creek Conference Center is situated on 130 acres of Missouri's scenic wine country, and features 10 fully equipped meeting rooms to serve groups of 10 to 100 individuals. Cedar Creek comfortably accommodates 80 overnight guests. For the convenience of Cedar Creek's professional clients, the facility features an office support center, a full range

of audiovisual equipment, and complete meeting planning assistance. Guests enjoy full-service dining featuring a variety of fresh, homemade selections.

Cedar Creek offers a variety of on-site recreational amenities for the enjoyment of its guests, including golf, tennis, swimming, hiking, and fishing, as well as a western town complete with an old-time saloon that has served as the site for many corporate social hours and theme parties.

THE PROGRAMS AT VATTEROTT COLLEGE ARE DESIGNED TO ACCOMMODATE THE BUSY LIVES OF WORKING INDIVIDUALS.

CITIBANK MORTGAGE

ITIBANK MORTGAGE LIKES TO KEEP ITSELF BUSY FINANCING the American dream. This St. Louis-based company— a subsidiary of Citibank N.A.—provides an array of mortgage, loan, and consumer credit products to customers across the United States. They focus on home mortgages—and service all the various

subsidiaries of Citigroup, Citibank's parent company.

"We are in the business of helping people fulfill their dreams," says David Lowman, president and chief operating officer of Citibank Mortgage. "And that doesn't mean just the first-time home buyer. It means every one of us who dreams about the next house we might own. We make people happy. That's really what we do."

The recent merger of Citibank with Travelers means new growth opportunities for the company. Citibank can now cross-sell to the Travelers customer base, while the Travelers sales team, along with the sales force of Primerica Financial Services, will help to distribute Citibank Mortgage products. As a result of the merger, Citibank Mortgage will also market mortgages through the firm Salomon Smith Barney. Significantly, all of the mortgages generated in

this way will be processed, closed, and serviced in St. Louis.

The merger has opened up another opportunity, as well, by providing mortgages, at a discount, to the combined employee population of the two companies. Altogether, that adds up to more than 130,000 employees in the United States. Citibank Mortgage

employs more than 2,400 who are based at the company's three offices in St. Louis.

This new business also translates into rapidly increasing profits. In 1998, the financial services industry originated more than $1.6 trillion in mortgages, substantially higher than a normal year's total of $750 billion. And Citibank Mortgage played a key role in this increase. The company had predicted 1998 mortgage volume of $10.5 billion, up from the $8 billion closed in 1997. But the actual total was more than $16 billion—doubling Citibank Mortgage's volume in only one year.

A BLUEPRINT FOR SUCCESS
Several factors have helped Citibank Mortgage achieve this kind of success. One is its centralized location. While some mortgage groups have operations scattered across the country, Citibank Mortgage processes all

MORE THAN 2,400 OF CITIBANK MORTGAGE'S EMPLOYEES ARE BASED AT THE COMPANY'S THREE OFFICES IN ST. LOUIS (TOP).

CITIBANK MORTGAGE PARTICIPATES IN THE MARCH OF DIMES WALK AMERICA IN DOWNTOWN ST. LOUIS (BOTTOM).

CITIBANK MORTGAGE EMPLOYEES
PROVIDE THEIR TIME AND EFFORTS AT
CHRISTMAS IN APRIL.

its loans in St. Louis. This centralized operation means huge economies of scale—which translate into lower costs. The centralization also means the management team can react quickly to business changes, without the need to contact branches or endure lengthy procedures.

Then there's the Citibank brand name, which is recognized around the world for its commercial stability and quality of service. Some 40 million people have Citibank credit cards, further underpinning this name recognition. "Another reason for our success is the terrific team we have assembled here in St. Louis," Lowman says. "This is a people business. Here you are interacting with the end consumer over a 45- to 60-day period. There are lots of places where something can go awry, but we have done a great job of meeting people's expectations."

FOCUSING ON QUALITY AND CUSTOMER SERVICE
Because of the ongoing need to meet customer expectations, Citigroup recently implemented a new corporate initiative: quality

training for all employees. Already, 900 Citibank Mortgage employees have attended an intensive, two-day seminar designed to underline the importance of customer service in their day-to-day work.

A further enhancement to this service will be a new software system, designed specially for Citibank Mortgage, which streamlines the loan origination process. Other technology-related improvements are also under way. Citibank Mortgage's 200-member technology group recently moved into a new, 50,000-square-foot facility.

REACHING OUT TO THE COMMUNITY
A critical part of serving the firm's customers is providing loans to groups that have been underserved in the past, particularly low- to moderate-income borrowers. In 1997, Citibank Mortgage established its Home Ownership Development Division to focus on community and fair lending efforts. In 1998, Citibank Mortgage met its fair lending targets, and the company will continue to expand these efforts, especially in areas where it has a banking presence.

True to its corporate values, Citibank Mortgage also believes in giving to the neediest in the community. The company itself annually donates $150,000 to area organizations, and even more in grant money through the Citicorp Mortgage Foundation. Employees are also heavily involved in outreach efforts. In 1998, the company had record United Way participation; every year, it is also one of the strongest supporters of the March of Dimes Walk America campaign. And a major drive at holiday time provides gifts, food, and clothing for the Hundred Neediest Cases program.

The company is also one of the four top contributors to Christmas in April, a program in which employees choose a Saturday and donate their time to upgrade people's homes. In 1998, the employees adopted eight houses; in 1999, they will sponsor 10 homes.

"We are proud of our employees, and we have aggressive growth plans for the future," says Lowman. "We have begun to take market share from others, and I think great opportunities lie before us. It is a very exciting time to be part of this organization."

McCormack Baron & Associates

on the site of a failed public housing high-rise development, stands a sparkling tribute to a new vision of city living: the mixed-income George L. Vaughn Residences at Murphy Park, begun in 1997 by McCormack Baron & Associates. There are some

THE QUALITY HILL DEVELOPMENT IN KANSAS CITY, MISSOURI, RECLAIMED THE WESTERN EDGE OF DOWNTOWN KANSAS CITY BY STIMULATING THE DEVELOPMENT OF 1,000 RESIDENTIAL UNITS AND 400,000 SQUARE FEET OF NEW OFFICE DEVELOPMENT (TOP).

MCCORMACK HOUSE IS THE FIRST EFFORT IN MISSOURI AT PROVIDING ASSISTED LIVING FOR FRAIL, LOW-INCOME SENIORS (BOTTOM).

THE RESIDENCES AT MURPHY PARK REPLACES THE FORMER VAUGHN PUBLIC HOUSING DEVELOPMENT AND SERVES AS A PROTOTYPE FOR THE NATIONAL HOPE VI DEMONSTRATION BY CREATING A NEW ECONOMICALLY INTEGRATED COMMUNITY ON THE NEAR NORTHSIDE OF THE CITY OF ST. LOUIS (RIGHT).

CRAWFORD SQUARE, LOCATED IN PITTSBURGH'S HILL DISTRICT, HAS CREATED HUNDREDS OF NEW HOUSING OPTIONS FOR NEIGHBORHOOD RESIDENTS AND THE DOWNTOWN WORKFORCE (LEFT).

400 units planned for Murphy Park, and with their stylish features; their attractive brick-and-siding facades; and the nearby playground, day care center, and swimming pool, these residences represent an important new anchor on the city's near north side.

In mid-town is another example of McCormack Baron's work: Westminster Place, a central-city development that combines rental housing, single-family homes, and a major retail center—all the elements of a successful urban neighborhood. This project, located adjacent to the site of the old Gaslight Square, is thriving, offering housing opportunities to families of various income levels, racial backgrounds, and ages.

The firm is managing the redevelopment of Forest Park Southeast, adjacent to the Washington University Medical Center. It is beginning work on a new, 500-unit development, Parsons Place, in the Emerson Park neighborhood of East St. Louis. And it has started a major project, due to be completed in 2002, in the center of downtown St. Louis: the redevelopment of the historic

Cupples Station warehouse district, which will include a Westin hotel, offices, retail services, and parking.

REBUILDING CITIES ACROSS THE NATION

Founded in 1973 by Richard D. Baron and his late partner, Terry McCormack, McCormack Baron is the premier U.S. for-profit residential development and management company committed exclusively to urban neighborhoods. The firm began by restoring historic buildings, then moved into multiblock development projects, including both rehabilitation and new construction. Thus far, the firm—based in St. Louis with a satellite office in New Haven—has completed 77 projects nationwide and has some 11,000 units in its management portfolio.

According to Baron, the company's ability to develop these projects is directly related to the commitment of the local community, both the public sector and private and/or philanthropic organizations. McCormack Baron is known for its creativity in putting together a blend of financing sources, including federal programs, tax-exempt financing, conventional loans, pension funds, foundation loans, grants, and equity from the private sector to bring a project to life. The firm also builds strong, interactive relationships with local governments and community-based organizations during the planning of each project.

"When the community is not interested in a project, we don't get involved," says Baron, company president. "Even when everybody is working together

R. PETTUS

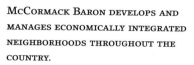

McCormack Baron develops and manages economically integrated neighborhoods throughout the country.

in a meaningful collaboration, it is still difficult, since we are trying to reverse what has usually been a pattern of disinvestment for many years. So we have to put together a comprehensive plan, then work jointly with the public and private sectors to oversee the recovery of a particular area."

McCormack Baron has taken its urban vision to cities around the nation. In Kansas City, it successfully put together an intricate financing plan to rebuild the historic Quality Hill neighborhood, a 19th-century residential district. Soon, the company will tackle Kansas City's 18th and Vine district, home of the American Jazz Museum.

In Pittsburgh, the firm built 60 single-family homes and 400 new housing units—some market rate, others affordable—in Crawford Square, a neglected downtown area in the predominantly African-American Hill District. "Work is continuing on the project," says Baron, "but already it has made an enormous difference in that area."

A Commitment to the City

Baron, who began his career in the late 1960s as a legal aid attorney, saw early on that many inner-city residents—particularly those in public housing—had to accept substandard living conditions. In their projects today, Baron and his associates offer residents the kinds of amenities that are typically only available

to those with higher incomes. Baron believes in the traditional notion of neighborhoods as places with people of diverse occupations and income levels living in quality housing.

"In Westminster Place, for example, we built some homes that sold for $80,000 and others that sold for $140,000," Baron says. "The difference is the same one you will find in suburban locations, if you had a two-car garage in one home and a one-car garage in another. But the quality of construction—the finishes in the unit, the washer and dryer, the dishwasher and range—are the same. We do not differentiate among the various housing units in a community."

Baron also believes in the importance of the area's surrounding development to a project—especially schools, social services, retail services, and employment centers. At Westminster Place, the company

built McCormack House, the first effort in Missouri at providing assisted living for frail, low-income seniors. Near Murphy Park, McCormack Baron has worked with the St. Louis Board of Education to renovate and revitalize the Jefferson Elementary School. Thanks to the firm's efforts, Southwestern Bell donated a state-of-the-art computer system, and the University of Missouri at Columbia is working with the Jefferson School faculty on new curriculum. Twenty other corporations contributed more than $3 million to the effort.

"Working in urban neighborhoods and rebuilding them, thereby reversing the years of disinvestment, is very exciting to me," says Baron. "I find the challenge in cities far more interesting and much more satisfying than anything I could have done as a developer in the suburbs."

Cupples Station is a 10-acre, mixed-use development in downtown St. Louis that will include a Westin Hotel as well as office and retail space. Completion of the project will occur in 2001.

BRIDGE INFORMATION SYSTEMS

ACH DAY, MORE THAN A QUARTER-MILLON FINANCIAL PROFESsionals in more than 100 countries receive vital market data, news, quotes, statistics, and analytics on global financial and commodity markets through the same source: Bridge Information Systems. This company, with annual sales of more than $1 billion, is the largest provider of financial information services in North America and the fastest growing in the world.

Through use of advanced technology and a series of strategic acquisitions, Bridge has helped redefine a rapidly changing industry with a business model that serves many different clients and supports many different products through a unified processing, delivery, and display architecture. As a result, Bridge is able to offer financial professionals and individual investors alike the industry's most complete range of products with the most complete coverage and functionality—all at competitive fees and the lowest operating cost for the customer. Bridge's three main business lines include financial information and news, trading and transaction services, and high-speed Internet services.

BridgeNews, Bridge's proprietary newswire service, is among the world's largest financial news organizations, with a 45-year journalistic tradition. A global network of more than 600 journalists breaks economic, government, financial, and commodity news that affects major and emerging economies and markets. It generates more than 6,000 stories and statistical items each day from around the world.

Bridge has more than 5,000 employees in more than 65 sales and marketing offices located in the Americas, Europe, the Middle East, Africa, and Asia/Pacific. Bridge was founded in St. Louis and still has a major presence here, with more than 850 employees in the area. A technology and trading center, located in west St. Louis County, contains the heart of the company's research and technology. Bridge's global communications network runs out of this office and connects to customers all over the world. Supporting the community, Bridge and its employees are actively engaged in a variety of St. Louis civic organizations and local charities.

"Our heart beats in St. Louis," says Tom Wendel, chairman and CEO. "We are a technology company and our technology center is here; we are a trading company and Bridge Trading is based here; we are an Internet service provider (ISP) and SAVVIS Communications is also here."

A HISTORY OF RAPID GROWTH

Bridge was founded in 1974 as a full-service stock trading firm, servicing professional money managers with the highest-quality trading execution, the fastest and most complete electronic market data, and in-depth research and analysis. During the 1980s, Bridge successfully pioneered a number of products, including a local area network (LAN)-based broker's workstation, an electronic trade order entry and routing system, and a computer-based order indication system.

Bridge Trading Company, established in 1974 to provide quality agency execution of stock trades in listed and OTC markets worldwide, today operates one of the largest floor brokerage networks on the New York Stock Exchange, with similar networks on the AMEX, Nasdaq, U.S. regional stock and options exchanges and markets worldwide. Bridge's suite of proprietary transaction services products provides professional investors with a quick and transparent means to execute trades, route orders, investigate order activity or advertise trades, and offers access to one of the industry's largest broker-neutral networks for secure, client-to-client connectivity.

Since 1995, Bridge has grown nearly ten fold. The firm has merged with seven independent market data and technology companies—including MarketVision, EJV Partners, Knight-Ridder Financial, Telesphere, and Telerate, Inc. (then called Dow Jones Markets)—expanding its services to include data, analytics, and news for the fixed-income, foreign exchange, money, derivative, and energy markets. In 1998, Bridge acquired the brokerage information business of Automatic Data Processing (ADP), which strengthened its position in the retail stockbroker market.

In April 1999, Bridge announced another important acquisition: SAVVIS Communications Corporation, headquartered in St. Louis. A leading national service provider of Internet access, SAVVIS offers high-performance communications solutions to the corporate and wholesale markets. Its network has been consistently

"Our heart beats in St. Louis," says Tom Wendel, Bridge Information Systems chairman and CEO. "We are a technology company and our technology center is here; we are a trading company and Bridge Trading is based here; we are an Internet service provider and SAVVIS Communications is also here."

rated number one for performance and reliability by Keynote Systems, Inc., a leading industry analyst. By combining with Bridge, SAVVIS has become the largest non-telco ISP in the world, offering service in 40 countries worldwide.

SYSTEMS FOR INFORMED DECISIONS

Bridge provides its information to customers through various delivery platforms: workstations, datafeeds, and Web solutions, all built on a common infrastructure. The company uses the full range of technology, including Unix, Microsoft Windows, Windows NT, and Java, each carefully crafted to maximize data delivery and functionality.

Bridge operates one of the most powerful communications networks in the industry. This network utilizes a broadband DS3 backbone and powerful switches, capable of processing thousands of transactions per second to deliver data at subsecond speeds. Together with SAVVIS, Bridge has created one of the world's largest providers of ATM–managed Internet Protocol (IP) networks, with more than 150 ATM switches owned and operated by Bridge throughout major cities in Europe, Africa, Asia/Pacific, and the Americas. Bridge's data processing center has scalable architecture that ensures virtually limitless capacity.

NEW FEATURES FOR THE FUTURE

Recently, Bridge unveiled several enhancements to its existing product lines, which feature fully integrated, open-architecture systems.

BridgeStation, for example, offers the industry's most comprehensive packages of market data, superior analytics, advanced charting capabilities, and news that use state-of-the-art technology and standard industry protocols. BridgeFeed is a high-performance, interactive digital datafeed that delivers global market information using advanced data management and delivery technology. BridgeActive1 is a revolutionary decision-support tool based on open standards that give total control to customize, integrate, and manage financial information. The Bridge Trading Room System (BTRS) tackles one of the industry's greatest problems: seamlessly integrating data and applications from multiple sources throughout the trading enterprise.

Telerate, the largest company under the Bridge umbrella, provides the world's most complete source of capital markets information. A range of package options is available, including Telerate Plus, which covers all the world securities markets—debt, equity, currency, derivatives, and more—and Telerate Energy, a real-time, one-stop energy platform.

Reaching out to clients on the Web, Bridge offers a complete financial workstation available through an Internet browser. BridgeChannel provides Internet access to data through realtime applets in a standard Web browser. This high-performance Web workstation incorporates rich data and indepth analytic tools into an easily accessible platform. Utilizing Java-based technologies, BridgeChannel's streaming data provides dynamic updates to the user, giving serious investors play-by-play coverage of the markets. Further, the functionality of BridgeChannel combined with Bridge's order routing and management tools is available in Bridge TraderChannel—a total trading solution that operates entirely through an Internet browser, making it a cost-effective solution for mid-size companies.

Bridge's high-bandwidth network also interacts with an array of portable, wireless communications devices on the market, including digital cellular phones and palmtop computers, giving investors access to financial information while on the go.

Bridge continues to expand its reach to offer the highest-quality products and services to an increasingly wider audience, affording high-speed access to information in versatile, cost-effective delivery options.

For example, individual investors can take advantage of Bridge's data, news, and charts on the Bridge Web site, bridge.com, or on PersonalBridge, a subscription service offering the most content-rich financial information individual investors can access on the Internet.

As the volume of financial information continues to grow, Bridge is using its technology advantage to improve performance and lower costs for its users. In doing so, the company strives to become the world leader in the global financial data distribution business.

"Bridge is geared to servicing the financial world, providing financial information and news, trading and transaction services, and network services that will lead market professionals into the new millennium and beyond," adds Wendel.

A TECHNOLOGY AND TRADING CENTER, LOCATED IN WEST ST. LOUIS COUNTY, CONTAINS THE HEART OF THE COMPANY'S RESEARCH AND TECHNOLOGY.

PPC International, L.L.C.

THE WORLD MARKETPLACE IS CHANGING, AS COMPANIES BASED in one country establish operations around the globe. But employees of these firms—wherever they are—still face the same kinds of personal problems: drug and alcohol abuse, marital and family tensions, and career and financial stress, among others. These issues often

affect the employee's productivity through increased absenteeism, reduced output, and even on-the-job accidents.

PPC International, L.L.C. (PPCI) offers a range of employee assistance program (EAP) services that address the needs of clients and their employees. Based in St. Louis, PPCI provides and supervises these services in 92 countries through licensee arrangements with local EAP organizations or contractual arrangements with private clinicians. Through its wholly owned subsidiary—PPC UK Limited—located in Oxford, England, along with an around-the-clock international call center, PPCI handles problem calls from all over the world. To its licensees, contractors, and subsidiaries, the company brings a strong record as a successful provider of EAP services.

"Today, companies have to become globally competitive to survive, so they must make the best use of their human resources. The kinds of EAP programs they need may vary because each country has its own employment laws, health

care systems, and cultural differences. But they all have problems that affect productivity. So if we can help them establish a culturally sensitive program, they can become more competitive by having more productive workers," says Carl R. Tisone, president and chairman of PPCI.

Local Roots, Global Reach

Founded in St. Louis by Tisone in 1974, PPCI has its roots in PPC, Inc., which became the leading U.S. employer assistance provider. The international arm of PPC, Inc. began in Puerto Rico in 1986, and operations in the United Kingdom began two years later. When PPC, Inc. (today a division of Magellan Health Services) merged with Medco Containment Services in 1992, he retained ownership of PPCI, and it became a separate company. Today, PPCI is still affiliated with PPC, Inc. as its U.S. provider of services. PPCI is focused on bringing world-class expertise to multinational companies that wish to deal with a single company in all their locations around the world. So

far, this specialty market has only a handful of competitors, which primarily operate in only a few countries or with expatriate employees of U.S.-based firms.

According to Vincent T. Volpe, CEO of PPCI, "We live in a world where everyone talks about branching out internationally, but this is not simply one of the things we are doing, it is the only thing we are doing. So many businesses find themselves dragged into international business because a domestic client has asked them to get involved. But we're here because global service is our mission."

CLOCKWISE FROM TOP:
FOUNDED IN ST. LOUIS BY CARL TISONE IN 1974, PPC INTERNATIONAL L.L.C. (PPCI) HAS ITS ROOTS IN PPC, INC., WHICH BECAME THE LEADING U.S. EMPLOYER ASSISTANCE PROVIDER.

PPCI'S INTERNATIONAL SERVICE CENTRE IS A STATE-OF-THE-ART FACILITY, PROFESSIONALLY MANAGED AND STAFFED 24 HOURS A DAY, 365 DAYS A YEAR.

PPCI PROVIDES ONGOING TRAINING TO MEMBERS OF ITS GLOBAL LICENSEE NETWORK.

A Full Range of Employee Assistance Services

PPCI offers an EAP that provides prepaid, solution-focused counseling for client organization employees and their families. Professionally trained clinicians are the counselors, and the number of sessions offered depends on the program model chosen by the client.

Along with counseling, the EAP includes other components that comprise a full management system. PPCI works with clients to develop policy and procedure statements that are customized to match the culture and language of each organization. During program implementation, PPCI trains managers and provides an employee communication campaign to promote EAP understanding and use. Finally, PPCI develops management systems to monitor EAP effectiveness.

PPCI offers two special services to its clients. One is its Expatriate Outreach Services, which is designed to support employees and their families from the time of their departure to a new assignment through the return to their home country. The other service is Critical Incident Stress Debriefing, which is designed for organizations that need professional counseling assistance in the aftermath of such events as industrial accidents, workplace violence, and natural disasters.

The Roots of PPCI

Tisone began workplace counseling in the U.S. Air Force in England and became an industrial consultant in Illinois in 1973. With his partner, Richard Hellan, he decided to form a private company and offer expanded services to companies in St. Louis. At first, they did fee-for-service counseling for companies with problem employees. But in 1976 a breakthrough occurred when Monsanto Company contracted for a full-service, EAP program. With word of mouth, their business grew until they were handling thousands of programs for companies across the United States.

"Over the years, we have treated every problem imaginable," says Tisone, "from homicidal threats, suicide, and serious drug problems to an employee who has broken up with a boyfriend or girlfriend and needs a little emotional support. We always wanted to identify emerging problems at an earlier stage, when they are much easier to treat and before the employee has to miss any work at all."

In 1992, the firm merged with Medco Containment, a pharmaceutical distributor, in order to strengthen its financial base. Medco asked Tisone to stay on as president to help PPC change focus from an EAP specialty firm to a managed behavioral health care firm that could also handle insurance benefits for each client. Tisone,

who was inducted into the EAP Hall of Fame in 1994, then left to focus on PPC International.

Today, Tisone has a vision for the future of PPCI. "Ultimately, it will become a multinational marketing firm and clearinghouse for its licensees," he says. As licensees sell multinational contracts, the contacts will come back through PPCI to be distributed to the other licensees. In a decade, the world will be dotted with affiliates and licensees, each working to help the others build their businesses."

CLOCKWISE FROM TOP LEFT: PPC UK LIMITED, LOCATED IN OXFORD, PROVIDES THE MOST PROFESSIONAL AND EFFECTIVE EMPLOYEE ASSISTANCE PROGRAMMING AVAILABLE IN THE UNITED KINGDOM.

PROFESSIONAL, QUALIFIED PPCI COUNSELORS ARE ALWAYS ON DUTY TO ASSESS THE LEVEL OF RISK, PROVIDE EMERGENCY INTERVENTION WHEN REQUIRED, CONDUCT AN INITIAL ASSESSMENT, AND DEVELOP AN APPROPRIATE SERVICE PLAN.

ACCORDING TO VINCENT T. VOLPE, CEO OF PPC INTERNATIONAL, L.L.C. (PPCI), "WE LIVE IN A WORLD WHERE EVERYONE TALKS ABOUT BRANCHING OUT INTERNATIONALLY, BUT THIS IS NOT SIMPLY ONE OF THE THINGS WE ARE DOING, IT IS THE ONLY THING WE ARE DOING."

UNIGRAPHICS SOLUTIONS INC.

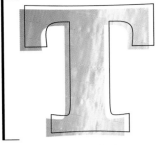

THE ENGINEER OPENS THE DOOR OF THE BUS AND LOOKS IN. He moves down the aisle, checking such things as the shape of the seats, the size of the windows, and the placement of the controls on the dashboard. But he doesn't like the windows; he thinks they should be smaller. What does he do—design a whole new bus?

All he has to do is press some computer keys and the job is done. That's because this is a virtual bus, which exists only on a computer screen. At one time, companies had to draw scale models on paper and then build physical prototypes. Today, they can perform three-dimensional modeling far more quickly and cost effectively, thanks to the innovative software of St. Louis-based Unigraphics Solutions Inc., one of the fastest-growing product development companies in the world.

"The virtual models that our customers build have all the characteristics of the physical product," says John Mazzola, president and CEO. "You can stress them and move parts around. What happens, for example, when you want to make an automobile with two doors instead of four? With our Unigraphics software, you can create the product, test it, change it, and build and rebuild it, over and over again. You can actually bring that product to market without a physical prototype."

A customer may also face the challenge of multiple parts—sometimes more than 10,000 in one assembly—from suppliers located around the world, making it almost impossible to know if the finished product will fit together the first time. Through its iMAN software, Unigraphics Solutions helps clients manage data from multiple sources to assure that the most recent changes are always a part of the various subassemblies, as well as of the master model. Unigraphics Solutions also provides the appropriate networking and computer capability to assure that all companies involved in the development of the product can work collaboratively on a global basis.

All of this capability is of little value, however, if a client's business processes are tradi-

tional and fail to take advantage of recent technological breakthroughs. Perhaps assembly has always occurred sequentially, with one department handing off completed product sections to another. Working in a consulting role, Unigraphics Solutions provides process re-engineering, helping the customer reshape its work flows and thought processes into a collaborative, team model that uses a cohesive set of competencies to successfully create a product.

"We don't provide shrink-wrapped answers to our customers," says Mazzola. "We offer our clients a broad array of software, consultative expertise, and competency in communications and networking. That's why we call ourselves Unigraphics Solutions—we bring all these capabilities to our customers."

A WELL-KEPT ST. LOUIS SECRET

Unigraphics Solutions is a leading global product development company with annual revenues of more than $400 million and a compounded average revenue growth rate of 22 percent. The company has more than 2,200 employees at 84 locations in 33 countries. More than 50 percent of Unigraphics' business is in North America; the rest is split between Europe and the Asia Pacific region. The company has more than 9,000 customers.

The Unigraphics product was first marketed in 1974 by United Computing. Two years later, McDonnell Douglas (now Boeing) bought the product along with key development personnel, but continued to use its own in-house CAD/CAM

MOTOR COACH INDUSTRIES' RENAISSANCE BUS IS CREATED VIRTUALLY IN UNIGRAPHICS—EXISTING ONLY ON A COMPUTER SCREEN. AS A RESULT, AN ENGINEER IS ABLE TO SEE BOTH THE EXTERIOR AND INTERIOR CHARACTERISTICS OF THE YET-TO-BE-MANUFACTURED PHYSICAL PRODUCT (TOP).

UNIGRAPHICS SOLUTIONS INC. IS HEADQUARTERED IN ST. LOUIS (BOTTOM).

Serving a Range of Markets

Today, Willis serves a variety of different industries, with a particular expertise in insurance and risk management requirements. Because of its global connections, the company can offer service, coverage, and rates that are not dependent upon the offerings of a single insurance company. The company has access to all the world's insurance markets and is one of Lloyd's of London's most important brokers.

As a global risk management firm, Willis works closely to evaluate risk and, in turn, develop risk-financing vehicles. The company also provides its clients with a variety of insurance products, including commercial property and liability, group health products, executive benefits, life, and disability. In addition, Willis offers several specialty resources, including safety and loss prevention; due diligence for mergers, acquisitions, and divestitures; business continuity planning; and crisis management.

The company maintains an Advanced Risk Management Services (ARMS) division supporting its local retail office network, which incorporates the Risk Management Consulting organization for Willis Americas. The focus of ARMS is to provide superior business solutions through leading-edge analysis and design of national and global risk management programs. ARMS is staffed by experts in corporate finance, actuarial science, computer modeling, captive assignment, and risk management.

By combining loss control and claims management services, Willis can work with its clients to provide a clear view of their exposures and the effectiveness of their management programs. The firm's Integrated Management Services Team provides this unique capability.

An additional resource available to clients across the country is the Willis National Benefits Resource Group. Operating from the centrally located St. Louis office, the group's staff of attorneys and legal assistants offer their expertise in the area of employment law, specializing in employee benefits.

In the area of employee benefits and compensation services, Willis excels, offering a full range of products and services. The company specializes in effectively managing its clients' benefits costs, creating custom-designed benefits packages that help attract and retain the best employees, and taking an active approach to a changing benefits environment.

Specific Industry Expertise

In certain industries with unique exposures, risk management solutions require specialization. Willis has responded to those industry challenges by establishing certain industry practice groups, each incorporating a network of insurance professionals dedicated to those industries.

For the construction industry, Willis Corroon is the unchallenged leader in construction insurance and surety bonding for large, Engineering News-Record (ENR) 400-listed companies, as well as smaller and midsize firms. The local service team and national Willis Practice Group offer contractors creative risk management and surety programs designed to grow their revenues and reduce costs. The company has its own Construction Industry Division (CID), the only group of its kind in the insurance industry.

Another primary focus of Willis is health care. The company has established a National Healthcare Practice Group, whose professionals are skilled in insurance, self-insurance, captives, reinsurance, and health care risk management consulting. Within the Missouri operations, Willis has further expanded its expertise in the health care field to meet the risk management challenges of the larger health care systems and expanding physician health organizations.

The company has many other areas of interest as well. It has developed a dedicated Environmental Risk Management Services Group, staffed by the country's leading environmental insurance, engineering, legal, and financial experts. Its Marine and Energy groups specialize in the energy industry, while other divisions serve the transportation and aerospace industries.

Willis remains committed to building strong, long-term relationships with clients and serving them in the most professional way possible. As a worldwide risk management practice, the firm uses all of its expertise to help its clients succeed.

WILLIS WAS ESTABLISHED IN 1990 THROUGH THE MERGER OF A U.S. INSURANCE BROKER, CORROON & BLACK, AND A BRITISH BROKERAGE, WILLIS FABER.

DOUGLAS ABEL PHOTOGRAPHY

I**N AN AGE OF COMPLEX, HIGH-TECH PROBLEMS, COMPANIES OFTEN SEEK** solutions from outside experts. Sykes Enterprises, Incorporated has been providing innovative solutions in information technology for more than 20 years. Today, SYKES is one of the world's largest suppliers of outsourcing services, with more than 11,000 employees worldwide and 1998 revenues of $470 million.

REAL PEOPLE, REAL SOLUTIONS

Sykes' strength lies in its people: project managers, application developers, software testers, systems analysts, technical support specialists, and more. The list is long and growing. What truly distinguishes the company is the quality of the employees it attracts. Sykes carefully selects each individual for people skills and provides in-depth training on specific technologies.

Headquartered in Tampa, Sykes has 17 branch offices throughout the United States. Branches provide staffing and business solutions, from the development of new processes,

JOHN SYKES IS THE FOUNDER AND CEO OF SYKES ENTERPRISES, INCORPORATED. THE COMPANY HE FOUNDED IN 1977 HAS GROWN INTO ONE OF THE WORLD'S LARGEST SUPPLIERS OF OUTSOURCING SERVICES (TOP).

SYKES' OUTSTANDING SERVICES HAVE LED TO PARTNERSHIPS WITH MANY FORTUNE 500 COMPANIES BASED IN THE ST. LOUIS AREA (BOTTOM).

products, and systems to documentation in all of its forms.

Sykes' localization services ensure that software, systems, and documentation maintain their integrity in various foreign languages and cultures. Foreign language services provide on-line help, hard copy, or code in 24 languages.

Through a unique partnering agreement with local communities, Sykes builds customer support centers that provide jobs and community spirit. These 13 centers have state-of-the-art computer systems, telephony, and fiber optics. They operate 24 hours a day, 365 days a year answering customer queries on more than 500 technical products.

Sykes' International Operations provides services to 21 foreign countries across five continents. This operation has grown from 100 employees in 1997 to more than 2,000.

AWARD-WINNING QUALITY

Sykes' Total Quality strategy guides the use of quality principles and practices in running the business. It ensures a focus on the Sykes definition of quality: "[to] provide external and internal customers with innovative services that satisfy their requirements and exceed their expectations."

Sykes' outstanding service has earned the Star Award for Sustained Performance Excellence for four consecutive years. And Sykes is ISO 9002 certified, an international standard of excellence.

A COMMITMENT TO ST. LOUIS

Sykes is proud to have a strong and growing presence in St. Louis. The St. Louis branch

office has been providing staffing and business solutions to Fortune 500 companies in the area since 1977.

Sykes' St. Louis application services range from systems design and application programming to conversions and project management. The typical staff member has six to eight years of data processing experience. The St. Louis office provides technical resources in the following disciplines: IBM mainframe, DEC, VAX/Alpha, Unix operating systems, client server development, and Internet development.

The St. Louis office also provides documentation resources. Sykes' writers combine information systems knowledge with communication skills and publications design expertise to produce clear, concise, and readable documents. All writers have experience in developing user documentation, systems documentation, standards, procedures, on-line help, and operating procedures.

Sykes works hard to make sure that each employee meets his or her professional goals, carefully matching clients with expertise. The St. Louis team works with each employee to formulate a career development plan. Ongoing training ensures exposure to the latest technologies.

LOOKING AHEAD

Sykes plans to develop new diagnostic tools for a multitude of uses, including telecommuting, home automation, and video-on-demand access. So when the digital home of the future becomes a reality, Sykes will be there—with the tools, and the people, to support the technology.

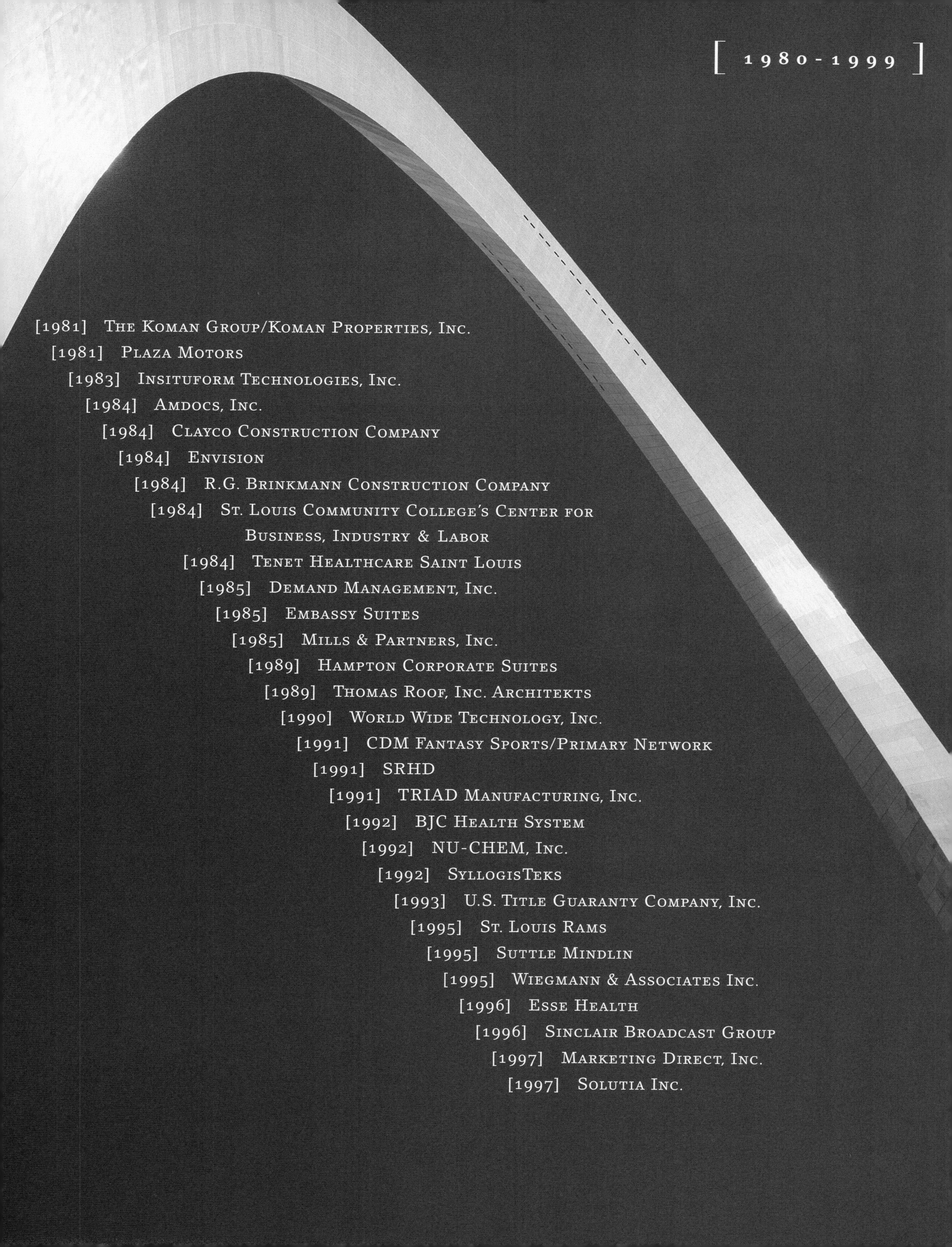

[1981]   THE KOMAN GROUP/KOMAN PROPERTIES, INC.

[1981]   PLAZA MOTORS

[1983]   INSITUFORM TECHNOLOGIES, INC.

[1984]   AMDOCS, INC.

[1984]   CLAYCO CONSTRUCTION COMPANY

[1984]   ENVISION

[1984]   R.G. BRINKMANN CONSTRUCTION COMPANY

[1984]   ST. LOUIS COMMUNITY COLLEGE'S CENTER FOR
BUSINESS, INDUSTRY & LABOR

[1984]   TENET HEALTHCARE SAINT LOUIS

[1985]   DEMAND MANAGEMENT, INC.

[1985]   EMBASSY SUITES

[1985]   MILLS & PARTNERS, INC.

[1989]   HAMPTON CORPORATE SUITES

[1989]   THOMAS ROOF, INC. ARCHITEKTS

[1990]   WORLD WIDE TECHNOLOGY, INC.

[1991]   CDM FANTASY SPORTS/PRIMARY NETWORK

[1991]   SRHD

[1991]   TRIAD MANUFACTURING, INC.

[1992]   BJC HEALTH SYSTEM

[1992]   NU-CHEM, INC.

[1992]   SYLLOGISTEKS

[1993]   U.S. TITLE GUARANTY COMPANY, INC.

[1995]   ST. LOUIS RAMS

[1995]   SUTTLE MINDLIN

[1995]   WIEGMANN & ASSOCIATES INC.

[1996]   ESSE HEALTH

[1996]   SINCLAIR BROADCAST GROUP

[1997]   MARKETING DIRECT, INC.

[1997]   SOLUTIA INC.

THE KOMAN GROUP/KOMAN PROPERTIES, INC.

THROUGH TWO SEPARATE BUT RELATED COMPANIES—THE Koman Group and Koman Properties, Inc.—the Koman family has become a major presence in the St. Louis real estate development market. ¶ The older of the two businesses, The Koman Group was founded in 1981 by William J. Koman, Sr. to acquire, develop,

lease, and manage local real estate. It has since developed more than 3 million square feet of commercial space in St. Louis. William J. Koman Jr., who joined the company in 1984, is now its president.

In 1995, James G. Koman, another of William Koman's sons, spun Koman Properties, Inc. off from the original company and became its president. It has already developed more than 1.5 million square feet of retail space. Currently, Koman Properties is involved in nine build-to-suit shopping centers, and has developed projects in various Missouri and Illinois locations, including Columbia and Jefferson City.

SIBLING COMPANIES

Like the brothers who run them, The Koman Group and Koman Properties are sibling companies, operating side by side, occasionally joining forces on specific projects. Their offices are also side by side in the City-Place One building, which The Koman Group developed. Together, the companies have developed more than $400 million in properties.

Along with a strong commitment to quality and integrity, they share the same advantages in dealing with potential customers. A major benefit is their flexibility: they have the ability to put together deals that do not involve outside investors who have no personal involvement in the project. Most business is done within the family, so that when customers talk to any Koman, they are dealing with a principal who will be included in the deal from beginning to end.

"Everything we do, we build, we own, and we manage," says James Koman. "That makes us different from the 99 percent of real estate developers in St. Louis who are fee developers; they build for other investors, then just walk away when the project is finished. We are managing and nurturing the project along, and we hope to maintain it forever."

THE KOMAN GROUP

Another major piece of The Koman Group portfolio is the CityPlace development in Creve Coeur, Missouri, off Olive Street Road near I-270. CityPlace One, built in 1989, is typical of the other buildings in the complex, which will be completed in 2001. Offices are lined with stained mahogany paneling; the lobby is lavishly decorated; and the building includes amenities such as a restaurant, health club, and shared auditorium space. Since the day they opened, CityPlace One and CityPlace Two have been 99 percent leased, and there is a waiting list of potential tenants.

Elsewhere, The Koman Group is involved in the St. Louis riverfront, as developer and part owner of the *Casino Queen*, a

riverboat casino located in East St. Louis, Illinois. The company is also coordinating the development of a hotel in East St. Louis.

Other successful projects include the regional headquarters of Aetna Casualty and Surety Company, Tandem Computers, Peabody Coal Company, Kroger Corporation, and Maryland Casualty Insurance Company, and the corporate headquarters of Arch Coal, Inc. The Koman Group has also developed or renovated retail centers from 30,000 to 400,000 square feet in size.

KOMAN PROPERTIES, INC.

Already, Koman Properties, Inc. has built or is currently in the midst of constructing a number of build-to-suit retail projects. Many of its projects involve well-known grocery store, department store, and pharmacy tenants. For example, it is currently developing nine Walgreens stores in Missouri and Illinois, each with a pricetag of $3 million to $5 million. It also has developed a number of neighborhood and large power shopping centers.

One of the power centers Koman Properties is building is Lincoln Place in Fairview Heights, Illinois, a 300,000-square-foot center anchored by Lowe's Home Improvement Center. Phase one was completed in fall 1997, and phase two includes a 130,000-square-foot addition. Total cost for the project will be $48 million.

In fall 1998, Koman Properties completed a $10 million, 75,000-square-foot shopping center, Maplewood Square, anchored by a Shop 'n Save grocery store. And in fall 1999, the company plans to finish work on the new State Street Center in East St. Louis, the first new shopping center to be built in this area in more than 20 years.

"In Maplewood and East St. Louis, we went into neighborhoods that were on the decline and made improvements that will probably become the catalyst for future developments," says Koman.

Koman's company is also engaged in expanding the CityPlace retail center on Olive Street Road near the CityPlace office complex. The existing center, currently leased to Kinko's, Metro Imaging, and Provisions Gourmet Market, is 42,000 square feet in size. A 25,000-square-foot addition will house a new location of Wild Oats Markets.

In the future, Koman Properties and The Koman Group will be taking on new projects: an office tower in Clayton, Missouri, and a hotel in Creve Coeur, Missouri, as well as retail developments in north city, the central corridor, south city, and downtown St. Louis.

"Under the direction and leadership our father has given us, we have evolved into a successful real estate development company in St. Louis," says James Koman. "We have determination, integrity, and commitment to the cities we build in, and we strive to honor those commitments—hopefully leaving St. Louis a better place in the process."

PLAZA MOTORS

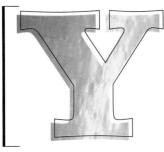

YEARS AGO, LUXURY CAR BUYERS WERE BRAND LOYAL. JOHN Capps, president of Plaza Motors, tells the story of his mother, who bought her first Cadillac and liked it so much that she continued buying Cadillacs for the next 40 years. Today, customers may love their Cadillac or Mercedes, but many also need or want something

different at various stages of their lives.

"Since customers today are not as brand loyal, we want to make them dealer loyal," says Capps. "And we thought we could do that by providing them with eight of the world's greatest luxury car franchises— Mercedes, Audi, Porsche, Cadillac, Land Rover, Infiniti, Lexus, and BMW—at one stop. Then, if we did a good job of taking care of them and earning their business, they would stay with us through the lifetime of their transportation needs whether they needed a sedan, convertible, or SUV."

At Plaza Motors, Capps and his team of 280 sales and service employees have worked hard to create the luxury car center of the nation, a business that inspires dealer loyalty among customers. The sales figures and revenue growth for the company are an index of its success. Since first opening in 1981, Plaza Motors has grown from $15 million in annual revenue to more than $200 million projected for 1999. Plaza is the largest luxury car

JOHN CAPPS (LEFT), PRESIDENT OF PLAZA MOTORS, AND GENERAL MANAGER TONY PANDJIRIS, A LONGTIME COLLEAGUE, HAVE BEEN WORKING TOGETHER SINCE THE COMPANY OPENED IN 1981 (TOP).

COLLISION REPAIR CENTER MANAGER MILO BOYLES (LEFT) AND PANDJIRIS CONFER INSIDE PLAZA'S STATE-OF-THE-ART, 80-BAY REPAIR FACILITY (BOTTOM).

dealer in St. Louis, and perhaps in the entire Midwest. One reason for the company's success is its strategic location. Most of Plaza's customers live within a six- to seven-mile radius of the dealership, which is located on Olive Boulevard at I-270.

Another reason for Plaza's success is the wide selection of automobiles, which are housed in four large showrooms with a total of 165,000 square feet on a 10-acre campus. Behind the showrooms is a $6 million, four-story parking garage— almost 50,000 square feet per floor. A large inventory of cars is always available for purchase or lease, protected from the ravages of weather.

TOTAL QUALITY CUSTOMER CARE

Perhaps the most important reason for Plaza Motors' success, says Capps, is its extraordinary

commitment to satisfying customers, both during and after the sale. The company's associates are on a first name basis with many clients, and all negotiations are done in a respectful, low-key, and dignified manner.

"Some 70 to 75 percent of our business is repeat business. To prosper and grow long-term, we need clients to continue to buy from us. So our mission has always been to make sure we create a strong bond with our customers by treating them very fairly and very well," Capps says.

After the sale, the company's service operation is an important ingredient in customer satisfaction. Sophisticated luxury cars—complete with computers and complex electronic devices— must be repaired by skilled technicians who take training updates each year. To perform routine maintenance and repairs, they need specialized diagnostic equipment. For collision repairs, Plaza Motors also has its state-of-the-art, $2.5 million Collision Repair Center with 50 repair bays and 30 refinishing bays.

The company was a local pioneer in providing amenities when a customer's car is being serviced. If needed, Plaza will pick the car up and deliver it after repairs are made. Plaza's staff washes each car—more than 200 each day—in the on-site car wash after it is serviced. In addition, a large fleet of loaner cars is maintained by the company to lend to customers while their own cars are being repaired. This level of customer service has won many awards. In customer satisfaction index polls conducted by car manufacturers, Plaza Motors routinely ranks in the top tier among car dealerships.

A HISTORY OF QUALITY

Capps founded Plaza Motors in 1981 after running another dealership—Northgate Porsche and Audi—and working for his father, George H. Capps, who owned a St. Louis Volkswagen, Audi, and Porsche distributorship that served a four-state region. John Capps loved the retail car business, and when a Mercedes dealership came available in 1980, he bid for it—and got it. By the time he had opened the doors of his new building in 1981, he had also bought back the Audi and Porsche franchises, and had handpicked an ambitious staff.

Plaza made a crucial decision: to try to carve out the luxury car market in St. Louis. Over time, the company bought Lindburg Cadillac, located downtown, and moved it to its campus. Plaza was the first non-Toyota dealer in the United States to be awarded a Lexus franchise. New franchises also came to Plaza for BMW and Land Rover; in the first year after acquiring the Infiniti franchise, it was the top Infiniti dealer in the entire country.

In 1998, Capps made another important decision: to blend Plaza Motors into the Asbury Automotive Group, which owns seven other megadealers in various cities throughout the United States. A significant owner now, Capps continues as president and CEO. For the future, he and his team plan to introduce leading-edge computer equipment at each sales associate's desk. Plaza plans to continue growing its pre-owned car business by providing a range of quality vehicles, new and used, in prices ranging from $10,000 to $150,000.

"Over the past 25 years in the car business, there have been seismic changes," says Capps. "Customers are much more educated about options and costs, and they have a very high expectation level for their dealership. We learned early on that you have to meet or exceed those expectations if you want to earn their business for a lifetime."

CAPPS (LEFT) AND TOM SCHULTZ, PLAZA'S PORSCHE, AUDI, AND LAND ROVER MANAGER, MEET IN THE COMPANY'S NEWLY REMODELED SHOWROOM AND CLIENT RECEPTION CENTER.

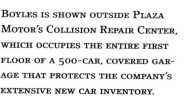

BOYLES IS SHOWN OUTSIDE PLAZA MOTOR'S COLLISION REPAIR CENTER, WHICH OCCUPIES THE ENTIRE FIRST FLOOR OF A 500-CAR, COVERED GARAGE THAT PROTECTS THE COMPANY'S EXTENSIVE NEW CAR INVENTORY.

INSITUFORM TECHNOLOGIES, INC.

THE SEWER INFRASTRUCTURE BELOW MANY CITIES IS AGING. Having already outlasted many of the roads, bridges, and schools constructed above them, many sewers are now approaching the end of their useful lives. Over time, these sewers become cracked or deteriorated and joints separate. If not treated, these problems can cause

pavement to collapse and place costly demands on the municipality.

Whereas pipes were once laid beneath undeveloped land upon which roads, neighborhoods, and high-rise office buildings would eventually be built, the challenge today is to repair these aging sewers without disturbing the environment above. That is exactly what Insituform Technologies, Inc. does.

For nearly 30 years, Insituform has been a leader in rehabilitating sewers and other underground pipes without digging or disruption. The company's flagship Insituform® process was developed in 1971 in the United Kingdom, and today has become the most widely used trenchless method of reconstructing sewers in North America, Europe, and Asia.

INSITUFORM TECHNOLOGIES, INC. IS HEADQUARTERED IN CHESTERFIELD IN A 60,000-SQUARE-FOOT RESEARCH AND DEVELOPMENT FACILITY (TOP).

AN INSITUFORM® TUBE IS INSTALLED BELOW BLOW STREET IN ST. LOUIS WITH LITTLE DISRUPTION TO THE NEIGHBORHOOD (BOTTOM).

With headquarters in Chesterfield, Insituform operates a global business of more than 1,500 employees dedicated to meeting the pipe repair needs of municipalities and industrial facilities. In Chesterfield, the company has a corporate campus consisting of its headquarters, an employee training facility, a regional operations center, and a 60,000-square-foot research and development facility.

Insituform is an integrated pipe rehabilitation company. This means the company develops, manufactures, and engineers the technologies that its own crews install. "Most installers of trenchless products are general contractors, who depend on others for the materials, methods, and technology they use," says Anthony Hooper, Insituform's president and CEO. "We are the only company to take full responsibility for every stage of solving a customer's piping problems, from product development to manufacturing, and from engineering to installation."

QUALITY MATERIALS, RELIABLE SERVICE

While Insituform serves a number of pipe rehabilitation markets—including water mains and industrial pipe—its primary focus is municipal sewer systems. Since its founding, the company has installed more than 40 million feet of product. Local customers include the Metropolitan Sewer District (MSD) of St. Louis, as well as municipalities in southeastern Illinois and in St. Charles, Jefferson, and Franklin Counties.

As more and more cities turn to trenchless methods for solving their sewer problems, they increasingly look to a company like Insituform for long-term, comprehensive solutions. Insituform can transform pipes that are collapsing or leaking into seamless, smooth vehicles that have enough strength to stand alone if sections of the host pipe deteriorate, resisting both soil loads and high-groundwater conditions.

The company's technologies can be applied to a wide variety of pipe shapes and diameters, as well as to pipelines made of virtually any existing material, including concrete, clay, brick, and steel. The company's technologies can also be used in sewers of varying shapes and even those with bends or changing dimensions.

The Insituform process involves the installation of a resin-impregnated felt tube into a deteriorated sewer. The tube is inserted into the damaged host pipe and turned inside out using water pressure. Once the Insituform® tube is completely installed, water is heated in an on-site boiler and circulated through the pipe to cure the resin and form a new pipe within a pipe. Insituform crews then use a robotic camera and cutting device to open feeder lines and reestablish service to local residents.

Residents are rarely inconvenienced for more than a few

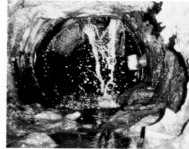

WHEREAS PIPES WERE ONCE LAID BENEATH UNDEVELOPED LAND UPON WHICH ROADS, NEIGHBORHOODS, AND HIGH-RISE OFFICE BUILDINGS WOULD EVENTUALLY BE BUILT, THE CHALLENGE TODAY IS TO REPAIR THESE AGING SEWERS WITHOUT DISTURBING THE ENVIRONMENT ABOVE. THAT IS EXACTLY WHAT INSITUFORM TECHNOLOGIES, INC. DOES BY LINING DETERIORATING SEWERS (RIGHT) WITH ITS INSITUFORM® PROCESS (LEFT).

hours, compared to the days or weeks it can take to replace a sewer using conventional pipe digging methods. Residents often do not even know that the sewer servicing their homes has been rehabilitated.

"Our goal is to make sure that residents, commuters, and business owners are inconvenienced as little as possible when we are working in their community. That's why we commit substantial resources to training our people in safe, efficient work practices," says Hooper. "We take pride in the service we provide to our customers."

AFFHOLDER, INC.
Since 1968, Affholder, Inc., a subsidiary of Insituform Technologies, has been installing new, large-diameter tunnels, using advanced technologies that cause little disruption to

the community. In St. Louis, Affholder crews are in the process of installing 28,700 feet of new, 10-foot-diameter sewer pipe that runs from University City under Forest Park to River Des Peres. This is a three-year project for the MSD.

Insituform continually focuses on finding new ways to make its rehabilitation processes even better and more affordable. Its employees continue to respond intuitively to their customers' needs.

"We work hard to develop products that address those needs, and we custom-engineer each project to meet their specific requirements," says Hooper. "Solving pipe problems is our business, and we believe the best way to do that is to take responsibility for the entire process, to ensure our customers' satisfaction."

FROM LEFT:
AN INSITUFORM CREW REPAIRS A SEWER WITHOUT DIGGING.

A NEW TUNNEL IS BORED WELL BELOW THE SURFACE OF FOREST PARK.

A TUNNEL-BORING MACHINE EXCAVATES AT A RATE OF EIGHT TO 12 FEET PER HOUR.

AMDOCS, INC.

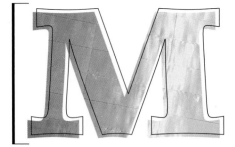

OST CONSUMERS HAVE NEVER HEARD OF AMDOCS— even in St. Louis, home to the company's North American headquarters and its subsidiary, Amdocs, Inc. Yet, the services provided by this leader in the supplying of information technology to the telecommunications industry affect the lives of many people every day.

Half the phone calls made daily in the United States depend on Amdocs software. Tens of millions of Americans receive phone bills that are processed with Amdocs software. And every copy of the *Southwestern Bell Yellow Pages* is designed, organized, and published using Amdocs software.

Amdocs provides information systems solutions in 15 different languages to more than 60 telecommunications companies in 25 countries around the world. Around half the company's business is in the United States; the company also boasts significant operations in Europe and Australia, with a growing presence in South America.

RAPID GROWTH TO FILL GROWING NEEDS

At the end of fiscal year 1998, the company, which now employs some 3,700 information technology professionals worldwide, had just over $400 million in revenue. And in June 1998,

Amdocs marked another milestone: a move from private to public ownership.

Rapid growth has always been the hallmark of Amdocs, which was founded in Israel in 1982 and expanded its operations to the United States in 1985. Southwestern Bell Yellow Pages was the firm's first U.S. customer—and soon became an Amdocs investor.

Today, Southwestern Bell, through its various entities, is Amdocs' biggest customer, representing some 15 percent of the firm's revenue.

At first, Amdocs produced software for the directory business—and it still has 50 percent of this market. But in the 1990s, the company changed its strategic direction, moving into the dynamic area of customer care and billing, with software that allows phone companies to be more responsive to their customers' needs.

And Amdocs does not simply sell the software. The company prides itself on providing a full-scale solution for the client by customizing the software, staying on long-term to support it, then further modifying and updating it to meet the customer's changing needs. Since the company began, it has never had a failed installation, and it has never been replaced by a third-party competitor.

Amdocs first came to St. Louis in 1984 to be close to Southwestern Bell. Now, the firm has some 300 employees here and a new, 80,000-square-foot building in Chesterfield, where it has consolidated its local offices and its state-of-the-art development center.

Both here and around the world, Amdocs will soon be branching out with new research and development efforts, largely in the area of churn control, fraud management, and data mining techniques for the telephone credit card market. Amdocs will also build on its past success, treating its customers to strong, personal service.

AMDOCS, INC. FIRST CAME TO ST. LOUIS IN 1984 TO BE CLOSE TO SOUTHWESTERN BELL. NOW, THE FIRM HAS SOME 300 EMPLOYEES HERE AND A NEW, 80,000-SQUARE-FOOT BUILDING IN CHESTERFIELD, WHERE IT HAS CONSOLIDATED ITS LOCAL OFFICES AND ITS STATE-OF-THE-ART DEVELOPMENT CENTER.

I N 1984, ROBERT BRINKMANN FOUNDED A CONSTRUCTION COMPANY that has grown to be a leader in the St. Louis building industry with a reputation for innovation and excellence. Today, R.G. Brinkmann Construction Company is a multimillion-dollar, full-service design/build firm whose commitment to value engineering has introduced new ways to deliver quality at a lower cost.

R.G. BRINKMANN CONSTRUCTION COMPANY

"Since day one, R.G. Brinkmann Construction Company has never lost sight of the fact that we are not only in the construction industry, but are also in the service industry," says Robert Brinkmann, president. "We don't just build one building and move on to the next. We negotiate more than 99 percent of our work—almost all of it from repeat customers who have grown to appreciate our personal service long after the project is completed."

A decade ago, the company decided to focus on efficiency to shave time off of projects without sacrificing quality. The result was a streamlined approach to each project that saves weeks and even months on construction. Projects are orchestrated to require subcontractors to perform work quickly and coordinate everyone's activities so projects run like clockwork.

HIGHLY QUALIFIED EMPLOYEES

"The essence of our success is built on the high standards maintained by Brinkmann's skilled construction staff that manage the projects," says Brinkmann. He hires civil engineers who understand the underlying structure of a building. Brinkmann also looks for employees who think creatively, work productively, and have a passion for the construction business.

That passion and innovative spirit are found in each Brinkmann project, many built under extraordinary time constraints. They also show in the breadth of construction projects completed by Brinkmann that touch nearly every market sector, including retail, manufacturing, warehouse distribution, institutional, and others.

One project that bears the Brinkmann innovative and quality trademark is the $28 million, 180,000-square-foot Brooks/WorldCom headquarters in Town and Country, Missouri. It was honored with a Readers Choice Award by *St. Louis Construction News and Review*. The five-story, two-building complex is linked by three bridges that span a 250-foot-long atrium. Despite the inherent complexities of the project, it was completed ahead of schedule.

Another recent project is the 16-screen, 2,800-seat West Park AMC Theater in suburban Creve Coeur, Missouri. The owners nearly canceled the project when construction bids came in $1.5 million over budget. Through site reconfiguration and other creative solutions, Brinkmann managed to cut costs so the $10 million project could proceed.

A third Brinkmann project is CityPlace Two, a $10 million, 120,000-square-foot office project for the Koman Group in Creve Coeur. In the retail market, Brinkmann also completed the 134,000-square-foot Schnucks Ladue Crossing Center, including a new Schnuck Markets store, finishing this eight-month, fast-track project in only five and a half months.

Brinkmann is also codeveloper of Chesterfield Grove, a $21 million, mixed-use development in Chesterfield. Today, this complex of buildings, which includes a Hilton Garden Inn, restaurants, retail shops, and office space, is the site of Brinkmann's new headquarters.

"SINCE DAY ONE, R.G. BRINKMANN CONSTRUCTION COMPANY HAS NEVER LOST SIGHT OF THE FACT THAT WE ARE NOT ONLY IN THE CONSTRUCTION INDUSTRY, BUT ARE ALSO IN THE SERVICE INDUSTRY," SAYS ROBERT BRINKMANN, PRESIDENT (LEFT).

A NATURE POND WITH LIGHT SCULPTURE ANIMATES THE BEAUTIFUL, 23-ACRE BROOKS FIBER CAMPUS AT NIGHT. R.G. BRINKMANN CONSTRUCTION COMPANY WAS THE GENERAL CONTRACTOR (RIGHT).

DEBBIE FRANKE PHOTOGRAPHY

SAM FENTRESS ARCHITECTURAL PHOTOGRAPHY

CLAYCO CONSTRUCTION COMPANY

CLAYCO CONSTRUCTION COMPANY IS A FULL-SERVICE, design/build general contracting firm with a growing reputation on the local and national level. In 1998 alone, Clayco worked in 22 states and two countries, producing a record 9 million square feet of new construction and total annual revenues exceeding $275 million.

Clayco's expertise and versatility are best described in the broad range of projects this fast-track company delivers. Along with the extensive list of successful design/build projects completed, Clayco's reputation as the nation's leading tilt-up concrete contracting company continues to grow. Clayco's expertise positions the firm to take on any kind of corporate structure: from a suburban office facility to high-profile corporate headquarters, along with warehouse distribution centers of up to 1.5 million square feet. Clayco continues to extend the scope of its work by taking on new categories such as education, banking, and athletic/sports facilities.

Some of Clayco's projects have received prestigious national awards. Its own St. Louis corporate headquarters, built of the firm's trademark concrete wall panels, has won several architectural design honors, including a national award from the Design-Build Institute of America (DBIA).

Another Clayco-built project, which also won a DBIA award, is the St. Louis Rams corporate headquarters and training facility in Earth City, Missouri, completed in 1996. This 168,000-square-foot building was particularly challenging because it has an unusual array of features: office space, media rooms, auditorium, indoor football field, training rooms with pools and saunas, and indoor basketball and racquetball courts. Clayco finished the project on a tight, fast-track schedule.

"Three simple philosophies have led to Clayco's success. First is to hire the brightest people in the business. Second is to have the best relationships with the subcontracting community through ethical practices and on-time bill payment. And third is to be selective in where we apply our craft, working for people we want to work for in situations where we can create and add value," says Robert Clark, chairman and CEO.

A DIFFERENT KIND OF CONSTRUCTION COMPANY

From childhood, Clark had always dreamed of owning a construction company. In 1984, fresh from his success at two other businesses, he decided to establish Clayco. His father, Harold Clark—owner of Clark Properties, a real estate rehabilitation business—gave him encouragement and advice.

From the beginning, Clark wanted to create a different, more open kind of business culture. He started an unusual profit-sharing plan in which employees share 25 percent of the company's pretax profit. And he also decided that all of Clayco's financial information would be available to all employees, so they would understand the company's strategy, every

CLOCKWISE FROM TOP:
CLAYCO CONSTRUCTION COMPANY'S OWN ST. LOUIS CORPORATE HEADQUARTERS, BUILT OF THE FIRM'S TRADEMARK CONCRETE WALL PANELS, HAS WON SEVERAL ARCHITECTURAL DESIGN HONORS, INCLUDING A NATIONAL AWARD FROM THE DESIGN-BUILD INSTITUTE OF AMERICA (DBIA).

MANY OF CLAYCO'S PROJECTS TAKE PLACE IN THE ST. LOUIS AREA. ONE RECENT EXAMPLE IS THE CORPORATE WOODS OFFICE PARK IN EARTH CITY, MISSOURI, WHERE SAVE-A-LOT, ONE OF CLAYCO'S REPEAT CUSTOMERS, HAS ITS CORPORATE HEADQUARTERS.

ANOTHER CLAYCO-BUILT PROJECT, WHICH ALSO WON A DBIA AWARD, IS THE ST. LOUIS RAMS CORPORATE HEADQUARTERS AND TRAINING FACILITY IN EARTH CITY, COMPLETED IN 1996.

EMBASSY SUITES, LOCATED NEAR THE RIVERFRONT ON HISTORIC Laclede's Landing, is more than just another nice hotel. In fact, it reflects the unique charm of its downtown surroundings and offers guests a real St. Louis experience. ❡ In addition to its ideal location and historic ambience, the hotel features a number of fine services

and entertainment options, all of which also make Embassy Suites a destination for both leisure and business travelers. Among its diverse amenities are an indoor pool, whirlpool, sauna, steam room, fitness center, game room, billiards tables, and the Dirtwater Fox Cafe and Lounge. Altogether, these extras allow guests to relax and have fun without ever leaving the hotel.

AN IMPRESSIVE TRANSFORMATION

FelCor Lodging Trust, a firm known for breathing new life into hotels nationwide, bought the Embassy Suites franchise through Promus Hotel Corporation of Memphis in May 1998. Both FelCor and Promus saw the potential of the 15-year-old St. Louis property and began an impressive transformation.

Today, the hotel's 297 two-room suites open onto an eight-story, enclosed atrium, where white wrought iron railings lend a New Orleans flavor to the lush setting. What's more, guests can lose themselves amid the hotel's garden courtyard, where fountains and waterfalls surrounded by greenery seem to bring the outdoors inside.

When it's time to venture beyond the hotel, guests ready

for fun or sight seeing don't have far to go. The Embassy Suites is just minutes away from river-boat gambling, the Gateway Arch, the America's Center Convention Center, and downtown shopping at St. Louis Center. Sports fans also enjoy easy access to nearby Busch Stadium, Kiel Center, or the TWA Dome.

GUARANTEED EXCELLENCE

For prices comparable to a single room at other hotels, the Embassy Suites provides a two-room suite with a wet bar; free, cooked-to-order breakfast; and manager's reception each evening with complimentary beverages. A new seafood restaurant—The St. Louis Fish Market—was added in early 2000. It is also the only chain that offers a 100 percent guarantee of excellence. If hotel services don't meet the guest's expectations, Embassy Suites adjusts the bill accordingly.

Business travelers find that the hotel pays close attention to their unique needs as well. Currently, 8,000 square feet of flexible meeting, banquet, and ballroom space are available, along with upgraded meeting rooms, suites, and public spaces that can accommodate groups

of up to 400 people. The Embassy Suites also boasts state-of-the-art communications systems—voice mail, computer modem connections, and two televisions with cable—in each suite for added convenience. And the hotel's Preferred Partners plan provides corporate members with preferential treatment and rates, including bonuses for company travel planners.

As the rapidly growing tourist and business trades create an ever greater demand for first-class accommodations in downtown St. Louis, the Embassy Suites is ready to meet the challenge with its refreshing charm and its exceptional service and amenities.

AS THE RAPIDLY GROWING TOURIST AND BUSINESS TRADES CREATE AN EVER GREATER DEMAND FOR FIRST-CLASS ACCOMMODATIONS IN DOWNTOWN ST. LOUIS, THE EMBASSY SUITES IS READY TO MEET THE CHALLENGE WITH ITS REFRESHING CHARM AND ITS EXCEPTIONAL SERVICE AND AMENITIES (LEFT).

EMBASSY SUITES, LOCATED NEAR THE RIVERFRONT ON HISTORIC LACLEDE'S LANDING, IS MORE THAN JUST ANOTHER NICE HOTEL. IN FACT, IT REFLECTS THE UNIQUE CHARM OF ITS DOWNTOWN SURROUNDINGS AND OFFERS GUESTS A REAL ST. LOUIS EXPERIENCE (RIGHT).

TENET HEALTHCARE SAINT LOUIS

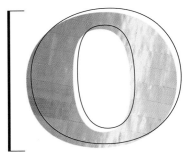

OVER THE PAST FEW YEARS, TENET HEALTHCARE SAINT Louis has emerged as a significant new force in regional health care, with a broad network of services located throughout the metropolitan area. Since it entered the community in 1984 with the purchase of Lutheran Medical Center (now SouthPointe Hospital),

the system has grown to encompass five academic and community hospitals, including SouthPointe Hospital, Forest Park Hospital, Des Peres Hospital, Compton Heights Hospital, and Saint Louis University Hospital; physician practices; home care and hospice; and two schools of nursing.

In all, more than 6,000 Tenet Healthcare Saint Louis employees work toward a common purpose: providing quality care to patients, often in partnership with other local health care providers, employers, insurance companies, and government agencies. The system is dedicated to quality care, devoting its resources to clinical and support staff, innovative therapies, and advanced equipment.

"In St. Louis, we want to help create a truly open, competitive marketplace where health providers compete based on quality, cost, and service," says

Matthew A. Kurs, chief executive officer of Tenet Healthcare Saint Louis. "By working harder than our competitors, we hope to become the best-value health care provider in this area."

A STRONG PRESENCE

Already, Tenet Healthcare Saint Louis can point to several medical distinctions. It has one of the area's largest networks of primary care physicians. Among its hospitals, it offers comprehensive psychiatric, heart, cancer, and orthopedic and geriatric services. And Saint Louis University Hospital, which has the most comprehensive organ transplant program in the region and one of the busiest Level I trauma services in the bistate area, has been ranked among the top 42 American medical centers in *U.S. News & World Report* in several specialties: cardiology/ cardiac surgery, endocrinology, gastroenterology, geriatric medi-

cine, neurology/neurosurgery, orthopedics, otolaryngology, rheumatology, and urology.

Through all its services, the Tenet Healthcare Saint Louis network has a substantial impact on health care in the area. Locally, its hospitals include 1,783 licensed beds and its medical group has approximately 100 physicians in 20 different locations. In 1998, Tenet Healthcare Saint Louis hospitals admitted approximately 39,000 patients and handled about 502,000 outpatient visits.

Tenet Healthcare Saint Louis also offers alternate ways outside the hospital to bring care to the communities it serves. The system's home care agency provides skilled services in the homes of patients. These services include nursing, physical therapy, occupational therapy, and speech therapy. Tenet Healthcare Saint Louis' Alternate Delivery Systems services also provide home infusion, private duty, homemakers, live-in companions, and Lifeline, an electronic system that enables people with a sudden medical need to summon help.

The system's Hospice Program takes a team approach to the care of terminally ill patients. An interdisciplinary hospice team cares for the dying patient and supports the patient's family.

Tenet Healthcare Saint Louis also makes a significant financial contribution to St. Louis by paying taxes that benefit the area. During the 1999 fiscal year, the system paid approximately $5 million in taxes to the City of St. Louis. In addition, Tenet Healthcare Saint Louis spends millions a year in routine capital improvements on its facilities, and has

POSTPARTUM OBSTETRICAL ROOMS AT FOREST PARK HOSPITAL—A TENET HEALTHCARE SAINT LOUIS HOSPITAL— ARE MODERN AND COMFORTABLE.

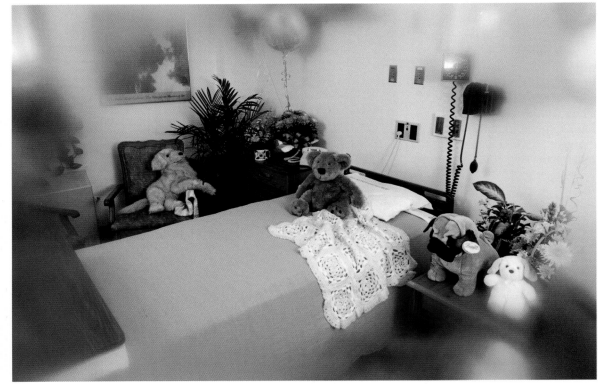

available about $100 million to incubate and launch programs with a goal of improving the health of the community.

Beyond that, Tenet Healthcare Saint Louis provides a generous amount of uncompensated health care to needy patients. By spring 1999, the system had exceeded its goal of delivering more than $16 million in community benefits, including caring for poor and uninsured patients unable to pay for their care.

"For all our patients, we believe in care that centers on their needs," says Kurs. "Our clinical staff members provide that kind of care by researching new medical techniques and procedures, developing innovative programs, and monitoring patient satisfaction. Because of our association with a national network, we can also import high-quality practices from 129 hospitals across the United States."

Tenet Healthcare Saint Louis entered the local market when its national corporation, Tenet Healthcare Corporation, purchased Lutheran Medical Center (now SouthPointe Hospital). In the years since, the system has made additional local acquisitions. In 1997, Tenet Healthcare Corporation bought the former Deaconess Incarnate Word Health System, consisting of several hospitals—Deaconess Central Hospital (now Forest Park Hospital), Deaconess West Hospital (Des Peres Hospital), and Incarnate Word Hospital (Compton Heights Hospital)—and The St. Louis Medical Group. And in February 1998, Tenet Healthcare Corporation purchased Saint Louis University Hospital, the teaching hospital for Saint Louis University.

SouthPointe Hospital

SouthPointe Hospital, believed to be the oldest hospital in one location west of the Mississippi River, has a long history in St. Louis. It was founded in a private residence at Broadway and Geyer Road in 1858 to care for the sick and injured. In 1864,

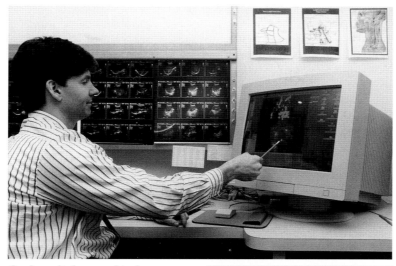

the hospital moved to larger quarters near Seventh and Sidney streets; then in 1878, it moved to its present location in south St. Louis.

Throughout this century, the hospital has been expanding. In 1968, it added a new residence hall and teaching facility for its School of Nursing, which offers students a diploma program. A nine-story community mental health center, parking facilities, and a four-story medical office building were added in the early 1970s. When Lutheran Medical Center became part of Tenet in 1984, the company undertook an extensive program of renovations.

Today, the hospital consumes two city blocks and consists of 11 buildings covering more than 500,000 square feet. SouthPointe Hospital is a licensed, 408-bed, full-service community hospital offering medical, surgical, skilled nursing, obstetrical, emergency, and psychiatric care. It is well known for its specialized services, which include the Center for Physical Rehabilitation, Continence Center, Continent Ostomy Center, Eating Disorders Program, Foot Care Center, Hand Center, Joint Diagnostic Center, New Start (a program for surgical weight reduction), Knee and Hip Center, and Skilled Nursing Facility.

Forest Park Hospital

In 1997, Tenet Healthcare Corporation dramatically increased

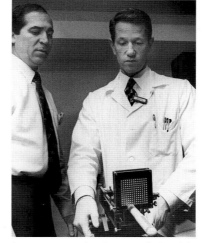

its presence in the area's health care community with the acquisition of several additional hospitals. The largest of these was Deaconess Central Hospital (now Forest Park Hospital).

Deaconess Central Hospital traced its roots to 1889, when the Evangelical Deaconess Society of St. Louis was organized by the Evangelical Synod, a forerunner of the United Church of Christ. The society founded its first hospital near Union Station on Market Street; its early staff members were the Deaconess Sisters, a group of women consecrated to the full-time Christian ministry of healing and teaching.

Over the years, that original hospital moved twice, finally building a facility on Oakland Avenue in 1930, which has since greatly expanded. Today, Forest Park Hospital employs some 2,000 full- and part-time staff. It offers an array of acute care services, including obstetrics/

Val Lowe, MD, assistant professor, internal medicine/nuclear medicine, Saint Louis University School of Medicine, demonstrates the use of positron-emission tomography, one of the tools used by Saint Louis University Hospital in the diagnosis and treatment of cancer (top).

Radiation oncologist Eric Sutphen, MD (right), and medical physicist David Keys, PhD, adjust an ultrasound probe used in prostate brachytherapy, an advanced cancer treatment offered at Forest Park Hospital (bottom).

gynecology, oncology, surgery, cardiac care, orthopedics, physical rehabilitation, psychiatry, and family medicine.

The hospital, which has 516 licensed beds, is a teaching facility, with physicians' medical education and nursing education activities on-site. On the same campus is the Deaconess College of Nursing, which offers associate and bachelor of science degrees in nursing. As a community service, the hospital also houses the Saint Louis Crisis Nursery, a temporary shelter for children.

Des Peres Hospital

Des Peres Hospital (formerly Deaconess West Hospital) is located in St. Louis County at I-270 and Dougherty Ferry Road. It has served communities in the region since opening in 1974. The facility has 167 licensed beds.

A wide range of medical and surgical services are offered, including heart care, encompassing cardiology, cardiac catheterization, and open-heart surgery; orthopedics, including prevention, surgery, rehabilitation, and therapy related to conditions of the bones and joints (total joint replacements and spinal surgeries are performed, as appropriate); comprehensive rehabilitation; psychiatric services, including geropsychiatry; a senior care center designed to provide support services to skilled nursing homes, residential care facilities, and retirement

communities; outpatient services; and an emergency department.

An important off-site component of the hospital is the U.S. Center for Sports Medicine, which is located in nearby Kirkwood. It provides diagnoses and care related to athletic injuries of both professional and amateur competitors, injuries occurring at work or in the home, and various other musculoskeletal conditions that may result from chronic disease or deformity. Capabilities include orthopedic surgery, complex fracture care, and rehabilitation; advanced arthroscopy and cartilage repair and regeneration; and body mechanics programs and exercise regimens.

Des Peres Hospital continues as a teaching center for physicians.

Compton Heights Hospital

Compton Heights Hospital (formerly Incarnate Word Hospital) offers compassionate, individualized care, springing from a strong religious mission that continues to this day. The Sisters of Charity of the Incarnate Word, who took respon-

sibility for the hospital in 1933, continue to guide the pastoral care department and maintain the hospital's spiritual tradition.

The 336-bed hospital provides the community with a strong list of services with particular focus on care for the elderly. Among them are cardiology; cardiopulmonary rehabilitation; geriatric medicine, and psychiatry; emergency care; orthopedic and other surgical procedures; a skilled nursing unit; respiratory care; a wound care center; audiology; and a comprehensive medical rehabilitation program.

Saint Louis University Hospital

In 1933, a new hospital was dedicated in St. Louis: Firmin Desloge Hospital, named for a local philanthropist whose family had donated $1 million to its construction. The landmark building, designed in the French Gothic style, has a 250-foot-high, pitched roof made of copper-covered lead.

Originally, the hospital was operated under the auspices of the Sisters of St. Mary, but in 1959, its administration shifted to Saint Louis University. A major

When an item shows the least sign of wear, Hampton Corporate Suites replaces it with a brand-new purchase. The older items—some used only for three to six months—go to several homeless shelters throughout the St. Louis area. The company is also active in other charitable causes, such as sponsoring special events at Saint Joseph's Home for Boys.

WORKING TO SERVE THE CUSTOMERS

To match a client with the right apartment, Hampton Corporate Suites offers personalized touring. Customers view three or four housing options to find the location they like best. During the placement process, the staff works quickly. Often, a request comes in and they have less than a week—sometimes as little as 48 hours—to locate an apartment and prepare it fully for the customer.

Once the client arrives, everything is in place. The kitchen is outfitted; other rooms are furnished and inviting. In the dining room, the table is set as though guests are coming for dinner. The bathroom has toilet paper, tissues, and soap. There's even a little food—candy bars, soft drinks, popcorn, and breakfast coffee—so guests don't go hungry before they can do some grocery shopping.

During the course of the rental, Hampton Corporate Suites supplies weekly cleaning and linen laundering for its clients. A 24-hour emergency line, monitored by a Hampton employee, is ready for unexpected problems, such as guests who get locked out of their apartments.

Although competition in the corporate suite industry is very strong, Hampton has a core of loyal companies who come back again and again for interim housing assistance. And the company has received many letters of commendation from guests who are pleased by its personalized service.

One client wrote, commending Hampton Corporate Suites on finding him an apartment within a five-minute drive of his job—and furnished with the traditional furniture that he liked best: "I wanted to . . . let you know how impressed I was with the service I received from your company . . . to commend you on a job well done and say thank you very much."

IN EACH APARTMENT, HAMPTON CORPORATE SUITES WORKS TO CREATE AN ENVIRONMENT THAT FEELS COMFORTABLE AND FAMILIAR, FROM THE STYLE OF THE FURNISHINGS DOWN TO THE KITCHEN UTENSILS.

ALTHOUGH COMPETITION IN THE CORPORATE SUITE INDUSTRY IS VERY STRONG, HAMPTON HAS A CORE OF LOYAL COMPANIES WHO COME BACK AGAIN AND AGAIN FOR INTERIM HOUSING ASSISTANCE.

THOMAS ROOF, INC. ARCHITEKTS

SINCE THOMAS B. ROOF ESTABLISHED THE ARCHITECTURAL practice that bears his name in 1989, he and his team of associates have assembled a diverse portfolio of projects, including retail centers, office developments, restaurants, and industrial facilities. Along the way, Thomas Roof, Inc. Architekts (TR,i) has also built a

A NEW IDENTITY WAS CREATED BY THOMAS ROOF, INC. ARCHITEKTS FOR THE 8301 MARYLAND AVENUE OFFICE BUILDING IN CLAYTON, MISSOURI. THIS 8,800-SQUARE-FOOT ADDITION AND EXTERIOR RENOVATION REFLECTS THE FIRM'S "CREATIVE YET CONSTRUCTABLE" DESIGN PHILOSOPHY (TOP LEFT).

THE EXPERIENCE OF BEING BOTH CLIENT AND DESIGNER FOR ITS OWN 8,500-SQUARE-FOOT OFFICE IN CLAYTON SERVED TO REINFORCE TR,i'S COMMITMENT TO BALANCING A PROJECT'S DESIGN AND BUDGET (BOTTOM LEFT).

client list that includes a prestigious group of developers and corporate customers.

The firm has grown substantially, and today, it has 30 employees located in a suite of offices in downtown Clayton. TR,i's work spans 35 states, and its reputation has spread; in 1998 alone, the firm grew by some 60 percent. One reason for this success is Thomas Roof, Inc.'s versatility. A full-service firm, TR,i has the expertise to go beyond basic architectural

services to help owners evaluate sites, maximize opportunities, and navigate the municipal approval process.

Also fueling TR,i's success is its company philosophy. The firm places a strong emphasis on service to the client and respect for the project requirements. From the very start of a project, TR,i works hard to acquire a detailed understanding of a client's business goals and budget.

"Our clients want to deal with an architectural firm that is not going to waste their time or push them in a direction they do not want to go. They want their project to be completed in a creative yet constructible way, without spending a lot of money on useless features. We work closely with each of our clients to understand their needs and to ensure that this happens,"

says Thomas B. Roof, principal and owner of TR,i.

The firm's employees also take pride in their continuing involvement with each project. From start to finish, the principal assigned to a job takes a personal, hands-on approach, carefully attending to it until it is completed and the customer is satisfied.

ARCHITECTURE FOR BUSINESS

TR,i's corporate motto—Our Business is Architecture for Business—points to the market it serves. Within this market, many of the firm's clients include national-level corporations that have sought an architectural firm to design a project within or outside St. Louis. An important area of TR,i's expertise is "prototypical site adaptation," according to Roof. "A client may

474

come into town with a prototype for a project, and we can take that and adapt it to given locations," he says.

Such well-known corporate clients as Extended Stay America, Walgreens, Applebee's, and Hollywood Entertainment have employed TR,i to design a number of their locations. The firm has also designed several natural-food markets for national customer Wild Oats.

St. Louis Projects

Another kind of client is the St. Louis developer or corporation looking for creative, local expertise. Over the past decade, Thomas Roof, Inc. has had an ongoing relationship with the Koman Group, a commercial real estate developer well known for its successful CityPlace development in Creve Coeur. Not only has TR,i designed two CityPlace office buildings, the firm has also been involved in another Koman project: the *Casino Queen*, a riverboat casino located in East St. Louis.

TR,i has also developed strong expertise in supermar-

ket design. For Dierbergs Markets in St. Louis, the firm has served as architect for two new stores, along with the Dierbergs corporate office building in Chesterfield and a 100,000-square-foot commissary in Bridgeton.

The firm is also experienced in shopping center design. TR,i has done design work for THF Realty's new Chesterfield Commons, a 120-acre retail and office complex. The firm also has been selected to join the development team for the new Brentwood Town Center redevelopment area, a large, mixed-use project on Brentwood Boulevard near Highway 40; and Gravois Bluffs, a 250-acre, mixed-use development in Fenton.

One-on-One Service

Although the firm is growing, it is committed to maintaining its hands-on approach to each project. And every job is a team effort, stresses Roof. "It's not 'mine' or 'his.' It's ours," he says. "A real collaboration of efforts and a sharing of ideas characterizes the work that we do."

The firm provides services that add up to a turnkey capability. For example, TR,i has an interior design staff to complement the work of the architects and provide full interior services. Additionally, the firm's experience with contractors—who often are on tight schedules— has given TR,i much practice in meeting client deadlines.

"Our business is all about trying to push the envelope and get as much creativity into the project as we can, within the budget that we have to work with," says Roof. "But we respect the client's economic formula because if that doesn't work, there is no project. So learning to be as creative as we can within the parameters that we are allowed to work within is a big part of the service we provide."

OVER THE PAST DECADE, TR,i HAS HAD AN ONGOING RELATIONSHIP WITH THE KOMAN GROUP, A COMMERCIAL REAL ESTATE DEVELOPER WELL KNOWN FOR ITS SUCCESSFUL CITYPLACE DEVELOPMENT IN CREVE COEUR (TOP LEFT AND OPPOSITE RIGHT).

THE GRANDVIEW PLAZA RENOVATION IN FLORISSANT, MISSOURI, IS AN EXCELLENT EXAMPLE OF TR, i BRINGING NEW VALUE TO AN EXISTING RETAIL CENTER (TOP RIGHT).

FOR DIERBERGS MARKETS IN ST. LOUIS, THE FIRM HAS SERVED AS ARCHITECT FOR THE DIERBERGS CORPORATE OFFICE BUILDING IN CHESTERFIELD, A COMMISSARY OF 100,000 SQUARE FEET IN BRIDGETON, AND FOUR NEW GROCERY STORES (BOTTOM RIGHT).

World Wide Technology, Inc.

WHILE MUCH OF ST. LOUIS IS SLEEPING, WORLD Wide Technology, Inc. (WWT) is helping a company customize 5,000 binders for an upcoming sales conference. The company is able to do this through custombinder.com, a powerful interactive electronic catalog

WORLD WIDE TECHNOLOGY, INC. WAS FOUNDED IN 1990 BY DAVID L. STEWARD. THE MUTLIMILLION DOLLAR FIRM OFFERS E-BUSINESS SOLUTIONS TO THE GOVERNMENT, TELCO, AND COMMERCIAL MARKETPLACE (TOP).

STEWARD GIVES MUCH OF THE CREDIT FOR WWT'S SUCCESS TO HIS EMPLOY-EES, WHOM HE DESCRIBES AS BRIGHT, YOUTHFUL, AND AMBITIOUS. HE BELIEVES THE MAIN ADVANTAGES OF BEING BASED IN ST. LOUIS ARE THE GREAT LOCAL UNIVERSITIES AND COLLEGES FROM WHICH HE CAN DRAW TALENT, AS WELL AS THE MIDWESTERN WORK ETHIC (BOTTOM).

WWT helped develop on the Internet that allows consumers to design custom-decorated binders and instantly send their requests to preferred dealers for price quotes. Helping companies gain a competitive advantage through Internet technology is what WWT does best.

Through its vertical Internet portals, fedbuy.com and telcobuy.com are helping government agencies and telecommunications specialists worldwide purchase products and services with credit cards and purchase order numbers. Customers also can check prices and availability, track orders, obtain order history, and gather industry information 24 hours a day, seven days a week, without waiting for a customer service representative.

This is the world of E-business, and the rapidly growing St. Louis-based technology firm is a leader in the field. It is estimated that by 2003, E-business will account for more than $3 trillion in commerce. Developing a globally networked business model and helping companies use the Internet are ways WWT

has established its reputation not only for anticipating changes in the technological landscape, but also for initiating those changes.

Founded in 1990 to market integrated technical solutions to federal government and Fortune 500 clients, WWT has become one of the fastest-growing Internet solutions integrators in the country. It now works within the government, commercial, and telecommunication marketplaces. The privately held company is a leading provider of E-business solutions that enable companies throughout the world to share, distribute, organize, and analyze information. In conjuction with providing e-business solutions, WWT's practice groups include business applications and consulting, systems and networking, Internet business solutions, and imaging and document management. Within five years of its founding, WWT became one of the top two federal suppliers in the St. Louis region, second only to Boeing. Clients such as AT&T, Southwestern Bell, GTE,

Bell Atlantic, Boeing, the U. S. Air Force and other Department of Defense agencies, Mercantile Bank, the U. S. Department of Agriculture, and Monsanto have turned to WWT to handle, design, and integrate their technological systems. WWT also has developed strong partnerships with industry heavyweights such as Lucent Technologies Inc., Sun Microsystems, Oracle, Cisco, and IBM. In addition, WWT is one of only 20 authorized Java centers in the United States. Java is a universal computer language that is designed to allow computers and other high-tech devices to communicate with one another faster and easier than before. Such partnerships have helped the company position itself as a model for 21st-century business.

FROM HUMBLE BEGINNINGS

WWT was founded in 1990 by David L. Steward. Union Pacific Railroad contracted with the auditing firm he established to look for undercharges in three years of billing. Steward reasoned

electronically, via their own designated area on the agency's Web site.

This people-oriented business is supported by sophisticated technology. SRHD uses advanced modeling analysis to look at databases, segment the market-place, target customers most likely to respond and buy from clients, and decrease the costs of marketing while increasing the results. Every employee has desktop Internet access and the latest in equipment.

For one longtime customer, Banc One Financial Services, SRHD provided a variety of successful services over a two-year period: list planning, analysis, and strategies; front-end profiling and modeling analysis; back-end analytics, including regression analysis; comprehensive turnkey pro-duction services; comprehensive creative services; and database planning and development for the firm's acquisition efforts. The outcome was even better than planned: Banc One grew its loan volume from $400 million in 1993 (the year the firm hired SRHD) to more than $5 billion in 1999. In addition, SRHD has provided similar services for others—often Fortune 500 companies—including Edward Jones, Fireman's Fund Direct, and a number of Banc One divisions.

"A client typically comes to us for one of two reasons," says Hoeft. "They may want new customers, or they may want current customers who are profitable to do more business with them. In either case, we offer a total solution. If they want new customers, we provide a way of accessing data and identifying which people they should and should not contact; if they want to expand their business with current cus-tomers, we identify which ones are the most profitable. And then we have some unique ways of tracking, reporting, and learning so that our customers are constantly getting smarter about their business."

A People-Focused Business

Strategy sessions with clients may take place in the office, but in keeping with its emphasis on relationships, SRHD may also go off-site for meetings that include some fun. Recently, com-pany staff members met with one client at Lake of the Ozarks, where they enjoyed leisure time together. Most important, they also had "some incredibly creative brainstorming sessions on solutions to their marketing needs," says Hoeft.

For the future, SRHD plans to make some exciting changes to its business. In conjunction with its parent company—Summit Marketing, a holding company that acquired SRHD in 1998—the firm plans to work toward providing clients with integrated access to direct marketing, sales promotion, licensing, kids' club programs, and event marketing solutions, all through a single source. SRHD is also looking at a number of acquisitions that will give it new, strategic capabilities in direct marketing—both data-base and E-commerce—that will extend the company's position as an industry leader.

"Our point of difference is this one-to-one service, our passionate caring for a client's success and for the customers they serve," says Hoeft. "We are building our company—our careers—on teamwork with our clients."

CUSTOMIZED, CREATIVE SOLUTIONS HELP SRHD'S CLIENTS ACHIEVE THEIR BUSINESS OBJECTIVES.

SRHD'S INNOVATIVE USE OF THE INTERNET FOR PRODUCTION WORK HELPS TO MANAGE ALL THE DETAILS— EXCEPT FOR GOOD, OLD-FASHIONED PRESS CHECKS.

PRO BONO CLIENTS SUCH AS THE MAGIC HOUSE CHILDREN'S MUSEUM AND THE ST. LOUIS ARTS AND EDU-CATION COUNCIL BENEFIT FROM SRHD'S MARKETING EXPERTISE, DEDICATION TO THE ST. LOUIS COMMUNITY, AND CHARITABLE CULTURE.

TRIAD Manufacturing, Inc.

WHEN MAJOR MANUFACTURERS DISTRIBUTE A NEW line of clothing to specialty and department stores around the country, they want it to look as enticing as possible to prospective customers. This means the merchandise needs a well-designed and well-produced

display fixture, such as a small enclave or vendor shop to create a kind of store within a store.

TRIAD Manufacturing, Inc., headquartered in St. Louis, is rapidly becoming one of the nation's leading manufacturers of custom wood and metal fixtures created to meet the design and merchandise needs of the retail market. These include nested tables, hang-and-fold units, kiosks, and interactive displays, among others. The company—which has satellite sales offices in New York, Minnesota, and California—also provides shipping, delivery, and installation across the United States and Canada, as well as to South America and Europe.

TRIAD's customer list reads like a who's who of the clothing industry, including Bugle Boy, Dockers, UNIONBAY, Duck Head, Arnold Palmer, Esprit, Liz Claiborne, Easy Spirit, and Fila USA. TRIAD also builds displays for retail giants such as May Company, Saks Inc., Federated Department Stores, Goody's, Sears, Target Stores, General Nutrition Cos. (GNC), Nine West, Cost Plus, Mont-

gomery Ward, Warner Brothers, and The Gap.

Sample fixtures are on display at TRIAD's corporate office and manufacturing facility on Semple Avenue in St. Louis. For Bugle Boy, the company has created a hang-and-fold unit with glossy maple veneer and aluminum trim; for Aerosoles

shoes, TRIAD has built a table out of wild cherry laminate. And for Nine West, it has developed a frosted glass-and-aluminum laminate table with an iridescent finish.

None of TRIAD's displays are standard, catalog-type items. Every one is custom designed by the client or by TRIAD's own design team. The pieces are then manufactured to these specifications at TRIAD's 500,000-square-foot plant, which has a staff of 275 employees.

"Our specialty is large-volume, high-quality fixture and vendor shop rollouts," says David Caito, TRIAD's president. "Recently, May Company bought the Jones stores. As corporate vendor for five of their programs, we'll ship to 10 stores, 10 products to each one. Or for UNIONBAY, we are doing their vendor shops: five different fixtures— a thousand of each—shipped around the country."

TRIAD MANUFACTURING, INC., HEADQUARTERED IN ST. LOUIS, IS RAPIDLY BECOMING ONE OF THE NATION'S LEADING MANUFACTURERS OF CUSTOM WOOD AND METAL FIXTURES CREATED TO MEET THE DESIGN AND MERCHANDISE NEEDS OF THE RETAIL MARKET (TOP).

THE NORTH FACE SHOP DESIGNED BY TRIAD HAS WON AWARDS (BOTTOM).

STARTING SMALL AND GROWING BIG

TRIAD started out small. In 1991, when Caito and his two partners, Mike McCormick and Don Bishop, decided to form the new company, they had no customer base, only $15,000 in savings, and a small, 5,000-square-foot, leased facility. But the team soon attracted two customers, Edison Brothers and Target Stores, and then each year added more.

TRIAD also added to the services it offered. Originally, the company only had an in-house metal division; whenever customers wanted wood cabinetry, TRIAD had to subcontract the work to other firms. One of those firms belonged to Jerry Vyskala, whose aggressive, hardworking attitude meshed well with Caito's and McCormick's. When Bishop left the company, Vyskala stepped in and became TRIAD's third partner. Today, Caito heads the sales, marketing, and financing end of the business; McCormick runs the metal division; and Vyskala manages the wood division. The entire manufacturing operation has been under one roof since December 1997, when TRIAD bought the Semple facility, which has since been extensively renovated and upgraded with state-of-the-art equipment.

AN AWARD-WINNING FIRM

Over the years, this privately held firm has grown substantially in sales: from $5 million in 1995 to $25 million in 1998. According to Caito, TRIAD expects to be a $50 million company within five years.

In less than a decade of existence, TRIAD has already won numerous awards for its work. In 1998, the company ranked as number 356 of the top 500 fastest-growing U.S. companies on the prestigious *Inc.* 500 list. In 1997, Ernst & Young gave TRIAD the Entrepreneur of the Year award, and in 1997 and 1998, the *St. Louis Business-Journal* recognized

TRIAD as one of the fastest-growing St. Louis companies. Trade magazines—*Display & Design Ideas* and *Visual Merchandising & Store Design (VM+SD)*—have also honored the firm.

A key to the company's success has been its ability to recognize emerging trends in the industries it serves, and then designing pieces that meet those needs. For instance, in 1993, TRIAD recognized that many department stores were implementing vendor shops within their stores. The firm was able to develop this line of business ahead of many of its competitors.

"Today, vendor shops are a hot line of business," says McCormick. "If you go into a department store, everybody has a little area—Donna Karan, Polo, Nautica, Tommy Hilfiger. We got into that arena with designs in hand—along with installation and delivery capa-

bilities—and we were very competitive with our pricing. Being a full-service manufacturer allowed us to expand rapidly."

Customer loyalty has also given the company an edge. Before Donna Karan awarded TRIAD a recent contract, representatives came to the firm to do a thorough walk-through inspection of its facility. They also checked the company's entire reference list, hearing only positive comments.

In the future, TRIAD expects to make some strategic acquisitions while continuing to attract new customers and serving existing customers, as well. "The key to our philosophy is servicing our customer," says Caito. "If we can do that in all aspects of our business—design, manufacturing, pricing, shipping, and meeting the clients' deadlines on time and without damage—then I know we will continue to be successful."

TRIAD—WHICH HAS SATELLITE SALES OFFICES IN NEW YORK, MINNESOTA, AND CALIFORNIA—ALSO PROVIDES SHIPPING, DELIVERY, AND INSTALLATION ACROSS THE UNITED STATES AND CANADA, AS WELL AS TO SOUTH AMERICA AND EUROPE.

WHEN MAJOR MANUFACTURERS DISTRIBUTE A NEW LINE OF CLOTHING TO SPECIALTY AND DEPARTMENT STORES AROUND THE COUNTRY, THEY WANT IT TO LOOK AS ENTICING AS POSSIBLE TO PROSPECTIVE CUSTOMERS. THIS MEANS THE MERCHANDISE NEEDS A WELL-DESIGNED AND WELL-PRODUCED DISPLAY FIXTURE, SUCH AS A SMALL ENCLAVE OR VENDOR SHOP TO CREATE A KIND OF STORE WITHIN A STORE.

BJC HEALTH SYSTEM℠

SINCE ITS FOUNDING IN 1992, BJC HEALTH SYSTEM℠ HAS focused on becoming the health care provider of the future. Its vision of health care delivery has placed it at the forefront of medical systems, both regionally and nationally, and made it a model for other systems that are grappling with difficult issues such as duplication

BJC HEALTH SYSTEM'S PARTNERSHIP WITH ITS PATIENTS AND FAMILIES MAKES IT POSSIBLE FOR THE ORGANIZATION TO LIVE ITS MISSION OF IMPROVING THE HEALTH OF THE PEOPLE IT SERVES (LEFT).

BJC'S RELATIONSHIP WITH THE RENOWNED WASHINGTON UNIVERSITY SCHOOL OF MEDICINE MEANS GROUNDBREAKING MEDICAL ADVANCES ARE AVAILABLE TO COMMUNITIES SERVED BY THE HEALTH SYSTEM (RIGHT).

of services and the growth of managed care.

BJC is the largest health care provider and employer in the St. Louis region, with more than 25,000 employees serving two markets: the St. Louis metropolitan area, including southern Illinois; and central Missouri. BJC is also one of the largest not-for-profit health care systems in the country, with $1.8 billion in annual net revenue and more than 100 delivery sites. Two of its hospitals—Barnes-Jewish Hospital and St. Louis Children's Hospital—continually rank among the best in the United States.

At its formation, BJC was the first health system in the country to link urban, suburban, and rural health care facilities with a medical school—namely, Washington University School of Medicine, rated as number four in the nation in 1999 by *U.S. News & World Report*. Washington University's physicians often appear in the national "Best Doctors in America" listings, and are known for their clinical excellence and cutting-edge research.

Since its founding, BJC has remained a pioneer. In 1999, BJC was rated number two in a list of America's top integrated health systems, selected for their wide geographic reach and coordinated systems of care. Across its facilities, BJC has combined previously separate efforts in clinical areas, such as women's and infants' health, behavioral health, and laboratory services.

In the future, BJC will continue this integration effort—from ambulatory and inpatient care to long-term and hospice care—enabling the system to provide a seamless range of services to its patients. Integration of services will also enable physicians and other care providers to deliver high-quality

care that meets marketplace requirements for efficiency and strict cost management.

As the 1999 recipient of the highly competitive National Quality Health Care Award, BJC is proving that coordinated efforts to improve health care can make a significant difference in an individual's health status. These efforts are a part of BJC's constant commitment to wellness initiatives and community outreach, unparalleled in the St. Louis region.

A RESPONSIBILITY TO THE COMMUNITY

BJC's mission—to improve the health of the people and communities it serves—drives every facet of the system's operations. Key to achieving the mission is community outreach.

Each year, BJC offers hundreds of events and programs, including health lectures, screenings, a free senior membership program, and the region's largest school outreach initiative. In 1998, for example, BJC conducted more than 1,600 community education events, attended by some 111,000 people. And the schools program reached more than 39,000 stu-

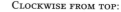

the balls flew directly over the BJC sign.

BJC works diligently to provide services to underserved members of the community. The system has bolstered health care in rural communities through clinics and continuing education programs for health care professionals. Recently, BJC agreed to a request from the City of St. Louis and the State of Missouri to assist in the management of ConnectCare at no cost. ConnectCare serves St. Louis residents with particular emphasis on health care for underinsured and uninsured people. And in 1998 alone, BJC Health System provided $28 million in charity care to those who couldn't afford the care they needed. Since 1993, BJC's charity care has totaled $171.2 million.

A HISTORY OF SERVICE

BJC was established in November 1992 when Barnes Hospital and The Jewish Hospital of St. Louis affiliated to form Barnes-Jewish, Inc. In June 1993, Christian Health Services merged with Barnes-Jewish, Inc., and the name was changed to

CLOCKWISE FROM TOP:
BJC PROVIDES HIGHLY SKILLED PEDIATRIC CARE THROUGH ST. LOUIS CHILDREN'S HOSPITAL, RECOGNIZED AS ONE OF THE BEST PEDIATRIC HOSPITALS IN THE COUNTRY.

FROM HOME HEALTH CARE TO A FULL CONTINUUM OF MEDICAL SERVICES, BJC STRIVES TO PROVIDE ACCESSIBLE, HIGH-QUALITY CARE.

BARNES-JEWISH HOSPITAL IS RANKED BY *U.S. News & World Report* AS ONE OF THE BEST HOSPITALS IN THE NATION.

dents through more than 700 programs.

School program topics include alcohol, tobacco, and drug usage; violence; nutrition; fitness; sexually transmitted diseases; HIV; smoking; and safety. A popular program involves displaying samples of diseased and healthy organs to demonstrate the effects of alcohol, tobacco, and drug usage. The school outreach program also supports school district employees. For example, BJC has held workshops for school nurses, helping them prepare for potential emergencies in their schools.

BJC partners with many kinds of community organizations—including churches, civic groups, schools, and businesses—to promote health and wellness. Over the past five years, BJC has offered programs and resources to pregnant teenagers and battered women; coordinated health awareness campaigns on issues such as gun safety, bicycle helmets, and seat belts; and conducted health education activities for schoolchil-

dren and older adults.

For adults 55 and older, BJC offers a free membership program, OASIS/BJC Plus. Through BJC Plus, members have access to fitness programs, health education, health insurance counseling, and discounts on items such as medications, medical equipment, and hearing aids. OASIS, a national education organization, provides stimulating programs in the arts, humanities, wellness, and volunteer services. OASIS/BJC Plus helps more than 105,000 older adults stay healthy.

In 1998, BJC embarked on a five-year partnership with the St. Louis Cardinals baseball team that links the two organizations in providing school programs aimed at improving the health, well-being, and future of area youth. The partnership also enables BJC to bring health and wellness messages to the crowds at Busch Stadium. When Mark McGwire hit his 62nd and 70th home runs during the 1998 season, BJC's name was seen in photographs and video clips worldwide as

BJC Health System. All three health care providers have deep roots in the St. Louis community.

Barnes Hospital opened in 1914, through the bequest of Robert Barnes, owner of a large wholesale grocery chain. The Jewish Hospital of St. Louis was founded in 1902 in response to the needs of 19th-century Jewish immigrants and physicians. And Christian Health Services (CHS) traces its origins to Christian Hospital, founded in 1903 by the Christian Woman's Benevolent Association.

In forming BJC, these hospitals brought other health facilities and services with them, including suburban and rural hospitals, home care and occupational health services, and long-term care facilities.

Over the years, BJC has grown through the addition of various other facilities. In 1994, Missouri Baptist Medical Center, founded in 1884, and St. Louis Children's Hospital, established in 1879, became members of BJC Health System.

PHYSICIANS: PARTNERS IN LEADERSHIP

BJC builds strong relationships with academic and community physicians and seeks their involvement in the leadership of the organization. Nine physicians are members of the system's board of directors. BJC offers the Physician Executive Leadership Course, a collaborative approach to health care management and leadership. Through the Center for Healthcare Quality and Effectiveness, BJC gives Innovations in Healthcare grants to physicians and other employees who want to study ways to improve patient care and make it more efficient.

Some 4,000 physicians are affiliated with BJC. These physicians provide the leadership for improvements in clinical care. For example, teams of caregivers have improved the clinical outcomes for congestive heart failure, coronary bypass, and pneumonia patients, among others. These results made BJC the recipient of the 1999 National Quality Health Care Award.

The training of future physicians is another focus at BJC. Two BJC hospitals serve as teaching facilities for the Washington University School of Medicine. Several other BJC facilities serve as clinical care training sites. Through these partnerships, BJC helped to educate more than 2,800 students in health-related professions in 1998.

This relationship with the School of Medicine also means that groundbreaking medical advances are available to communities served by BJC. In 1998 alone, BJC directed $27 million toward medical research.

A NEW LOOK FOR WASHINGTON UNIVERSITY MEDICAL CENTER

At Washington University Medical Center, BJC is creating the health care campus of the future by making an investment—unprecedented in the St. Louis health care market—of more than $300 million in physical improvements. During the next several years, this sweeping project will boast new, state-of-the-art facilities; renovation of existing facilities; and the demolition of older buildings that cannot be updated for 21st-century medicine.

A key element of the plan is to consolidate clinical care that today is scattered throughout the medical center. On the north end of the campus, a new ambulatory care center and a cancer center facility will consolidate

CLOCKWISE FROM TOP: BJC's PARTNERSHIP WITH THE ST. LOUIS CARDINALS LINKS THE TWO ORGANIZATIONS IN PROVIDING SCHOOL PROGRAMS AIMED AT IMPROVING THE HEALTH, WELL-BEING, AND FUTURE OF AREA YOUTH.

LISTENING TO PATIENT CONCERNS IS A FIRST STEP FOR BJC PROFESSIONALS IN PROVIDING HIGH-QUALITY CARE.

PHYSICIANS AFFILIATED WITH BJC AND THE WASHINGTON UNIVERSITY SCHOOL OF MEDICINE ARE KNOWN WORLDWIDE FOR THEIR CLINICAL EXCELLENCE AND CUTTING-EDGE EXPERTISE.

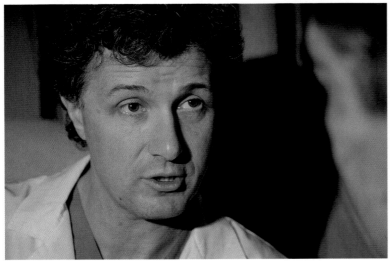

outpatient services and cancer research, diagnosis, and treatment into one patient-friendly, accessible location. Complex inpatient medical and surgical care will be concentrated on the south end of the campus. In addition, a new emergency, trauma, and urgent care facility—designed to accommodate the more than 80,000 annual emergency visits currently handled by two emergency departments—will be conveniently located at Barnes-Jewish Hospital on Kingshighway.

CORE SERVICES OFFERED BY BJC

BJC offers a full continuum of care. Inpatient care is available at 13 hospitals with more than 4,000 patient beds. From 1993 to 1998, BJC hospitals admitted more than 768,000 patients, handled 2 million emergency-room visits, and delivered nearly 67,000 babies.

BJC provides outpatient services in nearly 100 locations, serving more than 40 communities. In the area of long-term care, BJC operates five skilled nursing facilities for adults in need of intensive rehabilitation and extended medical and nursing care. For older adults, BJC runs a continuing care retirement community that offers independent apartment living.

For people who require medical assistance at home—such as skilled nursing, respiratory or rehabilitation services, or home infusion therapy—BJC Home Care Services has the region's most comprehensive program, including hospice services for adults and children. BJC Corporate Health Services handles work-related injuries and provides companies with pre-placement physicals and on-site wellness and ergonomics programs.

Through its own managed care products and relationships with area insurers, BJC has assumed financial responsibility for the health and disease management of several hundred

thousand patients. In tandem with Washington University School of Medicine, BJC sponsors Health Partners of the Midwest, a growing managed care plan. BJC also sponsors CarePartners, a Medicaid HMO.

BJC shares its health care knowledge and provides health care services to people and communities far beyond St. Louis. Through its International Healthcare Services, BJC works with hospitals and administrators in other countries to help them deliver high-quality care locally. BJC has the resources to provide everything from long-distance, one-on-one consultations to a highly skilled team of health care professionals able to help provide quality care in other parts of the world.

Patients come from many countries to receive care at several of BJC's hospitals. International Healthcare Services coordinates all aspects of the care these patients receive—from transportation and lodging to interpreter services.

Just as BJC's reputation for quality reaches far beyond St. Louis, so do its acts of charity. Donations of medical equipment and supplies have made their way to communities in Germany, Ghana, Honduras, the Philippines, Poland, and Russia. During the past three years, BJC and Washington University School of Medicine have led a nationally recognized humanitarian partnership to improve health in the Republic

of Latvia. BJC and its hospitals also have supported a number of international relief efforts.

BJC's mission promises to improve the health of the people and communities it serves. With good health, individuals, families, and communities can thrive. BJC's physicians and employees live the promise of health improvement every day as they bring their patients high-quality, compassionate care.

CLOCKWISE FROM TOP:
BY DEVELOPING EFFECTIVE LINKS BETWEEN BJC, PHYSICIANS, AND INSURERS, BJC IS PLACING HEALTH CARE DECISION MAKING BACK IN THE HANDS OF DOCTORS.

BJC PROVIDES AREA YOUTH OPPORTUNITIES TO LEARN ABOUT HEALTH CARE PROFESSIONS AND STRATEGIES FOR A HEALTHY LIFE THROUGH ITS SCHOOL OUTREACH PROGRAM, THE LARGEST OF ITS KIND IN THE REGION.

BJC PROVIDES HEALTH CARE SERVICES AT MANY OF THE AREA'S LARGEST COMMUNITY EVENTS, INCLUDING FAIR ST. LOUIS.

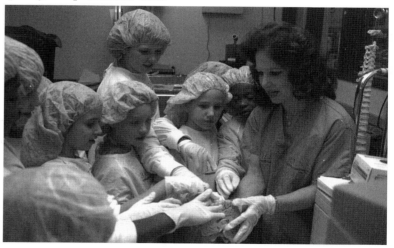

SYLLOGISTEKS

SYLLOGISTEKS®, A ST. LOUIS-BASED INFORMATION TECHNOLOGY (IT) firm, is reminiscent of those good old days when enthusiasm, integrity, and a good work ethic were just as important as the result of work performed. Those were times when employers knew each employee by name and expressed appreciation for their contributions to

the organization's success. SyllogisTeks prides itself on building long-term relationships with its employees as well as its clients—and in celebrating the everyday achievements and milestones of each individual.

"There are so many rewards that come to us daily in this job," says Thomas Smith, founder and chief executive officer of SyllogisTeks. "We celebrate every little success because they are all very important to us," adds Maurie Smith, president and chief operating officer.

SIMPLIFYING BUSINESS WITH TECHNOLOGY℠

Founded in 1992, the company's distinct name defines its business goal of simplifying business

with technology. SyllogisTeks is a derivative of two words: syllogistic, Aristotle's description of the most direct form of logic and the basis of the Western thought process, and technology.

To meet this goal, SyllogisTeks offers three major areas of IT specialization. The first is its staffing services division. The company provides clients with experienced personnel for such varied client-driven needs as Web development, E-commerce, systems and business analysis, imaging, software engineering, project management, information security, programming, help desk, technical communications, and systems administration. These proven professionals usually work at customer premises and are available for the duration of a project, on a six-month right-to-hire basis, or as permanent placements.

The second service area is networking technologies. The company serves clients on either a project or retained services basis for their network hardware, software, and support needs, and ensures that these solutions are implemented successfully. The range of services includes network design, planning, procurement, installation

and integration; performance management; network diagnosis and troubleshooting; conversions; technical support; and training. The company's extensive LAN and TCP/IP knowledge, resources, alliances, and expertise allow it to solve a variety of problems found in today's modern, high-performance networks. Representative projects have included implementation of Microsoft® Windows® NT Cluster Servers, thin client server computing, Web hosting, fire walls, proxy servers, virtual private networks, and Microsoft Exchange™ messaging and collaboration.

The third service area is SyllogisTeks' specialized software solutions practice. Here, it invests heavily in research and development activities to produce products and technology innovations for both internal and commercial applications. The company can deliver customer-specific turnkey applications and licensed software products. Developers in this unit typically work at company facilities, on their own enterprise level computer systems, and under company management and direction. The Microsoft® SQL Server-based front-office systems used by SyllogisTeks' staffing services division, and its proven IBM® mainframe software tool, Multiple Report Creation System (MRCS®), exemplify the range of the firm's resident software engineering capabilities.

THE BOTTOM LINE

SyllogisTeks is a company founded on four core values that are as important as its bottom line. The first is honesty: being open and honest with customers and employees as they work together. Second

and nurse case managers meet weekly in small groups to discuss care management issues. In these meetings, physicians critically challenge each other to create best practices in a real-time environment. With the autonomy they enjoy, physicians and staff collaborate and create ways to improve health, ultimately developing disease management protocols that improve health care for every patient.

EMBRACING TECHNOLOGY AND MANAGING INFORMATION

The future of health care lies in managing information. At Esse Health, physicians and staff use technology every day to communicate, analyze, and share information. In 1999, the company is installing an information system that will incorporate a complete electronic medical record for each patient. Eventually, through Internet access, this record will draw patients into a better understanding of and greater participation in their health care. This system will also expand the group's ability to evaluate and improve the care it delivers. For example, the group will be able to analyze the factors influencing the health of patients with chronic diseases. It will also help assure that patients receive appropriate preventive health services such as immunizations for children and mammograms for women.

In 1998, Esse Health launched the Esse Research Institute, a division headed by Scot Walker, Doctor of Pharmacy. Walker consults with Esse physicians on the most effective use of pharmaceuticals, which often present complex health care management issues. The institute also conducts drug studies and outcomes research to help evaluate the most effective treatment strategies for Esse Health's patients.

Pharmaceuticals also represent one of the fastest-growing costs in health care today. "Employers, insurers, and other

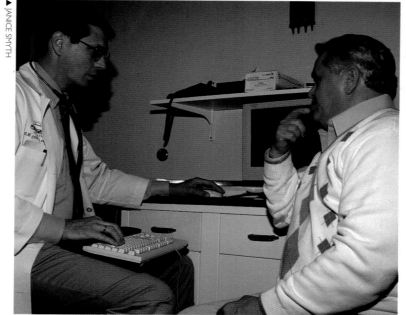

managed care organizations are constantly putting pressure on physicians to be cost effective in their treatment choices," says Willey. "The institute will help us be cost effective, but, more important, it will help us find ways to keep our patients healthier."

At Esse Health, learning about the latest advances in medicine is a high priority. The organization supplements its daily, informal learning opportunities with formal educational programs. In the fall of 1998, the company sponsored a clinical symposium on improving the quality of care while

managing costs. In the near future, Esse hopes to become accredited through the Missouri State Medical Association. This will allow the group to provide continuing medical education credits to physicians for the educational programs it designs and sponsors.

"Esse Health will continue to deliver the highest-quality health care. We will not rest on our current reputation for excellence, but we will strive for continuous improvement," says Willey. "Our primary focus is our patients, to whom we bring a renewed emphasis on service and satisfaction."

SINCLAIR BROADCAST GROUP

IN 1971, JULIAN SINCLAIR SMITH'S FIRST TELEVISION STATION, WBFF, went on the air in Baltimore. Over the years—especially after David Smith took over leadership of the business from his father in the 1990s—Sinclair Broadcast Group (SBG) has looked for ways to expand its broadcast holdings, in both radio and television. During this time, the firm made acquisitions in Baltimore and Pittsburgh, and in 1995, SBG became a publicly traded company.

"SBG knew that only those companies that were growing and consolidating were going to stay in business, so it wasn't a question of whether we should remain small or grow big. It was: Should we get big or get out of business? The Smith family—David Smith and his three brothers—really wanted to stay and become leaders in this industry," says Barry Drake, chief executive officer for SBG's Radio and Television divisions.

A ST. LOUIS MARKET LEADER

In 1996, SBG entered the St. Louis market with the purchase of River City Broadcasting, which owned one television station, KDNL-ABC 30, and two radio stations, KPNT-FM 105.7 (The Point) and WVRV-FM 101.1 (The River). SBG added to its St. Louis properties in March 1998 with the purchase of Heritage Media, which owned three radio stations: WIL-FM 92.3, WRTH-AM 1430, and KIHT-FM 96.3 (K-HITS). Only six months later, SBG signed a local marketing agreement to operate KXOK-FM, 97.1 (The Rock).

Overall, SBG has established itself as a leader in the broadcast industry nationwide, with 50 radio stations and 65 television stations in its portfolio. That makes SBG the seventh-largest broadcast group in the United States on the television side and the 10th largest in radio. Besides St. Louis, SBG is also located in such key areas as Kansas City, Buffalo, New Orleans, and Memphis. During 1998 alone, SBG added several new markets to its holdings: Greensboro; Greenville, South Carolina; and Norfolk, Virginia.

SBG's goal is to become the nation's largest independent broadcaster—and it is already well on its way. Currently, SBG television stations reach 22.5 percent of the country's households, a figure that exceeds the combined total of households in New York City, Los Angeles, Chicago, Philadelphia, and San Francisco.

"We look for opportunities in which we can have radio and television holdings in the same market," says Drake. "That gives us a promotional and sales advantage in approaching advertisers with broad programs and campaigns that encompass the use of radio and television. Instead of going in and talking about one television station or one radio station, we can

K-HITS, WHICH IS OWNED BY SINCLAIR BROADCAST GROUP, PRESENTED TWO FREE CONCERTS AT UNION STATION IN JULY 1998, DRAWING RECORD CROWDS.

JONATHAN POSTAL ▲

advanced production capabilities, a global sales force, and extensive data management expertise, Towery has emerged as a significant provider of Internet-based city information. In keeping with its overall focus on community resources, the company's Internet efforts represent a natural step in the evolution of the business.

The primary product lines within the Internet division are the introCity™ sites. Towery's introCity sites introduce newcomers, visitors, and longtime residents to every facet of a particular community, while simultaneously placing the local chamber of commerce at the forefront of the city's Internet activity. The sites include newcomer information, calendars, photos, citywide business listings with everything from nightlife to shopping to family fun, and on-line maps pinpointing the exact location of businesses, schools, attractions, and much more.

DECADES OF PUBLISHING EXPERTISE

In 1972, current President and CEO J. Robert Towery succeeded his parents in managing the printing and publishing business they had founded nearly four decades earlier. Soon thereafter, he expanded the scope of the company's

published materials to include *Memphis* magazine and other successful regional and national publications. In 1985, after selling its locally focused assets, Towery began the trajectory on which it continues today, creating community-oriented materials that are often produced in conjunction with chambers of commerce and other business organizations.

Despite the decades of change, Towery himself follows a long-standing family philosophy of unmatched service and unflinching quality. That approach extends throughout the entire organization to include more than 130 employees at the Memphis headquarters, another 60 located in Northern Kentucky outside Cincinnati, and more than 50 sales, marketing, and editorial staff traveling to and working in a growing list of client cities. All of its products, and more information about the company, are featured on the Internet at www.towery.com.

In summing up his company's steady growth, Towery restates the essential formula that has driven the business since its first pages were published: "The creative energies of our staff drive us toward innovation and invention. Our people make the highest possible demands on themselves, so I know that our future is secure if the ingredients for success remain a focus on service and quality."

TOWERY PUBLISHING WAS THE FIRST PRODUCTION ENVIRONMENT IN THE UNITED STATES TO COMBINE DESKTOP PUBLISHING WITH COLOR SEPARATIONS AND IMAGE SCANNING TO PRODUCE FINISHED FILM SUITABLE FOR BURNING PLATES FOR FOUR-COLOR PRINTING. TODAY, THE COMPANY'S STATE-OF-THE-ART NETWORK OF MACINTOSH AND WINDOWS WORKSTATIONS ALLOWS IT TO PRODUCE MORE THAN 8,000 PAGES EACH YEAR, CONTAINING WELL OVER 30,000 HIGH-QUALITY COLOR IMAGES (TOP).

THE TOWERY FAMILY'S PUBLISHING ROOTS CAN BE TRACED TO 1935, WHEN R.W. TOWERY (FAR LEFT) BEGAN PRODUCING A SERIES OF COMMUNITY HISTORIES IN TENNESSEE, MISSISSIPPI, AND TEXAS. THROUGHOUT THE COMPANY'S HISTORY, THE FOUNDING FAMILY HAS CONSISTENTLY EXHIBITED A COMMITMENT TO CLARITY, PRECISION, INNOVATION, AND VISION (BOTTOM).

DOUGLAS ABEL worked as a registered architect for 12 years while pursuing photography from both a creative and an architectural point of view. Today, he is self-employed as the owner of Douglas Abel Photography, specializing in architectural images. Abel's photographs have appeared in *Architecture* magazine and architectural marketing materials and catalogs, as well as Towery Publishing's *St. Louis: Home on the River*. A graduate of the University of Kansas, where he received bachelor's degrees in environmental design and architecture, Abel is a lifelong St. Louis resident.

LEON ALGEE is a freelance photojournalist who has done work for the Associated Press, *Suburban Journal*, *St. Louis Post-Dispatch*, *USA Today*, *Chicago Tribune*, and *Kansas City Star*, as well as for Saint Louis and Webster universities. He enjoys news feature and sport photography, and his work has also appeared in Towery Publishing's *St. Louis: Home on the River*. Algee is active in volunteer and community service work, particularly with the Mathews-Dickey Boys' Club. He is a St. Louis native and a graduate of Webster University, where he received a bachelor's degree in media studies.

SCOTT R. AVETTA, a St. Louis native with a degree in business management, is a freelance photographer with experience in professional sports photography. His clients include the St. Louis Ambush soccer team and the St. Louis Vipers roller hockey team. Avetta works for Ray Davis Photography, specializing in wedding, portrait, and event images. In addition, he enjoys photojournalism, nature, and abstracts such as reflections, windows, and doors. He is a charter member of the Missouri Nature and Environmental Photographers and serves as program cochairman. Avetta is also a member of the St. Louis Camera Club.

STEVE BAKER is an international photographer who has contributed to more than 100 publications. With a degree in journalism from Indiana University, he is the proprietor of Highlight Photography, specializing in assignments for clients such as Eastman Kodak, Nike, Budweiser, U.S. Olympic Commit-

tee, and Mobil Oil, which has commissioned seven exhibitions of his work since 1994. Baker is author and photographer of *Racing Is Everything*, and he has contributed to Towery Publishing's *Baltimore: Charm City*; *Chicago: Heart and Soul of America*; *Dayton: The Cradle of Creativity*; *Indianapolis: Crossroads of the American Dream*; *Jackson: The Good Life*; *Los Angeles: City of Dreams*; *Nashville: City of Note*; and *Celebrating a Triangle Millennium*. Currently, Baker resides in Indianapolis.

BILL BOYCE, a native of St. Louis, specializes in travel, wildlife, and sports photography. His clients include the St. Louis Convention and Visitors Commission and the Missouri Division of Tourism.

GARY BUDKE, an amateur photographer, first became interested in photojournalism after taking a workshop from *National Geographic* photographer Sam Abell. Now vice president of the Missouri

Nature and Environmental Photographers, Budke has won numerous awards from the St. Louis Camera Club.

DOUG CALDWELL received a bachelor of science degree in business from Eastern Illinois University. For the past 12 years, he has been a part owner of a regional distributor primarily involved in marketing specialty food ingredients and nutraceuticals sold to industrial food processors. Photography is a hobby that began seven years ago when Caldwell volunteered to pho-

tograph his sons' high school cross-country team. Since then, he has won numerous awards for his sports and architectural photography.

DAN DONOVAN specializes in photographing people for advertising, corporate, editorial, and entertainment clients. In his spare time, he likes to shoot abstracts in color, as well as read science fiction and watch auto racing.